Praise for Jean Nathan's
The Secret Life of the Lonely Doll: The Search for Dare Wright

Selected as one of the best books of 2004
San Francisco Chronicle
The Chicago Tribune
Toronto Globe

"An exhaustively reported, gracefully written biography . . . This biography left me wanting to know more—about Jean Nathan."
—*The New York Times Book Review*

"Compelling psychological biography . . . Nathan's meticulously researched, well-documented biography . . . illuminates Wright's tangled and tragic life, work, and times."
—*Library Journal*

"Compelling . . . [Nathan's] gift in this slender biography of a princess enchanted by a witch is to bring to life a mystery that is deepened, more than unraveled, in the telling."
—*Vogue*

"Hard to put down . . . This graceful biography elucidates and follows those emotional threads to create a read as compelling as Wright's photographs."
—*Chicago Tribune*

"[A] poignant and beautifully written book."
—*Philadelphia Inquirer*

"[Nathan's] sympathetic, graceful style seems appropriate for this private, elusive figure who kept such porous boundaries between her real and imaginary worlds."
—*The Village Voice*

"Highly entertaining . . . The psychological underpinnings make the book glide."
—*Bay Area Reporter*

"A compelling dissection of a dysfunctional mother-daughter relationship and the strange body of photographic collaboration that resulted. Even if *The Lonely Doll* was not part of the reader's childhood, Nathan's biography of Dare Wright is an absolute pageturner, and the most interesting biography I've read in ages."

—*Missoula Independent*

"Totally fascinating . . . *The Secret Life of the Lonely Doll* is dark, disturbing, and obliquely sensual. It is rich with wonderful photographs both of and by Dare Wright and those who peopled her world, but it reads almost like a modern novel."

—*Currents* (Cleveland)

"Well-written and absorbing."

—*The Oregonian*

"Nathan's dexterous writing sees around the corners of Dare Wright's life to show that behind her perhaps perverse books was a childlike effort at life that was both futile and bold."

—*The New York Sun*

"You'll be fascinated. . . . An amazing and compelling document of a life of public glamour and private madness."

—*San Francisco Weekly*

"Nathan gives us a riveting story that deserves to be told and pondered.

—*Tampa Tribune*

"A compelling, fascinating, and harrowing story . . . A treasure trove of photographs . . . *The Secret Life of the Lonely Doll* is proof real lives are often more interesting than anything fiction creates."

—*The Ottawa Saturday Sun*

"A great read!"

—*The Union* (Nevada)

"Unforgettable."

—*The Dallas Morning News*

"Nathan took a truly sad, and in many ways creepy, story and crafted from it a poignant and sensitive memoir of a gifted artist's life."

—Charleston City Paper

"Fascinating."

—Doll Reader

"Compelling."

—New York magazine

"Nathan has crafted an astonishingly complete portrait of an intensely private person. . . . Nathan's revelation of her own personal, emotional connection with *The Lonely Doll* reaffirms the lasting power that books can have in the life of a child."

—The Horn Book magazine

"Sensational though Nathan's subject matter is . . . she never descends into exploitation. Her deft handling of these horrors recalls David and Albert Maysles' 1976 documentary *Grey Gardens*."

—Time Out New York

"Masterfully researched and disquieting."

—Beacon Journal (Akron, Ohio)

The Secret Life of the Lonely Doll

The Search for Dare Wright

■ ■ ■

JEAN NATHAN

PICADOR

———

HENRY HOLT AND COMPANY

NEW YORK

www.picadorusa.com

Picador® is a U.S. registered trademark and is used by Henry Holt and Company under license from Pan Books Limited.

For information on Picador Reading Group Guides, as well as ordering, please contact the Trade Marketing department at St. Martin's Press.
Phone: 1-800-221-7945 extension 763
Fax: 212-253-9627
E-mail: readinggroupguides@picadorusa.com

Designed by Paula Russell Szafranski

Library of Congress Cataloging-in-Publication Data

Nathan, Jean Elson.
    The secret life of The lonely doll : the search for Dare Wright / Jean Nathan.
        p. cm.
    Includes bibliographical references.
    ISBN 0-312-42492-2
    ISBN 978-0-312-42492-3
    1. Wright, Dare. 2. Authors, American—20th century—Biography. 3. Children's stories—Authorship. 4. Wright, Dare. Lonely doll. I. Title.

PS3573.R53244Z78 2004
813'.54—dc22
[B]   2004042412

First published in the United States by Henry Holt and Company

First Picador Edition: August 2005

For W.E.N.

My childhood bends beside me. Too far for me to lay a hand there once or lightly. Mine is far and his secret as our eyes. Secrets, silent, stony sit in the dark palaces of both our hearts: secrets weary of their tyranny: tyrants willing to be dethroned.

—JAMES JOYCE, *Ulysses*

Contents

The Secret Life
of the Lonely
Doll

Prologue

Some books are undeservedly forgotten; none are undeservedly
remembered.   —W. H. AUDEN, *"The Dyer's Hand"*

It was on the first day of spring that the oddest
image floated into my mind: the cover of a children's book I hadn't seen or even thought of in over
thirty years. At first I could barely make it out. It was
no more than the image of a pattern, pink-and-
white gingham. But there it lodged and there it
remained; it felt as if it were a message, and from the
farthest edge of consciousness. Its insistence startled
me. I tried to tromp it down. I lived among the
grown-ups now. I was a journalist, fourteen years
into a career that had taken me from newspaper
reporter to magazine editor to freelance writer. On
this day, a deadline loomed. I had work to do.

But the image kept flashing in my mind, becoming clearer and clearer, like a photograph developing, until I could see that the gingham was a frame

of sorts, surrounding a photograph, a black-and-white photograph of a blond-haired wide-eyed doll, an open book between her outstretched legs. *The Lonely Doll*. That was the title. Encouraged, I strained to peel back the layers of memory, to summon up at least something about its narrative. But that was all I could come up with: the image of the cover, its title, and the fact that it had once fascinated me.

My first stop was one of the best children's bookstores in New York, a store known for its experienced staff. I asked the clerk behind the front desk if they had the book. It was out of print, he said, adding that it was just as well. He murmured something about it being "politically incorrect." Curious—were we talking about the same book?—I asked why. "The spanking scene," he scoffed.

I had no recollection of any spanking scene. Could he give me the information I would need to find the book elsewhere? Consulting his computer, he read it out to me and I wrote it down: "Dare Write, Doubleday, 1957." As I turned to leave, he called me back, pointing to a rack of business cards by the cash register. An enterprising book searcher whose specialty was children's books had placed the cards there. She might be able to help me.

The New York Public Library listed several copies of *The Lonely Doll* but none now fit to circulate; beside each notation in the electronic card catalog were the words "damaged" or "missing." This, the children's librarian told me, was the sign of a well-loved book. Children read their favorite books to death, she said. They are careless in their devotions. They rip the pages, scribble, and spill things on them. And they are demon book thieves. At least I had now cleared up the spelling of the author's last name. It was "Wright."

I had misplaced the book searcher's card but I did remember her name and found her number in the phone book. Unlike the bookstore clerk, she passed no judgment, but she surprised me too, offering to add my name to her long waiting list. I couldn't imagine why anyone else would be thinking of this book. And people willing to spare no expense: A copy in good condition could cost $200, she informed me. Should she go ahead and add my name to the list? I thanked her anyway, unwilling to pay such a sum to satisfy such an ill-defined curiosity. She asked if I would be interested in a paperback copy. That would run about $30, although the wait might be longer still. The price seemed more in line; I gave her my address and credit card number. As I put down the receiver, I felt an almost childish sense of disappointment at more delay, but also astonishment to learn that the book lived on in other people's consciousnesses.

Meaning to put the phone book away, I found myself turning absently to "Wright." And there, jumping out at me from blurred columns of type, was Wright, Dare, 11 East 80th Street, 249-6965. I don't think I could have been any more amazed if the address given had been, say, "Second to the right and then straight on till morning," Peter Pan's address on the island of Neverland.

In the weeks to come I dialed the number many times. There was never an answer. One day I set off for 11 East 80th Street, but on the way I lost my nerve. What would I do once I got there? Ring the doorbell? I decided instead to write a letter. In it, I explained that I had been a fan of her book as a child and asked if she knew where I might find a copy. Optimistically, I enclosed my phone number. As I addressed the envelope, it occurred to me that what I was really doing was sending a letter to my childhood, or trying to. But time passed and I heard nothing. My attempt to make contact through writing was proving as fruitless as my phone calls. Maybe this Dare Wright had died.

Some weeks later, a package arrived, wrapped in brown paper, actually a recycled grocery bag. As I tore it open carefully, I could see the pink-and-white gingham peeking through. There was the cover, just as I remembered it; there was the doll, a black ribbon tied around her high blond ponytail, her bangs, her gold hoop earrings, her gingham frock, the lace petticoat beneath it, the starched white apron over, and between her outstretched legs, ending in white socks and Mary Janes, an open book. It was all exactly as I had pictured it—down to the downward glance of her painted-on eyes.

I opened it slowly and began to read the story of a little doll named Edith who "lived in a nice house and had everything she needed except somebody to play with." I studied the photographic illustrations of Edith, eating her cereal "all by herself," wishing for company, and at night kneeling by her bed praying for friends. Even the pigeons she feeds on her terrace fly away as she begs them to stay and talk to her.

One morning, two teddy bears appear on the terrace. They tell her they've come to be her friends. Edith isn't lonely anymore as the bears move in, providing a home life and taking her on wondrous adventures around New York City and to the beach.

Then one rainy day, Mr. Bear, umbrella in paw, sets off on an undisclosed errand, leaving Edith and Little Bear on their own with only an admonition to stay out of trouble. Edith despairs, wondering how they will find a way to entertain themselves. "There's nothing for us to play indoors," she grumbles. Little Bear suggests they explore the house. Soon they discover, behind a set of louvered doors, a glamorous dressing room with a vanity table and a big round mirror. While Edith considers her reflection, Little Bear comes upon a woman's closet, filled with an enticing array of clothing, shoes, and accessories.

A frenzied dress-up session follows. Little Bear adorns himself with rhinestones and pearls; Edith dons a ruffled petticoat, a hat with roses and ribbons, and high-heeled shoes, but passes on the leopard handbag. In their excitement, they knock over a vase with one long-stemmed rose. The water spills into the jewelry box, but they are oblivious.

Wielding a lipstick, which he has helpfully swiveled out, the mischievous Little Bear goads Edith to try it on. She says she wouldn't dare. "You know what Mr. Bear would say." With that, he uses the lipstick to scrawl "Mr. Bear is just a silly old thing" across the mirror, when whose reflection should appear in the mirror . . . ? Spankings ensue—the lipstick is what really gets him—but Edith fears the worst is yet to come, that their bad behavior has jeopardized the whole arrangement. When the little ones clean up the mess and promise to be good, however, Mr. Bear gives his word that he and Little Bear will stay with her "forever and ever."

Yes, I now recalled the spanking scene, but it had been the dressing up that thrilled me most. I was surprised to see it lasted only a few pages. As I remembered it, the scene stretched on and on. Now I realized it did so only in my childish imagination. But even for a grown-up, this book was still full of wonder. The effect of time telescoped reminded me of a movie. And the setups for each of the photographs seemed obsessive, the effort required astounding.

I could recall the long-ago sensation, an almost erotic charge, that the photographs of the grown-up appurtenances—the bottles of perfume and nail polish, the jewelry in the box—elicited. It was all so sophisticated. My own home when I was five was filled with screaming babies, diapers, and an overwhelmed mother in practical shoes; this book was proof that glamour and elegance existed out there somewhere. And I remembered how I envied the characters their autonomous afternoon. I was never left at home alone, unwatched and unsupervised.

I knew I had once found this book deeply reassuring. And I knew my imagination, helped along by the realism of the photographs, had transformed the doll into a real little girl. But the warm associations I had carried for the book did not square with my new impressions. Decades on, the book struck me as dark and a little troubling. Had I never questioned to whom this doll and this closet belonged? The woman's identity, and her absence, is never explained. It might be Edith's mother, but from all indications Edith has no mother. And if she is a doll, where is the little girl who owns her, and where is the little girl's mother, whose closet this might be? The doll herself was unsettling too, oddly sexy with her lacy white underpants almost always in view, even when she isn't being turned over Mr. Bear's knee.

However intriguing, my reunion with *The Lonely Doll* triggered no eureka moment. Although I mined the book carefully for clues as to why it had so suddenly and involuntarily sprung back into my consciousness, I found none. As I placed *The Lonely Doll* on my bookshelf, it was with a nagging sense that I had missed something I was meant to find. But I had spent far too much time on this project already. I had to get back to work. I consoled myself that the book would be there on the shelf, slipped in securely between Virginia Woolf and Marguerite Yourcenar, should the need to revisit it ever overtake me again.

A few days later, I received a phone call from a woman who introduced herself as Brook Ashley. My letter to Dare had been forwarded to her in California by Dare's nurse, who also looked after Dare's apartment. She explained that Dare was in a New York hospital on life support; since she was incapacitated and had no living relatives, Brook had stepped in to look after her affairs as her legal guardian. Dare, whom she said was eighty-four, had been in this condition for more than two years. Brook confirmed how difficult it was to find the book. I explained that I had finally, just days earlier, received it in the mail from a book searcher. I started to thank her for her call but she kept talking. And as she did, I reached for a pen and paper—a journalist's reflex—and took down every word.

Brook's mother, an actress, had met Dare when they both appeared in a 1930s stage production of *Pride and Prejudice*. The two became lifelong friends. Brook's father had been Dare's lawyer. Brook had known Dare for as long as she could remember.

Dare had been a great beauty, a Renaissance woman with many talents. She had been a gifted artist since childhood; Brook had watercolors Dare had done in Paris when she was thirteen. Although Dare had trained as an actress, she had been "too humble" to pursue acting. She had gone on to work as a fashion model and later became a fashion photographer. Photography had led her to the books. There were nineteen in all, ten that featured Edith and the Bears.

Dare had never married. She had been engaged, but her fiancé, a Royal Air Force pilot, was killed in the war. She had remained naive about men and the ways of the world. "She has always kept the ingenuousness of a child," Brook said. "The reason Dare was able to touch a chord in the children who read her books is that in a way Dare never grew up. She never lost a child's capacity for wonder."

It was a fragmentary accounting though quite detailed, fascinating in all that it suggested and yet still mysterious. Whether this last was solely in Brook's telling, there was no way to know. I didn't probe, I only listened.

Without expecting or even wanting it, I knew I had stumbled onto the exact thing that drove my entire professional life: a good story. I felt excited as the possibilities expanded in my mind. I might like to write about Dare, I said. Brook had mentioned her hope to have *The Lonely Doll* reissued. If that happened, I could write about the synchronicity of my search for the book with the book's second coming. I sent off a package of writing samples to her the next day.

A few weeks later, Brook called again. She was coming to New York to begin packing up Dare's apartment. Did I want to meet her?

Five days later, I stood before a stately five-story red-brick townhouse half a block from Fifth Avenue and Central Park. Letting myself into a mosaic-tiled vestibule, I scanned the building directory, which, coincidentally, included the names of two acquaintances. Once I pressed the buzzer beside "D. Wright, 4A," the inner door clicked open and, over the intercom, a voice instructed me to take the elevator to the fourth floor. I boarded a tiny elevator with a manual gate.

A light-haired woman in a flowing summer dress was waiting on the fourth-floor landing. This was Brook. She ushered me into the apartment, and as my eyes adjusted to the dark, I could make out a pullman kitchen and a woman hovering in the background. She was introduced as Winkie Donovan, Brook's childhood friend and schoolmate at the Brearley School, who had come to help with the packing.

As we stood on the threshold of the living room, I took in what looked like a stage set, half struck, on which the curtain had come down long ago. The room had two windows, but they were so coated with grime that almost no natural light could penetrate. The furnishings looked to be either disassembled or broken, and everything was covered with dust. Even the fireplace was nothing more than a mantelpiece backed against a wall. Beside it were paintings, dozens of paintings; on the opposite wall, stacked against floor-to-ceiling bookshelves, were more. The books, the paintings, the fireplace—everything looked slightly artificial, like props. The effect was somewhere between a Potemkin Village and Miss Havisham's house. Pip's line from *Great Expectations* came to mind: "It was then I began to understand that everything in the room had stopped, like the watch and the clock, a long time ago."

The paintings were portraits, almost all of which featured the same subject: a striking blonde, viewed across a span of years. Here she was a rosy-cheeked toddler; here she was, older now, with a Dutch-boy haircut, standing straight and tall in a pink taffeta party dress; here, a moody teenager with a flower in her darker hair; on to womanhood, demure in a white gown, with a laurel wreath atop long flowing blond hair or looking over her bare shoulder in a black sleeveless gown and full-length black gloves, a red shawl clutched to her hip, a come-hither look on her face—unmistakably the same person. "That's Dare," I heard Brook say. "They were all painted by her mother." This was news. Brook's initial rundown had included no mention of her mother.

Not only was Dare beautiful, she looked very like the doll Edith, down to the blond hair, the bangs, the gold hoop earrings. One painting was turned, exposing the back of the canvas, on which I noticed a handwritten inscription: "To my good and precious child, Alice Dare Wright." It was signed "Edith Stevenson Wright."

Brook had a purpose in inviting me into what was left of Dare's world. She said she would like my help, when the time came, in arranging Dare's obituary. Handing me a one-page interview with Dare from the in-house newsletter of Random House, one of her publishers, she explained that was all there was in the way of official biographical information. She also gave me two black-and-white head shots of Dare, taken, she said, when she was in her sixties. Dare's long blond hair blew around her face, which, although heavily made up, was pale and ghostlike. The photos were arresting. She was still quite beautiful and strangely untouched by time.

Two months later, Brook called to say she was planning another trip to New York. Again, she invited me to meet her at Dare's apartment; again, Winkie was with her. When I arrived, they were sorting through a trunk full of what seemed to be old costumes, opulent fairy-princess gowns, of fine materials and beautifully made. Apparently, Dare had sewn them all.

As Winkie held up each item, pinning its shoulders to her own and striking a pose, she provided a running narrative. Miss Havisham's name was mentioned as she held up what looked like a wedding dress. And when they moved on to exquisite lingerie, neatly folded, seemingly never worn, Winkie surmised, "Probably from her trousseau." She called these discoveries, rich with possibilities for speculation, "Nancy Drew moments." Had I been the detective in charge, my greater curiosity would have been to find Edith and the Bears and the louvered doors leading to the Lonely Doll's dressing room. There was no such room in this apartment, but I did spot a dressing table in Dare's bedroom. On it was a lazy Susan with a framed photograph of a man, two pots of a makeup popular in the 1960s, a tiny doll and teddy bear inside a bell jar, and an unopened bottle of Joy perfume.

That day, Brook gave me a 12-by-15-inch green leather-bound scrapbook containing mementos from Dare's publishing career:

reviews and correspondence relating to the first twelve books and their jackets. I had never known of any books beyond *The Lonely Doll*; combing through the scrapbook I was struck by this record of accomplishment.

I was summoned for a third visit six weeks later. Brook had called from California to say that some things had been put aside for me, and I could pick them up at Dare's apartment.

I found the front door open and Winkie standing in a sea of boxes, waiting for the moving men to arrive. Most of "my" things were already packed, in boxes and in two battered suitcases bearing "DW" monograms and customs stickers, curling from age but still brightly hued, from places all over the world. On the couch were manila folders with "Jean?" scrawled across them, which Winkie now tossed in a shopping bag. She offered to help carry the load downstairs and into a taxi. We piled the boxes and the shopping bags on the front and back seats. As the driver hoisted the well-traveled suitcases into the trunk, I thought how odd it was that they would be making their last journey with a stranger.

Back at my apartment, day faded into night as I unpacked my treasures on the living room floor. It was light again when I had finished going through it all, paging through books that had belonged to Dare as a child, reading yellowed notes tucked inside as they fluttered out, deciphering her scribbles in the margins, skimming the books that she had grown up to write, poring over mock-ups of the works in progress. I noted that what appeared to be an earlier version of *The Lonely Doll*—it was no more than just the dressing-up scene—was titled "Spring Fever."

But most enticing were the photographs, hundreds of 11½-by-16-inch black-and-white prints. Sifting through this trove, I found an astounding visual record of a life, as if illustrations to an autobiography. But the text was missing. Lacking dates and identifications, these beautiful but mute images seemed pieces of an immense and mysterious puzzle awaiting assembly. There were photographs of a woman I assumed to be Dare's mother, photographs of a dark-haired man, and of a fair-haired man, sometimes in uniform, one of whom I surmised must be Dare's true love, the RAF pilot.

The majority were pictures of Dare. From her modeling days there were modeling cards, including a selection of shots of Dare in various looks and outfits, a list of her measurements, and her hourly rate. From the fashion photography days, there were behind-the-scenes shots of Dare photographing models. And from the period in which she focused on the books, there were pictures of her photographing the doll and the teddy bears. In one, her subjects sit in a rowboat, while Dare, camera poised, crouches down by the water's edge in a glamorous black velvet maillot.

There were magnificent photographs of what looked like Dare playing dress-up, in elaborate costumes, some of which I recognized from the trunk. But the most startling images were the ones depicting Dare playing, across a spectrum of ages, what could be described as "undress": posing naked or partially so. Posing, always posing, but for whom?

It was to the characters that had peopled Dare's world that I turned to unravel the mysteries. I began with a phone call to one of Dare's neighbors, an opera singer whose name I had recognized on the building directory, a woman I had once met. She suggested I call Dare's nurse, Christine Corneille, who cleaned her apartment from time to time to bring in extra money. In 1987, Dare had been hospitalized after an accident. When she was discharged, Brook had hired Christine, a nurse's aide newly arrived in New York from the island of St. Lucia. Dare was Christine's first assignment. The job was to have lasted three weeks but had continued, in some capacity, into the present.

Christine was thrilled when I divulged the reason for my call. She said Dare was lonely and would love to have a visitor. We agreed to meet at the hospital a few days later. The best way to get to Goldwater Hospital on Roosevelt Island, she informed me, was to take the tram, a gondola that traverses the 3,100 feet from 59th

Street in Manhattan to the island in the middle of the East River. On that November day, a cold wind was blowing off the water as I disembarked and followed a winding road up a hill to the hospital.

Christine waited for me in the front lobby. She was wearing a soft purple sweater and a cotton flowered print skirt and smiling broadly. Beckoning me to sit beside her on a couch, she was as sunny and warm as the afternoon was bleak and chill, cheerful even in such grim surroundings.

As Christine led the way through Goldwater's labyrinthine hallways, we dodged amputees in wheelchairs and howling patients being pushed on gurneys. This public hospital for indigent patients had in no way been sanitized for visitors. So few of the patients even had any. It was like a warehouse of the forgotten.

We stopped at a ward on the the third floor. From its doorway, I took in four beds and their occupants, all on life-support machinery. There was a terrible silence, punctuated only by the hum of electricity and intermittent alarms. In the bed closest to the doorway, tucked in tightly, was Dare. Her expression was blank and her head, propped up on pillows, looked waxen; she was hooked up to an intricate network of tubes. The resemblance to Edith was unmistakable, but this was the horror-story version, a gold hoop earring in one ear, the other missing, the high ponytail gathered to one side in a long yellowing white braid. Still, despite all this, she retained a fragile beauty. And somehow, despite the maze of tubes, Christine had managed to wedge a teddy bear in the crook of each arm. Even though it was evident that she was sleeping, one eye remained tantalizingly open. Christine called it her "camera eye." As I turned away, my gaze lit on the bedside table. Resting on it was a copy of *The Lonely Doll*.

I had brought along two of her photographs. In one she was accompanied by a dark-haired man, whom Christine identified as her brother. In the other, she was with the RAF pilot. At Christine's urging, when Dare woke up, I held the photographs before her. She looked at them, smiled, and closed her eye. A few moments later, I noticed a tear, a crocodile tear as it is called in children's books, coursing slowly down her cheek.

I decided to try reading to her from *The Lonely Doll*. Holding up the book so that she could see the photographs, I began. What she actually registered or recognized of her own words and images was impossible to know, but her face broke into a wide smile.

Over the next four years, I would cross the river to Goldwater many times, bearing photographs, books, flowers—and tales, with which I regaled her, of my talks with and visits to those whom she had known. As I collected their remembrances, I was filling up note-book after notebook.

The Lonely Doll had fallen out of print in 1991. Six months after my first visit to Dare's apartment, I learned of the book's planned re-issue by Houghton Mifflin. Anita Silvey, the editor who brought this about, first discovered the book when she served as editor of *Children's Books and Their Creators*, an 800-page compendium that Houghton Mifflin published in 1995. She had polled hundreds of people to decide which twentieth-century children's books, authors, and illustrators to include. Although she hadn't been familiar with *The Lonely Doll* when she began, she soon found, she said, that "inevitably, *The Lonely Doll* would be one of the books at the top of their list. It seemed to be a book that entered into the conscious-nesses of the children who read it in a particularly strong way."

Convinced that the title should be included in her compendium, she assigned a biographical entry on Dare Wright. The writer came up empty. Not long after, Silvey was named publisher of children's books at Houghton Mifflin. Her first order of business was to bring *The Lonely Doll* back into print.

By September 1998, many former readers were revisiting the book. References to it sprang up on the Internet. These self-appointed critics seemed to find the book more troubling than they had remembered. One posting on Amazon.com, headed "Hello, Freud," declared: "This is not a children's book. . . . This is an autobiographical therapeutic photomontage which is deeply disturbing. A must-read for all those who wish to understand how and why people punish children through deep psychological manipulation." At the time, such analysis struck me as unfounded as the bookstore clerk's objection to the book on the grounds of its political incorrectness. I felt protective of this touchstone of my childhood, even if I myself was finding signs that the world of the book and its author might be far darker than I anticipated.

By buying the paperback copy of *The Lonely Doll*, I had missed the author photograph and the jacket copy on the hardcover version. In that photograph, Dare appears enviably glamorous, dazzlingly beautiful, and intensely self-possessed. Resting a Rolleiflex camera on an outstretched leg, holding it steady with long manicured fingers, she sits on a ledge peering down into the camera's viewfinder. She wears blue jeans and a white turtleneck. Like Edith's, her long blond hair is tied up into a high ponytail.

The biography beneath the photograph reports that Dare was born in Canada, raised in the United States, and lives in New York. She began her career as a fashion model and "then went around to the other side of the camera" and had been a successful freelance photographer ever since. It goes on to explain that Edith was her doll from childhood and describes Edith's happy ending, ". . . she was a lonely doll until a few years ago when Miss Wright helped her brother to choose a bear for a small friend. They came home with two bears, and Edith looked so happy with them that Miss Wright kept Little Bear. After a good deal of shopping for an animal with the right expression, her brother found Mr. Bear, and the family was complete. Out came Miss Wright's camera, and the book began."

If this rendition was true, and if the reviewers of *The Lonely Doll* whose work I found in the scrapbook were correct in saying, as many did, that in her book, Dare Wright had "recaptured her happy childhood," where did this disturbing book come from?

As in all good children's stories, Dare had eliminated a mother from the proceedings. There was no way to know then what a profound achievement this had been for her. Or how miraculous it was that her brother should come to buy her a bear. Or that the book was a restaging of her childhood's traumas.

When *The Lonely Doll* floated back up into my consciousness, my only intention had been to find the book. Along the way, my mission became to rescue Dare Wright—who once told an interviewer that her idea of the "greatest luxury was to go out leaving all the electric lights burning"—from the dark.

Dare, I was to discover, had lived in her own version of Wonderland. As I followed the trail, trying to reconstruct and then make sense of the world I had stumbled into, I thought of those Japanese paper nuggets, compressed and flat, that expand and assume forms when steeped in water, the ones Proust wrote of in *Remembrance of Things Past*, the ones I played with as a child. Before my eyes, a life was taking shape. Dare Wright had once told me the story of Edith and the bears. Now she was telling me another story. I just had to write it down.

CHAPTER ONE

Beginnings

To be born is to be wrecked on an island.
—J. M. BARRIE, from the preface
to R.M. BALLANTYNE's *The Coral Island*

The sole autobiographical record Dare Wright
left behind is concealed in her photographs and in
the nineteen books she wrote and illustrated for
children. She kept no diary, wrote few letters, and
spoke of her past in only the most selective terms.
Musing on Dare's origins, a woman who worked
with her in the 1950s, when Dare was a photographer for *Good Housekeeping* magazine, remarked, "I
have no sense of what came before. Maybe Dare was
born in a seashell."

Based on so many of her photographic self-
portraits, Dare too viewed herself as a sort of sea
creature, but one trapped—whether caught in a net,
twisted up in driftwood, or tangled in the remains of
a shipwreck. In some, she appears to be a mermaid,
posed as if washed up on a beach by a stormy sea,

abandoned, left for dead. Her naked body lies partially draped in seaweed, conch shells are caught up in her long blond hair, and bluish scallop shells cover her eyes.

While the woman she became inspired romantic notions of her origins, there was no seashell birth, not even metaphorically, no Venus-like floating to land on a gentle breeze. Rather, she was born in a storm, the kind that separates the branches from the tree, like the driftwood in which she photographed herself enmeshed or, in her family's case, the kind that separates parents from children and from each other. The storm had been gathering even before Dare's birth in 1914. Beset by financial troubles, mismatched and disillusioned with one another after four years of marriage, her parents' relationship had all but capsized. Her father, Ivan Leonard Wright, once a promising actor and later a drama critic, was stumbling professionally and had retreated into alcohol. Her mother, Edith Stevenson Wright, a talented portrait painter, swung between efforts to rescue her family financially and her own retreats into fantasy.

Edith, almost always known as Edie, was born in 1883 in Youngstown, Ohio, the first child of Samuel Henry Stevenson, a steelworker, who had come to this country from England as a young boy. He met Alice Madolia Gaither as she waited on line in his father's butcher store, sent in by her mother to do her family's shopping.

As Sam and Alice Madolia shuttled between Youngstown and Toronto, Canada, following work opportunities for Sam, two more children were born. By now, their first-born's extraordinary artistic gifts had caught her parents' attention. Edie recalled her "almost hypnotic fascination," even as a young child, with the human face. She told a story of becoming so fixated on the beautiful features of a playmate that she collided with a tree and skinned her own face. This fascination found expression in a preternatural drawing facility, an ability to reproduce in drawing almost anything she encountered. Although Edie took pride in her gifts and basked in the praise they elicited, she was also conscious that what made her special made her different, setting her apart from her peers and arousing resentment and jealousy in her younger sister and brother.

In 1896, when Edie turned thirteen, her parents enrolled her in the Central Ontario School of Art and Design in Toronto. When her family returned to Youngstown in 1900, Edie stayed behind in Toronto to begin an apprenticeship to J. W. L. Forster, a well-known Canadian portrait painter.

Edie reveled in the life of Forster's studio, the proximity it provided to the wealthy, high-born friends and patrons of her mentor. She had grown ashamed of her humble origins, of her father's lowly work as a manual laborer, and of her pretty but ambitionless mother's union with an immigrant butcher's son. Edie was far prouder than her mother of Alice Madolia's more distinguished lineage. Her English forebears were among the country's first settlers, arriving in the Jamestown Colony in Virginia in 1620. When the Gaithers later settled in Anne Arundel County, Maryland, they gave their name to Gaithersburg, Maryland.

Two years into Edie's apprenticeship, Forster painted his nineteen-year-old student, a beguiling and self-possessed beauty, her hair a mass of auburn curls with golden glints. Edie's looks and stylishness were attracting attention in Toronto society as well. A December 1902 social column in the *Toronto Globe* took notice of "Miss Edith Stevenson, the pretty 'belle of the ball,' in white satin Empire gown with sash of pale blue satin, her fair curly hair being dressed to complete a charming effect" at a dinner dance. So did an up-and-coming twenty-three-year-old actor, Ivan Wright, among the three hundred guests that evening. As he slipped into a seat beside her at the candlelit table, Edie was as transfixed by Ivan's beauty—his handsome face, his softly chiseled, almost feminine features—as he was by hers. Having recently fallen in a bicycle race and injured his hip, Ivan had been forced to take time out from his thriving acting career and, on this evening, to sit out the after-dinner dancing. But his gaze never left the ball's belle.

Ivan, also a first child, had been Emelene Mallory Wright's

Edie in her teens, circa 1896, as an art student at the
Central Ontario School of Art and Design in Toronto.

consolation when her second child, Irene Dare, died of "congestion of the brain" at the age of ten months. Ivan would remain Emelene's favorite, even after two more sons were born. Although coddled and indulged, he chafed at his mother's overprotectiveness. In marriage, he saw an escape; in Edie, he saw a dreamy free spirit whose talent matched his own. Always impatient and impulsive, he felt they should marry as soon as Edie's apprenticeship was over. Edie, more practical, thought they should wait until they had both become more established professionally, especially as Forster was encouraging her to continue her studies in Europe. And, too, Ivan's future was uncertain. His hip injury was not healing properly. By 1903, unable to walk without limping, he realized he would have to find a more sedentary profession than acting. Having written stories and poems since childhood, he began his reinvention as a literary man, casting himself as a drama critic, the best way to bridge his interest in the theater in view of his physical limitations. In a burst of ambition, following a successful debut in various Toronto newspapers, he decided to head to New York to ply his trade. Edie could join him there after her European studies. Preparing for their separation, Edie painted Ivan's portrait to remember him by and gave him her self-portrait so he could do the same.

Ivan did go to New York, but Edie's plan to study in Europe was derailed by her father's death in a gruesome steel mill accident. Sam Stevenson's obituary, December 25, 1903, in *The* (Youngstown) *Vindicator* reported that the forty-one-year-old was "fatally crushed" after catching his sleeve in a steel rolling machine. It omitted the detail that he was also decapitated.

Sam left $225 in savings and an equal amount in debts. Alice Madolia decided her daughter's portrait painting was the only hope for the family's financial future. She insisted that Edie, who had just turned twenty-one, return to Youngstown. Edie made no secret of her bitterness at missing the chance to study in Europe. But however resentful she felt, she proved practical and industrious. To advertise her talents, she asked a downtown pharmacy if she could place a pastel portrait of her sister, Algeo, in their window. It quickly drew in her first customer, the owner of the steel plant where her father had worked, who commissioned her to paint a posthumous portrait of a friend from a photograph. Her patron pronounced the portrait a triumph and spread word of Edie's talents. She was soon supporting her family by painting Youngstown's "Princes of Steel," as she called them: wealthy industrialists, their families, and friends.

Patrons offered to underwrite her European studies, but Edie always demurred, feeling a sense of responsibility to her family. A later newspaper article described this period: "Edith Stevenson had her job cut out for her—to support her mother. Not for her Paris or Rome, vie de bohème, and the companionship of other aspiring artists. For her—hard work in Youngstown."

If Edie was meeting her responsibilities, Ivan was in free fall. When drinking failed to anesthetize the chronic pain in his hip, he finally sought medical attention. The doctor ordered an operation to remove a part of his femur that had become tubercular. His father insisted he return home for the surgery. He left New York for Toronto in 1906.

Confined to bed for a yearlong convalescence at his parents' home, out of which his father ran a pharmacy and his mother a boardinghouse, Ivan whiled away the hours drinking, writing poetry—and being fussed over by his mother, his Auntie Mer, and Lady Letty Blaine, a wealthy and much older Englishwoman lodging at the Wrights' who had succumbed to Ivan's considerable charms. Despite these feminine attentions, Edie, whose self-portrait he hung in view of his bed, remained uppermost in his thoughts. He fired off love letters and poems, one of which, "The Want of You," became his first to be published, appearing in a 1906 issue of the *Toronto Mail and Empire*. A lamentation in Ivan's typically overblown poetic voice, he describes himself as "Mad with demand and aching with despair" at his "want of" Edie.

In spite of Ivan's entreaties to return to Canada, Edie had

accepted a patron's offer to send her to New York. An introduction to an art dealer led to a solo exhibition at the William Schaus Gallery at 415 Fifth Avenue. She remained in New York for two years to carry out commissions and to take classes with Kenyon Cox at the Art Students League. Edie's mother, who had accompanied her elder daughter, stayed on as her chaperone, knitting in a rocking chair in the corner of Edie's 57th Street studio to discourage her sometimes lecherous patrons' advances, and, as was explained to Algeo, "to do all the mundane things, so Edie is free to paint." Algeo, who had married in 1905, was jealous of this arrangement; she felt her mother belonged in Toronto to help her with her growing family.

Ivan, too, was becoming increasingly impatient with Edie's extended stay in New York. Fretting that she might slip away, he enlisted his aunt to write to Edie at the beginning of 1907. She did so, saying, "I do think my dear Baby is the most fortunate being to be able to claim such a treasure as you. I think tonight he was almost overcome, he loves you so dearly, he worships you madly. . . . Dear Edith, you are getting a treasure in my dear spoiled Baby."

This was soon followed by Ivan's own entreaty, a poem he called "An Appeal of Spring," which was published in the April 1907 issue of *Canadian Magazine*. Its four stanzas appeal to a fairy princess for answers to nature's mysteries and ends with the questions:

Will you tell me, brown-eyed dreamer,
All the things I wish to know;
Why in summer all is sunshine,
And in winter all is snow?
Will you tell me, too, my Princess,
That you'll wear this symbol ring,
Violets with it entwining—
First sweet certainties of spring?

Ivan's fairy princess did agree to marry, but it wasn't the poem that seduced her. It was Ivan's clear promise that he would provide for her as her father had not, beginning with an extended honeymoon in Europe. After their marriage, he assured her that she would no longer have to paint for money but could pursue her art for art's sake.

For a time, Ivan immersed himself in preparations for his future role of husband and provider. Although the surgery rendered him, in Edie's later description, "quite lame"—he would limp and require a cane for the rest of his life—as soon as he was ambulatory he bought, with financial help from Lady Blaine, a falling-down house on the Kings Highway in Thornhill, a village outside Toronto, and began its renovation. He also secured a steady job as editor of *The Toronto Star Weekly*'s theater pages.

All that was needed now was the bride, but a career opportunity for Edie once again intruded and the wedding was postponed. The city of Youngstown had offered her a $10,000 commission for portraits of the judges of the Mahoning County Bar, past and present, to be hung in the city's new $4 million courthouse. In April 1909, Edie arrived in Youngstown to paint the living judges. The posthumous portraits could be painted from photographs in Thornhill, near Ivan, who had already lost *The Toronto Star Weekly* job with which he had planned to support his wife-to-be.

At the end of October 1910, Edie's eleven portraits were hung in the courthouse rotunda under a quotation etched in stone from Abraham Lincoln's speech at Cooper Union, "Let us have faith that right makes might, and in that faith let us to the end dare to do our duty as we understand it." Six weeks later, Edie and Ivan were married in Toronto's All Saints Church in an evening wedding described as "brilliant" by *The Vindicator*. The guests marveled at Edie's exquisite wedding dress, a crystal-embroidered gown over Chantilly lace and marquisette and a silk tulle veil hemmed with seed pearls, and at the sophistication of her traveling costume for the three-day honeymoon to New York: a suit trimmed in white fox and a cloth turban trimmed in beaver and osprey feathers. No

The studio photographs that accompanied the newspaper
announcement of Edie and Ivan's engagement, 1910.

one imagined that Edie, with her mother's help, had sewn it all. The dinner that Edie's mother gave after the church service was paid for out of Edie's savings. Ivan contributed plain gold cuff links, engraved *W-S*, which he gave to his best man and his three ushers.

Although the couple planned to settle in Thornhill after a year-long trip abroad, they never made it overseas. The responsibilities thrust upon Edie by her father's death and her subsequent professional successes had turned her into a pragmatic and ambitious woman, leaving Ivan to wonder what had become of his "brown-eyed dreamer." And her edges did not soften in the bedroom. Edie's attraction to her husband was evidently more aesthetic than physical. It took weeks to consummate the marriage, which did nothing to increase Edie's fondness for what she called "the messy mechanisms of coupling." In this respect, Ivan accommodated her by taking a series of jobs out of town. In the first year of their marriage, he was gone as much as he was home. In the second, during which he worked for an Ottawa newspaper, he was away steadily, except for one visit to Thornhill, during which a child was conceived. By April 1912, Ivan was managing a stock theater company in Ottawa and absent for the birth that month of Victor Blaine Wright— named for Ivan's middle brother, Victor Clair, who had died the year before at the age of twenty-eight, and Lady Blaine. He did, however, pen a long poem expressing the "joy" he felt at the arrival of his "bouncing baby boy." It was the last poem he ever wrote.

This could not have been the picture of marriage that Edie had envisioned. Not only was she forced to continue painting for money, she was also saddled alone with a small child while her absent husband went through jobs—and alcohol—at an alarming rate. Even the promise of Ivan's looks had not held up. He was hardly recognizable when he arrived home for a short visit to meet his son, his body bloated and his face puffy from drinking. For a time, the physical handicaps that left him struggling to stand up to Edie creatively and financially had inspired him to strive harder. By this juncture, however, he seemed no longer to care.

The more dismal the reality, the harder Edie worked to block it out. If the picture was far from ideal, there was nothing to stop her from painting it otherwise. Edie constructed an elaborate "Mother Stork's Baby Book," assiduously chronicling Blaine's development. Whenever Ivan returned home again, he could see all he had missed: baby's first bottle, baby's first bathtub bath, baby's first step, even regular cuttings of Blaine's curly brown locks, which she sewed onto its pages with blue ribbon.

Now it was Edie's turn to worry that Ivan was slipping away. And just as he had tried to woo her back from New York with flowery poems during their courtship, she sent him alluring photographs of herself in glamorous getups: a cloche hat, pearls, a fur-trimmed coat opened to expose a breast on which her lace-gowned baby nursed. While Edie might be indomitably pragmatic and strong, she also had a tendency to retreat into fantasy. But the role of wife or mother requires more than dressing up and posing. Dressing a child in exquisite clothes, all of which she sewed herself, did nothing to ensure that his emotional needs were met. Other than these photo opportunities with his mother, Blaine spent most of his time shunted off to the nurse Algeo had hired to help care for her own children. As the wife of a successful dental surgeon, Algeo could afford such luxuries.

In the spring of 1913, jobless again and no longer able to afford the cheap hotel room in which he had been living, Ivan did return to Thornhill. The welcome was not warm; Edie realized it was his desperate straits—not her charms—that had brought her husband back. As alcohol had once fueled Ivan's poetry, it now fueled unreal dreams of quick financial fixes that, like a mirage in the desert, only he could see. Still confident of his seducer's charm, he pursued these schemes. If he couldn't support his family, perhaps his exquisite sixteen-month-old son could. And so he carted Blaine off to New York, using money Edie had earned painting portraits, to make the rounds of his friends in the movie business, contacts he had made during his stint as a theater critic there. From New York, he wrote to Edie that Fox Pictures intended to sign Blaine. Nothing ever came of this or of his next scheme: his reinvention as a gentleman farmer. Toward this end, he roped his two brothers-in-law, Algeo's husband, Ted Zinkan, and Edie's brother, Fred Stevenson, into a partnership to buy a 150-acre farm on Yonge (pronounced *young*) Street. Zinkan, the only partner with ready cash, would put down the first year's payment, although it would serve only as a sometime country retreat for his family. Zinkan would leave its management and the livelihood it would generate to Ivan and Fred. By January 1915, when it would be Ivan's turn to put down that year's payment, he assumed his share of the income from the farm would cover it.

For a time, Ivan seemed back on his feet. In January 1914, Edie, Ivan, and Blaine moved to the Thornhill farm. That March, Edie became pregnant again. Later that spring, the Wrights made a trip to Youngstown to visit Edie's prosperous Uncle Charlie Gaither, the inventor of an early car and now Youngstown's first car dealer, and to see his grand new mansion, Craftstone, on 150 acres in Boardman, just outside of town. No one had a home like it, with its rustic fieldstone exterior, oak woodwork interior, and state-of-the-art features, a central vacuum system, and a built-in refrigerator with icemaker, run electrically by a motor in the basement. Charlie, his new wife, Clyde, his daughter Maude, and Edie's grandparents all posed on the front-porch steps with Edie and Ivan for a family photograph. Edie, glowing, sports a maternity dress of her own design with laces on the side designed to be let out as her belly grew. Tenderly, she holds Maude's hand in hers. Ivan, playing the role of good husband and proud father-to-be for his in-laws, sits back in his chair above his wife with his arms around Edie's grandmother and grandfather. He appears to be on top of the world.

But back in Thornhill that summer, things hit bottom. Ivan was feuding with his brothers-in-law, who foresaw that he would never have the means to make his $5,000 payment. Realizing that he had miscalculated the amount of time it would take for the farm to become profitable, Ivan wrote in desperation to Lady Blaine, since returned to England, asking for a loan. While Edie let out her laces, Ivan became increasingly frantic as he waited for the money to arrive.

Alice Dare Wright, named for Edie's mother and Ivan's sister who had died in infancy, was born on December 3, 1914. Any joy in their second child's birth was overshadowed by their financial straits. Lady Blaine's money had not materialized. And if Ivan expected Ted Zinkan to bail him out, he had miscalculated there as well. Forced to take over or lose the farm altogether, Zinkan decided to keep the farm. But in order to do so, he had to sell his family's home in Toronto. Furious with Ivan, he ordered the Wrights to leave. Edie, still in her confinement, let Ivan do their bidding. But she, too, was furious. She had sacrificed study in Europe to support her brother and sister when they were in need, and now that she was, they had failed to come to her rescue. She never completely forgave Fred, and her relationship with her sister, intensely rivalrous always, took one step closer to its eventual breaking point. When Ivan heard of a job managing a newly opened theater in the town of Medford, Massachusetts, just north of Boston, they moved within a few weeks.

The first years of Dare's life involved constant moves and an often-absent mother. Edie's attempts to keep the family together financially necessitated long separations. Sometimes she took one of the children with her, but on most of the 1915–1916 trips to Youngstown and Toronto, where portraits by Edith Stevenson Wright were in demand, she left both children with Ivan.

On one 1916 trip to Youngstown, she took the four-year-old Blaine along, thinking to introduce her son to past patrons as an excuse to solicit work. To Blaine's relief, the plan achieved its end quickly, as he soon tired of being trotted around to the homes of wealthy Youngstowners and admired in the black velvet Little Lord Fauntleroy suit his mother had sewn for the occasion. While she carried out the ensuing commissions, Edie left Blaine in the care of her aunt, Daisy Whiteside, and her husband, James, with whom they were staying. The Whitesides were aghast at Blaine's bad behavior. Their daughter, Alice Pearl, known as Allie, recalled him "racing madly around, never still," brooding and pouting when a grown-up would attempt to mete out discipline. One Sunday, James Whiteside was driven to the limit when Blaine, inspired by a *Katzenjammer Kids* comic strip Allie had read to him, persisted in head-butting the newspaper Whiteside was trying to read, in imitation of the goat in the comic. Allie was stunned to witness her usually placid father scream at Edie, "Can't you discipline this boy?" Edie did have a problem with discipline; she seemed to view her children as inanimate creations and acted confounded when they behaved like real-life children or needed attention. When they exhibited distress, she observed them coolly. On a visit to her sister in Toronto, Edie came across Dare, parked in a baby carriage, alone and bawling. Instead of attending to her baby, she snapped photos with her Brownie camera, later captioning one: "Crying. Isn't she sweet?"

On her next trip, Edie left both children behind with Ivan in Milford, Massachusetts, where they had moved when Ivan lost his job in Medford. Through a wealthy sculptor she had known in New York, Edie had found Ivan a job as caretaker in exchange for a house in which they could live. Edie returned home a month later to find the house a pile of charred remains and Ivan and the children living with neighbors. All of Edie's paintings there, the ones she had kept for herself, were destroyed in the fire. Although the local newspapers reported the cause as an overheated furnace, Edie told her aunt she believed Ivan was drinking and smoking in bed.

Seeking, as always, to present a better public picture than the true one, Edie took the children to a photography studio to sit for a portrait, carefully selecting the clothes for the occasion: for herself a voluminous white chiffon dressing gown, trimmed with satin and marabou feathers at neckline and cuffs; Blaine in a sailor suit; Dare in a smocked dress over a lace petticoat.

Studio photograph of Blaine, Dare, and Edith Stevenson Wright, Milford, Massachusetts, early 1917.

Dare and Blaine on Long Island Sound just before the Wright family was separated, summer 1917.

In April 1917, pronouncing himself fed up with the provinces, Ivan decided they were moving to New York City. The closest they managed was Huntington, Long Island, 32 miles away, where Ivan's Auntie Mer was now living and could provide a free place to stay. Ivan's stabs at finding newspaper work in the city proved fruitless, and in four months Edie came up with only one portrait commission. Soon their credit was no longer good. When Ivan was offered the editorship of the newspaper back in Milford, Edie implored him to take the job. Writing of this period years later, she recalled, "He refused, saying it was too small for his talents, that New York was the place for him. I begged—said we could live without everything, or anything just so we could stay together. He brushed it aside and said I should go visit my sister until he found the New York job." In fact, as soon as he had shipped her and the children off to Thornhill, Ivan decamped, taking the Milford newspaper job after all. He planned to work just long enough to bring in some money to finance a move—on his own—to New York City.

When Edie and her children appeared on their doorstep, the Zinkans were quite prepared to turn them out. They had not forgiven Ivan for defaulting on his farm payment. Edie's mother, now living with them, intervened, insisting they be allowed to stay. Still, tensions ran high. The Zinkans berated Edie, making much of Ivan's continued pattern of irresponsibility and inability to provide for his family. Edie later wrote of the "intense" humiliation she felt at throwing herself on their mercy with two children in tow.

Determined to bring in some money to contribute to the household, Edie loaded up on commissions. In free moments, she painted portraits of the Zinkans' two children, an attempt to please her hosts. And always, she managed to keep up a picture-perfect exterior. A Toronto newspaper arts columnist took note of the "young and lovely . . . wife of Ivan L. Wright, the litterateur" sketching out of doors, "a sunny-headed baby for her subject." Although Ivan was still her husband, nominally at least, their only contact that year was an envelope he sent without a return address. It contained a $5 bill.

Two months into their stay, Algeo decided that Edie wasn't limiting her charms to journalists. Convinced that her sister was trying to steal her husband, she accused Edie of writing love letters to Ted Zinkan and ordered her to leave.

Seemingly deserted by her husband, ousted from her sister's home, Edie had no place to go but Youngstown. But as Blaine, now five, had not been well received on the earlier visit to the Whitesides, Edie asked if she could leave him with her mother at the Zinkans. Algeo would agree only if Alice Madolia promised to take full charge of the young boy. Her mother, caught between feuding daughters, agreed.

In later letters to Blaine, Edie steadfastly maintained, "These times mean nothing to you because you don't remember much." In fact, they could not have meant more. The scenes—tantrums thrown in his desperation to be taken with his mother and adored sister, which intensified as the morning of Edie and Dare's departure arrived—were forever etched in his memory.

Soon after Edie and Dare left, Alice Madolia fell ill. Adamant in her refusal to care for Ivan and Edie's son, Algeo shipped Blaine off to Ivan's mother, Emelene. Unable to contend with her grandson's obstreperousness, Emelene ordered Ivan to come to Canada to retrieve him. Ivan, preparing to leave Milford for New York, had no choice but to take Blaine with him.

Ivan had found a position as a copy editor on the *New York Tribune*. His night-shift job provided a solution of sorts to the babysitting problem. He would bathe and put Blaine to bed in their boardinghouse room before leaving for work. By morning, when Blaine awoke, Ivan was back home. No provisions were made if Blaine were to need anything in his absence. And in the daytime while Ivan slept, Blaine had to learn to entertain himself quietly or risk his father's wrath. All the while, Edie assumed Blaine was still in Canada with Ivan's mother.

When Edie and Dare arrived in Youngstown, in September 1917, it was arranged that Edie's Uncle Charlie Gaither, rather than the Whitesides, would take them in. There was more room at Craftstone, which had become an even more magical setting since Edie's visit with Ivan. The grounds had been landscaped to include a lily pond fed by an artesian spring, gardens and orchards had come in, and a working farm, with a full complement of farm animals, had been added. Charlie fit the rescuer bill; he was a generous and welcoming host. But his childless second wife, Clyde, as plain and down-to-earth as Edie was not, disliked her husband's niece and was no fonder of her daughter. In the summer of 1918, sensing they had worn out their welcome, Edie decided she and Dare would move to the Whitesides.

The Whiteside home was less grand but the atmosphere was more salubrious. As soon as they moved in, Edie painted a portrait of their daughter, Allie, then twelve, as a gesture of her gratitude. Allie, who would later become a teacher and writer, was in awe of her cousin Edie, twenty-two years her senior. She wrote of how thrilled she had been at Edie's discovery that the red dye that rubbed off the crepe paper they were using for Christmas decorations made the perfect rouge. She was equally fascinated with Edie's cosmetics bag, hung out of arm's reach in the bathroom. "She must have felt that I would be overwhelmed with the temptation to know what was in it," Allie later wrote, "and she told me in a stern, firm tone, 'If you touch my bag, a little red devil will jump out and bite you.' I never did touch it, though the sight of a little red devil was rather tempting, but her really cross look held me back. I loved her so much and I wanted to please her by being good."

When she was off painting, Edie left Daisy and Allie to care for her daughter. On November 11, 1918, Allie took Dare, three weeks shy of her fourth birthday, out for a walk in Youngstown. An ordinary errand—"Mother handed me a little list and a coin purse, adding, 'Take Dare with you, she needs some fresh air' "—turned memorable when "a cacophony of earsplitting noise . . . church bells, school bells, tower bells, factory whistles, even housewives on their porches ringing dinner bells" erupted around them. Her charge, "the nicest sort of little companion, always described as 'such a good child,'" with her "solemn little face, big quiet eyes, and so well-mannered that I always enjoyed taking her for walks . . . looked up very anxiously into my face for explanation and reassurance. I said, 'The war is over.'"

Edie had been through a war of her own, but hers was not over. In less than two years, she had lost her home and her sister—the two would never talk again—and been separated from her husband and her son. Her maternal grandparents had died within two weeks of each other in the spring of 1917, and two months before the Armistice, her mother had succumbed to uterine cancer at the age of fifty-seven. Shuttling between the homes of relatives, she had worn out her welcome at all but one. Edie had nothing left but her talent, her beauty—and her daughter.

One last bomb was to fall. Florence Jeanette Cobb, who had spent the war in France as an interpreter and doing work for the Red Cross, had moved into the boardinghouse at 346 West 76th Street where Ivan and Blaine were living. "Of Florence it can be said: For all 'she has a voice of gladness and a smile,'" noted her entry in Bucknell University's 1906 yearbook. "Sprightly, agile and happy, she lends a silver hue to the seeming clouds which occasionally envelop the more sombre of the choice spirits among whom she flits—surely a gladsome benediction." It was to be for Ivan. Florence was instantly charmed by her father-son neighbors. "On the other side of my room was the bath," she later wrote to Blaine. "Ivan gave you a bath every night before he went to the *Tribune*. You rebelled at his methods sometimes but always obeyed. I could hear your conversations very often and very often they were funny." Ivan had found a new "brown-eyed dreamer."

In exchange for his portrait, David Fitch Anderson, a Youngstown trial lawyer known as "the Black Hornet" of the Mahoning County Bar, agreed to handle Edie's divorce. Edie's biggest concern was that the news be concealed from her patrons. Anderson, whose law firm also had offices in Cleveland, suggested the divorce could take place more quietly there if she were willing to take up temporary residence in that city. And so it was that in February 1919, a few weeks after her thirty-sixth birthday, Edie, leaving Dare in the care of the Whitesides, boarded a train for Cleveland and checked into a room at the Hotel Griswold.

In Anderson, Edie had found an able protector. Thanks to his connections to wealthy Clevelanders, she worked steadily while there. The divorce petition, filed that April, charged Ivan with "gross neglect" of his marital duty and sought custody of Dare. No reference was made to Blaine; by default, custody of his son would go to Ivan. Edie also requested that Ivan "be restrained from in any way interfering" with herself or with Dare, over whom she would have "sole charge and control." The divorce was handed down at the end of October, granting all of Edie's stipulations.

Edie had been away for eight months, leaving Dare, not yet five, to wonder if she would ever be reclaimed. And even when Edie returned to Youngstown, two more months would pass before she retrieved Dare from the Whitesides. Unlike Clyde Gaither, their willingness to help proved unlimited. Edie moved into a boarding-house alone. Her failed marriage had struck a massive blow to her idealized sense of herself. She needed to take stock of her life and pick up the pieces. Ashamed, wanting to avoid any reminder of her black-sheep status, she could regroup best in solitude.

Edie referred to the years between her marriage in 1910 and the divorce in 1919 as "the beginning and ending of all I wanted of life." Overblown words, perhaps, but expressive, too, of the anguish she was feeling. A new Edie emerged from this period, pragmatic, as before, but hardened and even more cut off from the world that had hurt her so. If the events were not in her control, the story was. The "facts," as she disdainfully called them, humiliating as they were, needed to be disguised—or embroidered upon. As she knew from her portrait painting, facts were mutable: Strategically placed brushstrokes could make a female subject's jewels appear larger or a male subject taller.

She took to signing her paintings "Edith Stevenson," an attempt to touch up the portrait of her life, to cast it in a more acceptable light. Dare—and the matter of Dare's last name—proved a sticking point, however. The existence of a son could be left out of the story entirely, but where had the daughter come from? "Wright" went back on the paintings, "Married" or "Widowed" on the official records. With Ivan out of the picture in New York, there was little chance that she would become caught up in these lies.

Edie did confide a truer than usual version of her circumstances to one portrait subject, Emily Arms, the twenty-nine-year-old daughter of a Youngstown steel magnate. Touched by Edie's predicament, Emily invited Edie and Dare to come live with her. They spent the entire year of 1920 with Emily, the longest consecutive time Dare and Edie had spent under the same roof. But Dare's days were spent not in the care of her mother but of Emily's live-in maid or Emily herself. Dare was too young to participate in the ballet classes that Emily gave in her home, but she watched and helped Emily decorate tutus for her students' recitals.

This felicitous arrangement came to an abrupt end in December 1920 when Emily announced her engagement and her plan to leave Youngstown. Buoyed by the professional success she had enjoyed in Cleveland, Edie decided she and Dare would move there. It would be a way to leave the past, the whole unworkable story, behind.

After the separation, Ivan made no effort to stay in touch with Dare. For a time, Edie did write to Blaine, and the children exchanged presents and cards. For Christmas 1919, Blaine, then seven, sent Dare, five, a book called *Tales from the Secret Kingdom*, a collection of fairy tales interspersed with verse poems, which closed with a poem called "Good Company":

And when we part at our journey's end
And the giant is safely slain,
We'll make a vow at the wishing well
That we will meet again.

In May 1920, Blaine, a second-grader at the Collegiate School, wrote to thank his mother and sister for the Valentine cards they had sent to him. It was the last time he ever addressed Edie as *Mother*. Shortly after this, Edie learned of Ivan's intention to marry Florence. She wrote to Ivan that neither he nor Blaine should ever contact her—or Dare—again.

Ivan and Florence were married in New York on November 19, 1920. Blaine, eight, had been sent out of town to stay with friends. When he returned, Ivan picked him up at the train station. On the way home in the taxi he told his son that he had married Florence, whom he was to call "Mother" from then on. Under Ivan's strict discipline and Florence's loving tutelage, Blaine finally developed the veneer, at least, of good behavior. From that period on, he was known for his perfect manners, especially toward women.

Edie was thirty-seven when she moved with Dare to Cleveland. There was talk that she had affairs with various portrait subjects. While her good looks and coquettish behavior did reel in admirers, she rebuffed their advances. "I had opportunities to get Dare a stepfather," she later wrote, "but feared it might turn into unhappiness for her—so I remained single." More likely she was concerned that another relationship would turn into unhappiness for herself. Although she yearned to be rescued by a man, she remained terrified by the prospect of sex and intimacy. But she liked to know that she was desired. She told a story of being taken to dinner by a wealthy man just after settling in Cleveland. He had held out a handkerchief brimming with jewels, but she wouldn't take them. The inference was that she would rather struggle financially than align herself with another man—and that she was desirable.

The men Edie allowed to court her were rich, powerful, and "safe," either married or homosexual. These men were useful, and her ability to manipulate them was critical to her success and well-being. But what really interested Edie was her painting. After Ivan, she threw herself into her work, out of financial necessity, certainly, but also because she found gratification there. As a portrait painter, Edie "created" people, the same line of work, she liked to point out, as God himself. There was power in that, even if the people she created were inanimate. It was better that way. Inanimate people could not hurt you. And they could be controlled.

CHAPTER TWO

Cleveland

Once there was a little doll. Her name was Edith. She lived in a nice house and had everything she needed except somebody to play with. She was very lonely! —The Lonely Doll

Starting with the family's expulsion from the Thornhill farm when she was three weeks old, Dare had lived in a state of constant upheaval, with her caregivers changing even more frequently than her surroundings. Along the way, her father and brother had vanished. Over time, their recollection would become more and more shadowy, until she could no longer be certain whether they were real or whether she had imagined them. All she had left was her mother, and even that was an unreliable proposition. Dare had become a perfectly behaved house guest and an expert traveler, quietly entertaining herself by making up stories as she looked out train windows or sat waiting for Edie to finish an appointment.

As Edie and Dare began their new life in Cleveland, Dare felt comfort in having her mother, until then almost always out of reach, by her side. And yet she felt torn as she watched her mother close the door on the past and on the subject of the family's missing members. She pined for her father and for Blaine, but she was learning to keep those thoughts to herself for fear of rousing her mother's fury. There was so much to learn and so much at stake. Dare studied her mercurial mother's every move and every mood, waiting for cues, wanting to be directed, to know what was expected of her—and to get it right.

On the advice of her lawyer, David Anderson, Edie rented an apartment in Cleveland Heights, about a forty-five-minute streetcar ride from downtown. Building on Anderson's connections and on her own from her work for Youngstown's courthouse, Edie's first commissions in Cleveland were portraits of lawyers, judges, and politicians. The courthouse job had established her reputation for painting posthumous portraits. There was big business in "deaders," as she called them privately. Although she preferred to paint from life rather than a photograph, Edie was shrewd enough to recognize that a subject's social prominence was more important than whether or not he sat for her.

Anderson was also behind her most important career break in Cleveland. He suggested that his friend Daniel Rhodes Hanna, Sr., commission Edie to paint a posthumous portrait of his father, Marcus Alonzo Hanna, a coal and iron tycoon who had gone on to become an important player in city, state, and national politics. Mark Hanna had organized Ohio governor William McKinley's run for the presidency in 1896 and he was in his third term in the U.S. Senate when he died in 1904. His son Daniel Sr. parlayed the family fortune into a sideline newspaper empire, purchasing the *Cleveland Leader* in 1910 and, in 1912, the *Cleveland News*. The Hannas could not have been better-placed patrons. Commissioning further portraits—Edie would paint five generations of Hannas—providing entrée to their circle, ensuring she was written about in their newspapers, and giving her studio space in the monumental Hanna Building downtown, the family helped Edie's career immeasurably.

Acting as the breadwinner required no adjustment for Edie; it was a part she had played since her father's death and throughout her marriage. The adjustment to her new role as the sole caretaker of her daughter—without the help of relatives, friends, or their maids—might have been the bigger challenge, except that Edie never really took it on. As she picked up her paintbrush and directed her gaze toward her daughter, until now a blank canvas she hadn't completely considered, she saw valuable potential in what was reflected back. As perfectly behaved—and malleable—as Blaine was not, Dare could be cast as a caring helpmeet in ways that Ivan never could. Dare was prepared to give anything to secure her newfound place in her mother's orbit, even if it meant concealing her real self and her feelings. It was far more important to try to anticipate and adapt to Edie's needs, however confusing they were to navigate.

While she worked, Edie needed to be left alone, undisturbed. Sometimes she would not even speak to Dare for the entire day. But when she had washed her brushes at day's end—or, spent from her creative labors, asked Dare to do it—Edie needed replenishment and companionship. For these, she turned to her dressing table mirror and her daughter. Replacing her paint-smudged smock with a glamorous white dressing gown, she took her place on the bench of her vanity table and beckoned Dare to her side. Dare watched as her mother performed her toilette, counted as she gave her auburn tresses, now cut into a fashionable bob, their hundred strokes, and listened as her mother unburdened herself of whatever was on her mind. For Dare, these were treasured moments—unless the subject turned to her father. It was agonizing to witness Edie's fury at Ivan. If Dare spoke, it was only to compliment her mother, to please and appease her, efforts to keep her mother's anger at bay. But as she studied her mother admiring herself in the mirror, Dare saw Edie from a new angle. Until then, she had told herself that invisible hands had spirited her father and brother away. Now, she wasn't so sure. She realized that Edie had played a part in their loss, and this made her not a little afraid.

Edie painted the first portrait of Dare in Cleveland just after their arrival. Seated on the floor in an organdy party dress, Dare clutches her knees, an open book resting on her thighs. She appears to be reading intently, her eyes trained downward on the book (the pages of which she was prohibited from turning, lest she break the pose). Half her face is concealed in shadow. A light seems to shine on the other half, as if illuminated by Edie's gaze. Dare lived in constant fear that that gaze might—at any moment—be directed elsewhere, especially if she were to reveal to her mother any intimation of what was really going on inside, how sad and lonely she felt. If there was reassurance in being looked at, it was not the same as being looked after—or being truly seen.

The next three years of Dare's life, between the ages of six and nine, years when most children are beginning to move away from their mothers into a world of their peers, were spent in an almost airtight isolation with Edie. Dare had become exquisitely attuned to her mother's requirements, playing handmaiden to Edie's queen as Edie created their own private universe, constructed with real-world skills and helped along by a prodigious gift for make-believe. Only the practical exigencies of the outside world were allowed to intrude. In their private world they were not defined by anyone else's judgment, or by the shortcomings and cruelties of a husband or relatives. Edie was not the black sheep who had failed at marriage. Dare was not the child abandoned by her father or the sister who had lost her brother.

A paragon of industriousness, and wildly inventive, Edie invited her daughter's participation in creating this new private world. She instilled in Dare the means to explore the power of her own creativity. She taught her not only to read and write but also to draw, to paint, to do carpentry, and to sew. Edie's view of the world as a canvas for her composition extended to their physical selves and to their surroundings. Dare was an avid and able student: together, they made all their own clothes, highly original and dramatic gar-

Portrait of Dare painted by Edie shortly after their arrival in Cleveland, 1921.

ments but always beautiful. The attention to appearance was not just in preparation for the public gaze; their game of dress-up was part of a private ritual. Through it, Edie found a passport to other realms, away from steel mills belching filthy black smoke, frigid winters, and pinched circumstances. Sometimes, Edie would record these dress-up flights of fantasy in paintings of herself or Dare.

Together, too, they "dressed" their habitats, with as much energy, ingenuity, and style as they did themselves. If their clothes looked like costumes, their environment resembled a stage set. Its construction, requiring practical skills and labor in which no proper queen or fairy princess would engage, did not deter them. Edie taught herself and Dare to do whatever was necessary. They painted the rooms, designed and built cabinetry and furniture, upholstered and sewed drapery. If the "real" thing could not be achieved, the illusion could. Without means to afford marble floors in the black-and-white checkerboard effect that Edie so admired, it was Dare who thought to paint the wood floor black and stencil white squares over it.

What were the sources of Edie's vision? Did her female patrons sleep in taffeta-canopied beds, primp at vanity tables, walk on marble floors, and draw cream-colored quilted draperies closed when they retired for the night? Where else might she have seen these elements of luxe interiors? In movies? In magazines? Or paintings? Regardless of their provenance, these features would become standard in all their subsequent apartments.

Edie's interest in domesticity did not extend beyond physical appearances. She was uninterested in food and its preparation. Most meals were taken in inexpensive sandwich shops in Cleveland Heights and downtown, where, in 1922, the Stouffer family, several of whom Edie painted, opened the first in a chain of restaurants. And her methods of child rearing were all her own. She seemed to believe that only "bad" children needed supervision; Dare, "such a good child," did not. She crafted unlikely child-care arrangements.

The obliging owner of the Korner and Wood bookstore downtown did not object to a little girl sitting for hours in the back of his shop, copying out the texts of his wares. *Robin Hood* was Dare's favorite. Back home, she bound the neatly transcribed pages in a doeskin cover that she secured with matching ties.

But mostly, when Edie had to be out in the world, Dare was left at home alone. There, she learned to find comfort and companionship in her books and her dolls, and to fire up her imagination. If Dare's first dolls were improvisational, homemade by her mother, with dresses sewn from remnants of the fabrics used for their own clothes, the books Edie bought Dare when she was feeling flush were the real thing. The first two purchased in Cleveland were a collection of the Grimms' fairy tales and a picture book called *The Lovely Garden*, the story of the much-beloved Princess Yolande who lives on the Island of Can-be-done, whose "sweet smile seemed to say: 'What am I here for if it is not to make others happier?'" The book's message was reminiscent of her mother's inscriptions on the backs of her portraits—"To my Good and Precious Daughter"—directives on how to act and so meet the conditions of Edie's love. The mechanics of fairy tales carried a message too. If princesses could be put to sleep to awaken unharmed, perhaps fathers and brothers could also. If princesses could escape punishing circumstances, perhaps Dare could too. She found comfort in their reassuring endings, in which, through ingenuity or simply by goodness prevailing, Hansel and Gretel, Rapunzel, and Snow White found solutions to their dilemmas.

Free of the chaotic influence of Ivan and her troubled little boy, doted on by her compliant and perfectly behaved daughter, and admired by her patrons (among them the heads of the forerunner of Republic Steel and of Sherwin-Williams), Edie was thriving in the new life she had made for herself and Dare on their Island of Can-be-done. For the first time since before her marriage, she could pursue her art and her career without disruption. Edie always spoke of success as "being on top." She may not have been on top yet, but she was well poised to get there.

Dare's development, never the focus for Edie, was more of an afterthought. In September 1921, nine months after their arrival in Cleveland, Edie enrolled Dare in first grade at Coventry Elementary, a public school close to their apartment. But Dare's attendance was sporadic. She missed not just days but months of school each of the three years she "attended" Coventry. Her permissiveness verging on neglect, Edie left it to her daughter to decide how she would spend her day, and Dare had little desire to venture forth from her mother's orbit. Edie could justify Dare's truancy by telling herself that she had the important aspects of Dare's education well in hand. Moreover, at public school Dare was not fraternizing with the children from the families Edie cared about, the socially prominent Clevelanders who came to her for portraits. Their daughters, she learned, attended the exclusive Laurel School, a day school for girls that also took in boarders.

Dare's self-sufficiency was assumed. No provisions were made for her to meet and play with other children. An exception was a 1922 Easter egg hunt held by Dan Hanna, Jr., and his first wife, Ruth, a former Ziegfeld Follies showgirl, in the backyard of their Cleveland Heights home. At this gathering, Edie told her hosts how surprised she was to see her seven-year-old daughter, usually so shy, disappear to the bottom of the garden with another little girl, to play as well as she could in her velvet-trimmed party coat with fur buttons and an elaborate Easter bonnet. Edie later invited Dare's new friend to lunch, hiring a maid for the occasion, but the child was never invited back. Edie had learned she was only the daughter of Hanna's chauffeur. Three more years would go by before Dare would experience sustained socialization with her peers.

As for her own social life, Edie refused most invitations, even if she did love any excuse to dress up and any forum in which to be admired. Patrons sought her out to join their circles, but she told them she had no time for such distractions. But she had plenty of time for the press, whose pursuit of the mediagenic artist was constant. These emissaries from the outside world were greeted—and confused—by the commingled smells of turpentine and oil paints and a woman dressed as though she never touched them; "petite, devastatingly feminine and with ringlets of blond hair," one journalist wrote, "she appeared at first meeting as a woman meant for luxurious and idle living." Edie, intolerant of dirt and disorder, began each interview with an explanation of the airless atmosphere. "Do come in," she told one reporter. "It is very warm here, I know. But if you open the windows, there is so much soot." (Cigarette smoke was apparently a different matter. The closed windows trapped the smoke of the Lucky Strikes and Chesterfields to which she had become devoted.) And instead of discoursing on art, "lights, nuances, color values and such, [she] tells us at once how to successfully wash a pair of washable kid gloves!" But their sympathies were ensured when she revealed that her husband had died young.

Edie welcomed the journalists' attentions and almost always manipulated them masterfully. A fateful exception was an interview with Maude Truesdale, a *Cleveland News* writer, for a series on Cleveland's pioneering women. Although complimentary of Edie's professional achievements, and admiring of the youthful appearance in which she took such pride, Truesdale's portrayal managed to run down Edie's professional and domestic setup. She described Edie's apartment as being as "unlike a studio as could well be imagined." And she painted a dejected picture of the artist's daughter, who should have been at school, relegated to the floor in a corner behind the easel. "Her little girl with a white cloth about her head upon which her mother had pinned a cross cut from red paper was playing Red Cross nurse to some decrepit dolls." Within weeks of the article's publication, Edie had signed a lease on a proper studio in the Fine Arts Building downtown to begin that September, when Dare would be entering the fourth grade at the Laurel School as a

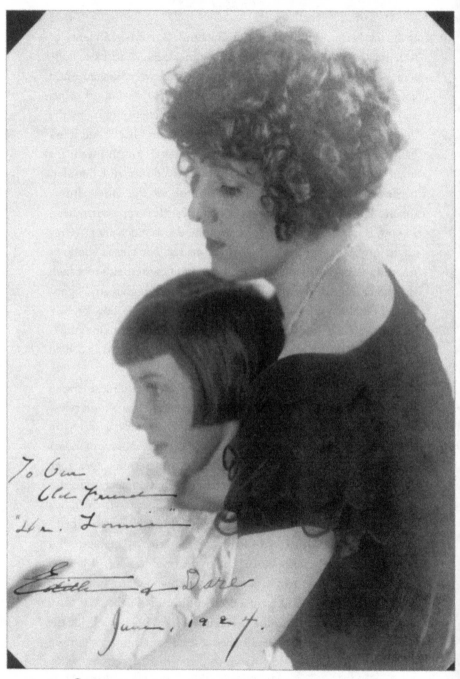

Studio photograph of Dare and Edie, taken in Cleveland, June 1924.

boarding "dormitory girl." She also made sure that no one could ever again describe Dare's dolls as decrepit. At the Halle Brothers Department Store, Edie bought, on the installment plan, an exquisite 22-inch-high Italian-made Lenci doll. At $12.50, it was the most expensive one in the store.

In presenting the doll to Dare, Edie made much of the extravagance of this gift and of the doll's beauty. She told Dare it looked like her. But with a curly mohair wig and painted-on face, the doll looked nothing like Dare, whose straight hair Edie cut in a Dutchboy style. It was Edie whom the doll most resembled. Together they decided on its name. They chose "Edith."

Dare was thrilled by this addition to the family circle. Edie had her Dare and now, in Edith, Dare had a Dare, a confidante and companion of her own. But her happiness was short-lived when Edie informed her that she would soon be leaving for boarding school. The doll, she realized, was to be not a family addition but a substitute for the original Edith. Dare did not protest or rebel. Instead, she gave her mother the reassurance for which she herself so longed. She promised Edie that she would make her proud by her performance at Laurel and assured her of her love. Edie reported to her cousin Allie that Dare had told her, "You seem so wonderful to me. Everything you do and have seems perfect." Typically, Edie described the decision to send Dare to boarding school as being in Dare's best interests "so I can work and know that Dare is safe."

If the fall to come was a dreaded prospect, the summer ahead was not. Edie's seductive side was on full display. After moving to a new one-bedroom apartment closer to Laurel, Edie took Dare on her first vacation, to Cedar Point, a resort about 60 miles from Cleveland on Lake Erie. Edie adored real travel as much as her imaginative flights. She loved especially preparing for a trip and planning the costumes. While Dare romped in the water, Edie, in an elegant dropped-waist jersey dress, not exactly beach wear, did watercolors on the shore. The Brownie camera with which Edie usually photographed her portraits had been brought along. When Edie asked a passerby to take their picture, Dare assumed a pose far more spontaneous than those usually set up by Edie in her studio: She threw her arms around her mother's waist and peered up at her adoringly.

Back home, they prepared for Laurel, but the school's strict clothing regulations left Edie little room to maneuver. Students were required to wear uniforms: a dark green skirt, white middy blouse with a green tie, and tan cotton stockings. As no stipulation was given regarding undergarments, Edie decided they would sew matching panties and camisoles out of flowered and textured materials, rather than the usual boring white cotton. (These became the envy of Dare's schoolmates.) They also sewed in the required name tapes, even though the company had misspelled the first name and the order had come back "B-a-r-e Wright." Dare found this riotously funny, until she realized that Edie intended to use them anyway. Dare's name—spelled correctly—and the dorm's address also adorned the engraved stationery that Edie gave Dare as a parting gift. Dare's pleasure in this gift was fleeting when she realized that, apart from her mother, there was no one else to write to.

On a Sunday morning that September, Edie, carrying Dare's suitcase, and Dare, carrying Edith, made the two-block walk from Patrician Apartments to the Laurel dorm. To Dare it felt like walking the plank. Being separated from her mother and plunged into a strange new universe of girls who, in most cases, had been together since kindergarten, was terrifying. Here, as at Coventry Elementary, were children who had stay-at-home mothers, fathers who worked and provided, and siblings. This was true even of the small group of dormitory girls, 40 among a student body of 350. That Dare's family life was so completely different only intensified her feelings of separateness and loneliness. But if she felt sad or ashamed, these feelings could be concealed. Almost instinctively, or maybe as she had seen her mother do, she silenced her schoolmates' whispers by cultivating a persona to protect herself, behind which she could hide. She would be aloof, self-contained. It was a guise successfully maintained for the next nine years, defining her as mysterious, intensely alluring—and very hard to reach emotionally.

There were advantages to a childhood spent in deciphering what was expected and trying to please. Dare excelled both in her schoolwork—she rose quickly to the top of her class—and on the playing fields. And yet she was not successful in forming close personal attachments. Drawn in by her prettiness and her charm, her classmates noted that she couldn't seem to follow through on the response they elicited. However persistently her classmates sought out her friendship, their attempts to get too close invariably failed. Among themselves, they decided that interaction with other people was hard for her. They explained it away by speculating on what a strange life she must have with an exotic artist mother who neither looked nor behaved like their own. On Edie's rare appearances at the school, the younger girls decided she must be a queen of some sort. The average woman neither dressed nor comported herself this way.

Missing Edie, Dare comforted herself as she had always done, retreating into her imagination, telling herself stories revolving around her life's central characters, attempts to work out solutions to her dilemmas. One such story, her first published effort, appeared in *Laurel Leaves*, the school yearbook, in the spring of 1925, the end of her first year at Laurel. On the surface, "An Imaginary Story: The Little Green Door" borrows from fairy tales, but between its lines it reveals the real preoccupations of its ten-year-old author.

Once, long ago, there lived two children, a boy and a girl who were nine years old, and twins. Their father was the king. In one of the highest towers of the palace there was a little green door. These two children had been forbidden to enter this door. One day they were wandering through the castle and they came upon the little green door. The boy said, "Come, let us go through this door." But the girl said, "No, we must not. Father told us not to." At last, however, the boy coaxed the girl to go with him. So they went in and shut the door. They found themselves in a very large room. Suddenly an old woman appeared who asked, "Who are you who dare enter my room? But as you have, you shall hear my story." And she led them into another room. The king was worried when his children did not appear and he started to search for them. In his search he came upon the door and entered. The old woman came hobbling out. The king said, "Old woman, who are you?" Just then the king heard voices. He asked the old woman whose they were, and she said, "Oh, those are only my children." The king said, "Will you not let me see them?" The old woman called the children rather unwillingly. When they appeared she suddenly ordered them to go back. Then the king called out, "Give me my children, old woman." But the old woman said, "Not until you have covered this floor with something that is the color of gold." So the king had everything that was the color of gold brought to the room. When everything was there, a very small place was still uncovered. Then the girl cut off a lock of her golden hair and covered the vacant space and immediately the old woman and all the gold vanished. The king and his children went downstairs and lived together happily.

All Dare's anxieties and conflicts were poured into its narrative: her fear—or fantasy—that her father was searching for her and unable to find her, her worry that her brother's bad behavior had led her astray and had caused the family to be separated, and above all her concern that she had somehow transgressed by going with her mother in the first place. It suggests she felt stolen and punished by Edie, the "old woman" who had imprisoned her and forced her to hear her story.

It was the first time in her life that Dare allowed herself, in terms however disguised, to express her inner turmoil—and to protest. But if this was an angry dig at her mother, it was also a way to assure herself that there was still hope for a solution. As in her adored fairy tales, the story arrives at a happy ending. Like Hansel and Gretel, Dare's characters outsmart the wicked old witch who has entrapped them. And like Rapunzel, the girl finds the means to escape her imprisonment in her physical self, in golden hair so valuable and powerful it might actually fill up the empty space left in her life by the disappearance of her father—who, like the supply of golden things, had fallen short—and reunite the children with him. In the story, she could be the thread to bind them all together. All she needed to sacrifice was a small part of herself, one that would grow back.

In real life, Dare's blond hair could not save her for much longer. It was turning darker. This upset her, particularly as Edie communicated her displeasure with this development by continuing to paint her now brown-haired daughter as blond. These physical changes, unlike her behavior, were out of Dare's control. And it wasn't just her hair. Her little girl's body was also undergoing unwelcome changes. Might Edie view this as a betrayal? Dare soon discovered a way to stem the tide. It drove her, after obediently cleaning her plate as was required, from the dormitory dining room to the bathroom. When one of her classmates found her vomiting in a toilet stall, Dare told her she was only spitting out the bread crusts she could not abide. She said she had devised a method by which she could hide the crusts in her cheeks until she could excuse herself from the table. From then on, Dare would have episodes of bulimia and anorexia at times of stress.

Above all, "The Little Green Door" expressed how fixated Dare remained on those who were lost and how fervently she wished to be reunited with her father—no ordinary man but a king—and her brother—no ordinary sibling but a twin. Dare did confide in some of her classmates about her brother, but never in a way they could be sure was factual. Sometimes she spoke of having a brother she had never met. Sometimes she even said he was her twin. By now, Dare knew the truth about the divorce and Ivan and Blaine's whereabouts, but she also knew that Edie, who had finally settled on the story that she was a widow with one child, never spoke of them publicly. However confusing Edie's tendency to alter the facts, Dare's complicity could be taken for granted even if she didn't understand the sense of shame Edie was masking or why the truth was unacceptable. Dare, too, began to lie when asked almost any biographical detail, as though her life were not a real story that belonged to her but a fiction that, like her blondness, belonged to her mother.

Ivan's second marriage was far happier than his first. Still, professional satisfaction and stability continued to elude him and his drinking problem accelerated with the years. In 1921, he had left his job at the *New York Tribune* to begin selling insurance policies for the Travelers Insurance Company. Seeing that he longed to return to a life in the theater, Florence suggested they economize so that Ivan could leave the job he found so deadening. They moved from Manhattan to Brooklyn and in 1924, Ivan did leave Travelers to form Ivan L. Wright Productions. His first play, *New York Exchange*, opened on Broadway to abysmal reviews on New Year's Eve 1926. Five days later, Ivan was dead at the age of forty-seven. His obituary in *Variety* reported he was "stricken during rehearsals . . . the illness proving fatal." It did not specify the illness; his death certificate gave the cause of death as "Epidemic Encephalitis, contributory: Nephritis, chronic." Relatives and friends wondered whether Ivan's sudden death had, in fact, been a suicide. Blaine did tell one close friend that it was. If this were true, Blaine never mentioned it again and Florence took the secret to her grave.

Within days of Ivan's death, and just as school was starting its second semester, Florence enrolled the fourteen-year-old Blaine at the private Collegiate School, using Ivan's life insurance money to pay the tuition. Despite an exceptionally loving and responsible step-mother, nothing could soothe Blaine's anger and pain at the loss of both his parents. At the end of Blaine's semester at Collegiate, his report book came back with failing grades in every subject but English. He scrawled *I am glad that I am smarter than these idiots* across the book's blank Scholarship Honors page and finished his second-ary education in public school. To support them both, Florence found a job at Travelers with the help of Aloysius MacGuire, known as Mac, a former colleague of Ivan's who had been their friend. Mac moved in with Florence, and they remained compan-ions for the rest of their lives. She told a niece who questioned why they did not marry that she had cherished Ivan and wanted to keep his name.

Florence would always cherish Blaine, too. But while she was attempting valiantly to shepherd him through a difficult adoles-cence, there is no evidence that Edie even knew that Ivan had died or that Florence had been left with the sole responsibility for Edie's son. Even had she known, it is doubtful that she would have allowed this to alter her increasingly glittering course. Blaine's real mother had other things on her mind.

With Dare out of the way at Laurel, Edie was able to take full advantage of opportunities due in large part to Noel Lawson Lewis, an editor at *Cleveland Town Topics*, a weekly magazine considered the bible of Cleveland's social and cultural life. Lewis, smitten as much by the artist as by her art, championed Edie, whose work he considered "not excelled by that of any other woman artist in this country and by only a few men."

A steady stream of Cleveland's elite arrived for sittings now held in her convenient downtown studio, a converted Hanna Building office suite, given to her in 1925 by Dan Hanna, Jr. While most women painters of the day were focusing on flowers, Edie was well established as an accomplished creator of powerfully dramatic por-traits, in full control of her medium. Some called her a female John

Singer Sargent. This may have been overstatement, but what could be said was that her ability to capture not only the look but a great deal of the personality of her sitter was indeed uncanny.

In the summer of 1927, after painting Dare in her sleepaway camp uniform, a full-length portrait titled "At First Camp. Pure Joy!"—in case Dare was in any doubt as to how to view this experience— Edie, now forty-four, fulfilled her longtime dream of going to Europe. From Venice, she sent Charlie and Clyde Gaither a picture postcard of herself in St. Mark's Square with a pigeon perched on her hand. She wrote in her most expansive hand: "Europe is wonderful— like a new world—feel as if I have gone to the moon or Mars. Love Edith."

Upon her return that fall, more new worlds beckoned. Lewis set in motion what would prove the most important commission of Edie's career. He asked Cleveland Congressman Theodore Burton to propose to President Calvin Coolidge that Edie paint his portrait, to be underwritten by *Town Topics* and donated to the city. It would be hung in the Cleveland Auditorium where Coolidge had received the presidential nomination in 1924.

After meeting with Edie for forty-five minutes at the White House, President Coolidge told Burton he would sit for the portrait. Lewis stood by and watched as the local and national press pounced on the story. The commission assured, Edie shrewdly put it off for several months in order to capitalize on all the publicity. Her work was more in demand than it had ever been. There was prestige in being painted by the woman who was to paint the president.

Coolidge sat for Edie over three weeks in the White House in February and March 1928, although she had turned down the president's offer to sleep there as well. Edie explained this decision in a letter to Allie. "All day in the White House is quite enough— besides, I have to wash my gloves and stockings, don't I? And get my breath." Instead, *Town Topics* paid for her to stay at the Carlton Hotel nearby. When friends and reporters later expressed astonishment that she passed up the chance to stay in the executive mansion,

Edie regretted her decision. It would have made a much better story. From then on, she simply pretended she had.

In all her letters, Edie swings wildly between moods and topics. In the Washington letters, she alternates between anxiety, a sense of feeling inferior to her task, and a tone of superiority. The president, she laments, "thinks early rising the thing. He had me painting at eight this morning." (This meant getting up at 6 A.M. to prepare herself.) She describes herself as "more dead than alive." But by the next paragraph she is effusing that Underwood and Underwood, the Washington photography studio, has taken a hotel suite next to hers to photograph her—with "moovie [*sic*] lights. They make me look like Mary Pickford, Ina Claire, and Norma Talmadge all in one."

As for her work, she is consumed by self-doubt, continually referring to her effort as "a mess." And she complains that she is unused to having an audience while she paints. "This thing of being Court Painter with the court at my elbow—help!! But I suppose we can get used to anything. I feel beaten all over after two days [waking] at six." Her nerves, she writes, are causing stomach distress, but she consoles herself that "nerves can't last forever and my grandchildren will be glad—perhaps Algeo's won't mind claiming me either." Deflated again, she writes, "Too utterly tired. I think it's a mess. He [Coolidge] thinks it's 'coming nicely.' Oh, Hell!! I was too tired to begin with—I am sick of being worked to death." But a few sentences later, she gushes: "The president is a peach! The president is really my friend and I find new things about him daily and he talks and smiles for me now." She is flattered by the interest he is taking in the painting. "He kept running in three times a day to look at my creation—and he told Senator Burton that 'the charming little Mrs. Wright' was painting what promised to be the best portrait ever done." An aide told her that "'since their occupancy of the W.H. no one had so captivated the whole family and staff as I had done.' I certainly had no thought of 'charming' anyone—eight hours on my feet and no powder puff—just agony."

That April, after finishing the portrait in Cleveland, Edie brought it back to Washington for the unveiling at the White House, along with several other portraits for an exhibition that the Carlton Hotel had planned. Otto Kahn, the financier and philanthropist, attended the unveiling and was among those who made their way to the Carlton to see more. He would become her next champion, and in the years to come this connection would lead to dozens of commissions that would take her to New York, Paris, and Los Angeles long after the portrait that led to all this had been destroyed; in 1935, a careless smoker dropped a cigarette in the sofa in the Public Auditorium over which the Coolidge portrait was hung. In the Cleveland *Plain Dealer's* account:

> The flames melted the varicolored oils that had been used by Edith Stephenson [sic] Wright. . . . The oils dripped on to the burning davenport and left nothing in the portrait frame but a blank canvas.

In interviews about the Coolidge portrait, Edie was asked repeatedly how she dealt with the legendarily laconic president. One reporter wrote:

> To get this silent man to talk she asked him how he felt about women with careers. He did not approve, he told her, and added that women belonged at home. She agreed with him. "Well then," he said, thinking he had her cornered, "how do you reconcile that attitude with what you're doing?" "I love my work but I didn't want it as a career," she answered. "The career is for economic reasons, Mr. President."

The career was paying off. Having missed companionship during her first European jaunt, she took Dare, thirteen, with her when she returned in the summer of 1928. They traveled throughout France, Switzerland, and Italy. For the summer of 1930, she again took Dare, this time to Paris so that she could deliver a posthumous portrait of Myron T. Herrick, a Clevelander who had been America's

Venezia, Aug 1928

Edie and Dare in Venice on their first European trip together, August 1928.

ambassador to France when World War I broke out as well as during the postwar reconstruction period. Then it was on to the Riviera. They sailed home from that trip on the *Île de France,* an opulent ocean liner with trendsetting Art Deco interiors.

These glamorous interludes with her now internationally celebrated mother fell in sharp contrast to Dare's more forlorn existence as an abandoned dormitory girl at Laurel. The school took its in loco parentis responsibility seriously. While day students could spend evenings in the bosom of their families and weekends at ice skating or dancing parties with children from other schools, dormitory girls lived in cloistered regimentation. After supper, they were shepherded back into the main school building, now silent and dark, to do their homework. For diversion, they were invited to listen to the school's live-in principal read aloud from *Paradise Lost.* The older girls were allowed to go to four movies each term, if accompanied by a chaperone. To take advantage of this privilege, Dare had to borrow money from the school for bus fare and the movie ticket. In the sometimes long periods that went by without seeing her mother, Dare would return to her dorm room to find embarrassing notes on her bed from the school secretary reminding her of her debts. Dare slipped these dunning notes between the pages of her schoolbooks, concealing them from her roommates.

While Dare must have recognized the awe her summers provoked in her impressed—even envious—schoolmates, who marveled to see her photograph in the newspaper boarding ocean liners with her exotic mother, it meant less than they could have imagined. For a long time, Dare had taken pride in having grown up, as she called it, "under an easel." It was all she knew. But as she saw how other girls lived, it only confirmed her longing for what *she* considered most exotic: an unbroken family. Even the other dormitory girls had families to fold back into during school breaks. Dare would struggle to hide her disappointment to learn that Edie would be traveling when it was time for her to come home for vacations or at the end of the school year. On some of those occasions,

Marguerite Vliet, Dare's first Laurel roommate, invited Dare to stay with her family at their luxurious home in Kirtland, 20 miles from Cleveland. On other school vacations, Dare stayed by herself in her mother's apartment, under strict orders not to leave, watched over only by the images of forbidding-looking men resting against a wall or staring out at her from the easel.

Dare was also reined in by a sense of guilt. Edie made much of her sacrifice, being forced to work so hard for their support. It was confusing, then, to hear on her mother's return from a 1931 trip to Paris of the parties and champagne suppers in Edie's honor, how she learned the tango at a swank nightclub, "dancing blisters" on her feet. Or how on the crossing home on the S.S. *De Grasse* she took first prize at a shipboard masquerade party for her costume, a blue Louis XV robe de chambre and powdered hair.

Only once did a classmate visit Dare's home. Edie told Dare she could invite Mary Yost, Dare's roommate in the eighth grade, to spend the weekend at Patrician Apartments. When the girls arrived, however, Edie announced that she had been called out of town unexpectedly. She said Mary could stay, but only if the girls promised not to leave the apartment. On the second day, with Mary as ringleader, they ventured out into the hallway where, stripped down to their underwear, they held a fencing match using umbrellas as foils.

While Laurel could provide a replacement family of sorts, surrogate sisters in her classmates and mother figures in her teachers, Dare mostly pulled away from them, fearing such an alliance would constitute a betrayal of Edie. One teacher, though, pursued Dare relentlessly. Jane Douglass Crawford joined the faculty in 1930, Dare's sophomore year, as a teacher of "Spoken English" and head of the drama club. The withdrawn but appealing student caught Jane's eye and soon became her obsession.

Jane had been drawn to the theater as a way to escape her own unhappy childhood. But unlike her favorite student, she had neither

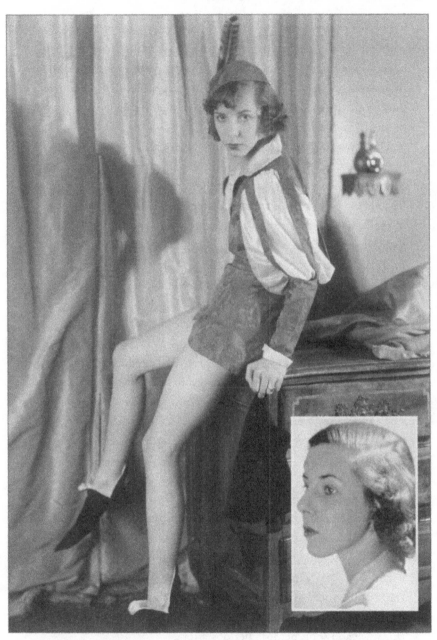

Dare in costume for a Laurel drama production and (inset) as she appeared in a *Cleveland Bystander* article announcing Laurel's 1933 Cum Laude Society Awards.

a pretty face nor an attractive figure, so she had found her place as a teacher rather than as a performer. Observing Dare, she believed she detected a natural-born actress. At Jane's insistence, the reluctant Dare joined the drama club, and Jane cast her in starring roles in every school production. But aside from her ability to take direction, Dare's gift was more for make-believe and playing pretend than the other attributes acting requires. Her shyness was always an impediment. Her voice rarely rose above a whisper. Her self-consciousness was underscored by her habit—which would persist lifelong—of putting a hand over her mouth when she spoke. Fiercely devoted to Dare, Jane worked to help her overcome these handicaps; hesitantly, Dare went along. Like her teacher before her, she too found the theater provided a sense of family, a structured place to belong, a prescribed role to play—and endless opportunities for dressing up.

But when Dare told her mother about her new teacher and her acting pursuits, Edie's reaction was predictable. From the very first, she detested this woman who sought to control her daughter. Edie had already cast Dare in the only role she wanted her to play: that of her mother's "good and precious" model daughter.

As their Laurel years drew to a close, Dare's classmates made plans for college, in those days little more than a stepping-stone to marriage and starting families. Dare, too, had starting a family in mind—or, in this case, piecing one together again. First, she would need to find her lost brother. She told no one at Laurel of this plan, and certainly not Edie. Her determination to find Blaine overrode even her fear of leaving her mother or of venturing into the world beyond. Apart from finding Blaine, Dare had no clear notion of what she would do once she had entered that world.

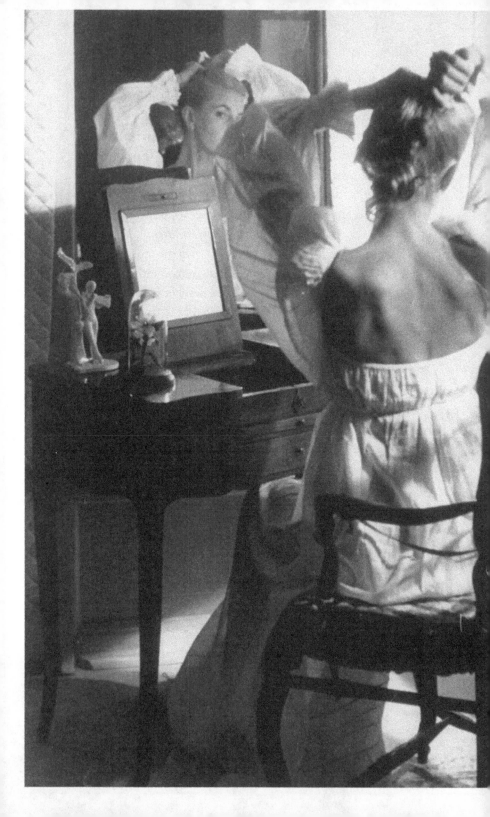

CHAPTER THREE

New York

Edith clapped her hands with joy. "You must have found me because I wished so hard," she cried.   —*The Lonely Doll*

When the editors of Laurel's 1933 yearbook drew up a composite of the Perfect Senior, she was given "Dare's brains." Dare graduated among the top five in her class of forty-two students. That her daughter's intellect was considered exceptional seemed to make no impression on Edie. What Edie valued was Dare's goodness and her appearance, reflected by the senior quote she picked out for her daughter from Sir Walter Scott's *The Lady of the Lake*:

> *And ne'er did Grecian chisel trace*
> *A Nymph, a Naiad, or a Grace*
> *Of finer form, or lovelier face.*

"I don't know what Dare will be," Edie had told *The Clevelander* magazine in 1930, "but if she wants to be a painter, I hope she won't paint portraits. It's a long, long road, and a hard one, for anyone, but especially for a woman." Asked about her daughter's future, Edie's answer was typically more about herself.

As Edie offered Dare no guidance about her future course, others were only too happy to step in. Jane Douglass Crawford, convinced that she had created a promising actress, pushed Dare in the direction of drama school, specifically the American Academy of Dramatic Arts in New York City, where she was angling to get a job. Mary Yost, Dare's former roommate, who was finishing her first year at Wellesley, pleaded with Dare to go to college. Mary had always been impressed by Dare's intelligence and considered acting a dead end.

Edie had nothing but contempt for Jane, and, as for a college education, Edie had managed fine without one. At Dare's age, Edie had lived in New York and studied at the Art Students League That was what Dare would do. Tugging back, Jane urged Dare to consider a compromise. She suggested Dare attend both art and drama school, one in the morning, the other in the afternoon, and this was the plan with which Dare left Cleveland for New York in October 1933. As both schools were on West 57th Street, she took an inexpensive room at the 1,250-room West 57th Street "clubhouse" of the American Women's Association, "an organization of young working women." No one had bothered to find out whether it was even possible to attend both schools simultaneously. It was not.

Dare began classes at the A.A.D.A. But with enrollment down because of the Depression, hiring had been suspended; Jane was forced to remain at Laurel, and Dare felt lost. She left after one term. A few weeks later, she enrolled in a life drawing class at the Art Students League. On the first day, George Bridgman told his students, "You are here to become good draftsmen. I teach you the facts. Then you take these facts and apply them. . . . Later, when you have a story to tell, you will be able to tell it." Dare already had these facts. She had been exceptionally well trained by Edie, as her childhood drawings, paintings, and watercolors attested. What she lacked was a story that was hers to tell. She lasted only one term there, as well. In six months in New York, Dare had run aground. And she had fared no better in her search for Blaine. All she could think to do was to look for him in the phone book. He was not listed.

Using her tuition money on a train ticket to Cleveland, Dare showed up at Edie's studio. She found her mother overwhelmed by work and terrified at the prospect, given the times, of not finding more. Dare had only to listen to Edie's worries to know this was no time to play dress-up. The real world had intruded, and Edie was in practical mode.

Dare returned to New York, ashamed to tell her mother there was really nothing to go back to. She spent the next year forcing herself to go on auditions. Acting, at least, unlike painting, did provide a story, the lines to recite and the persona to step into. In the summer of 1935, she finally landed her first part in a professional play, a dramatization of Jane Austen's *Pride and Prejudice*. Her part as a Bennet family maid, so minor that she had no name and only one line, required her to walk across the stage set of the Bennets' living room in Act I and extinguish the candles on the mantelpiece. In Act III, she announced to Mr. Bennet the arrival of "Mr. Darcy, sir, and Mr. Bingley." The production opened in Washington, D.C., on October 22, 1935, and on Broadway November 5, where it ran for six months. Dare was asked to stay on with the production for a ten-city tour that fall and to understudy the part of Jane Bennet. She never had a chance to play Jane, but midway through the season she was given a slightly bigger role, that of Maggie, the Irish maid of the Bennet girls' Aunt Gardiner. She also played Agatha, a woman in a party scene, again a part with a single line.

She may have had two roles when the company arrived in Cleveland for four performances at the Hanna Theatre on December 14, 1936, but she was hardly a star. Nonetheless, Edie, by now her own experienced press agent, pitched the story of the Broadway star's homecoming to her Cleveland press contacts, dangling before them a risqué photograph of her daughter posed atop a bureau, the ties of her gladiator-type sandals winding up her bare legs and a button-down shift open to her crotch. Edie also provided the information with which the accompanying squib was written, including the invented detail that Dare had spent an entire year at drama school.

Edie attended each performance, seated in the front row, accompanied by a coterie of patrons. After the curtain, she entertained the company at her studio. Jane Douglass Crawford, who was still teaching at Laurel, attended the opening night, sitting separately from Edie's entourage and making notes scrutinizing Dare's performance. All her criticisms related to Dare's problems with audibility and projection. "More breath," she recommended. "Sustain the thing to the end."

In a one-page essay on Dare's life, her cousin Allie Whiteside (now Jorg, having married in 1930), the self-appointed family chronicler, gave Dare's acting career a single sentence: "While attempting acting, Dare made friends with a real actress, named Eugenia Rawls." Rawls was indeed a "real" actress; she had just concluded a two-year Broadway run in Lillian Hellman's *The Children's Hour* when she joined the cast of *Pride and Prejudice* and would go on to a successful acting career. For Dare, a subsequent friendship with Genie Rawls and, to a lesser degree, several others in the cast, was the only truly lasting dividend of *Pride and Prejudice*. She continued to go on auditions, but no part came her way. Discouraged, she again headed home to Cleveland.

This time, she found Edie in far better form, and packing—for Hollywood. Sam Katz, a movie theater magnate whom Edie had painted in 1931 in New York, now a production executive for Metro-Goldwyn-Mayer, had commissioned Edie to paint a portrait of his new wife, the actress Sari Maritza. He offered to cover all her travel and living expenses and to arrange other commissions if Edie wanted to plan an extended stay. Edie gave up her apartment and stored her belongings in her studio. Thinking that Katz could help Dare break into the movies, Edie decided she should come along.

They stayed in Los Angeles from mid-1937 until mid-1938. Katz made good on his promise to arrange other commissions, but Dare's only role in Hollywood was that of Edie's companion. Katz, tied up with preproduction on *The Wizard of Oz* and battling with his boss Louis B. Mayer to cast Judy Garland as Dorothy, was not moved to take on Edie's daughter as a project.

For Dare, this period felt like a replay of her earlier years. Edie spent her days carrying out her commissions and most evenings being entertained by her patrons. To pass the time, Edie suggested Dare occupy herself by painting still lifes as gifts for her Cleveland patrons. Dare did paint one—for Noel Lawson Lewis—but, left alone in the hotel room Katz had provided, she was lonely and bored. The mirror beckoned. She could give herself the appearance, at least, of a Hollywood starlet. Plucking out her eyebrows, she replaced them with thin and exaggerated penciled arches, and experimented with lip- and eyeliner. With a paste of Clorox and soap powder, she lightened her hair, taking care not to go too far, to avoid the scalp burns and brittle hair that this method often produced. She then set it in tight curls.

Edie was impressed, even covetous, of her daughter's new look. Together they worked out a shade for Edie she called Titian Red, a strange copper-colored dye, and she too plucked out her eyebrows and lined her lips and her eyes. To commemorate their new looks, they visited a photography studio to have their portraits done.

While Edie had some sympathy for Dare's disappointment at her unfulfilled acting career, the stage had never been part of her vision for her daughter. Edie's bigger concern was Dare's negligible income. She suggested that when they left California, Dare register with a modeling agency to bring in money between acting jobs.

The magazine caption for Dare's first New York job describes not only the outfit Dare wears but the model herself. "Dare Wright is a girl of many talents: actress (understudy in *Pride and Prejudice*); portrait painter; Hollywood find (she refused a contract in favor of more stage experience); and currently our nomination for Model

The studio shots documenting Edie and Dare's Hollywood "transformations," Los Angeles, 1937.

No. 1." The story of the movie contract refusal was pure invention. Dare was not painting portraits. As for "Model No. 1," the magazine hype was wrong on this point too. But Dare quickly found more work as a model than she had as an actress.

On Edie's return from Hollywood in June 1938, she moved into a suite at the Hotel Cleveland in Terminal Tower on Public Square while maintaining her studio in the Hanna Building. "The court painter to Cleveland," as she was frequently referred to in the press, made the Hanna Building the exclusive kingdom over which she reigned, part queen, part damsel in distress. Her servants were the building staff who worked night and weekend shifts to run a manual elevator for her exclusive benefit and forwarded her mail whenever she was out of town. Her courtiers were the professional men with offices there, doctors, dentists, and lawyers. Edie bewitched these solid stand-up men with wives and children, who might have found fulfillment enough in the grind of their workday lives but missed the glitter someone like Edie could provide. They revered her talents as a painter and commissioned portraits of their families. The highlight of their day was to be invited for 5 P.M. cocktails in her studio or to the unveiling of a portrait.

These men provided Edie—and Dare when she was in town— with both free professional services and invitations to their homes. Their children called Edie "Aunt Edith" and found her—and Dare—as fascinating as their fathers did. Marion Broadbent, the daughter of Dr. Holly Broadbent, an orthodontist whose office was in the Keith Building across the street and who had straightened Dare's teeth free of charge, was painted by Edie in 1939. To the fourth-grader Marion, Edie and Dare seemed to be "more like playing a part than real people." Their very lives seemed make-believe. But Edie's gifts for getting by struck her as very real. She thought of her as "savvy," as someone who "knew instinctively how to do things." Or to work with what she had. Even though the economy had improved, the Depression had muted Edie's opportunities.

Commissions from Europe and Hollywood were no longer coming in. For now, Cleveland's elite was all that was left to cultivate.

Edie's days followed a disciplined and mostly solitary routine. There were no cooking facilities in either the studio or her hotel room. For lunch, she descended to the coffee shop in the Hanna Building lobby; even though she carried the food back up to the studio, she was invariably done up to the nines. Dinners were taken at the Fred Harvey's restaurant in the Cleveland Union Terminal adjoining the Hotel Cleveland. She timed her nightly entrance to avoid the dinner rush, but stragglers stopped and stared when Edie appeared in her mink coat, her curls coiffed and her face meticulously made up. She always sat at the counter with her back to the room, leaving her fur draped over her shoulders. As Edie could walk from her hotel room to the restaurant through interior passageways, no coat was necessary. Perhaps it served as a sort of protective armor or as the badge of her achievement. Regardless, no other Fred Harvey's patrons dressed like this.

To Edie's regular waitress, Amelia York, Edie seemed very lonely. She spoke incessantly of missing her daughter. She invited Amelia to her hotel room several times and expressed interest in painting her portrait, although she never did. But she was generous and attentive in other ways. Amelia had admired Edie's gold charm bracelet, and one evening Edie presented Amelia with a charm bracelet of her own; over time she bought her many charms to go on it. Once when Edie left her lipstick behind on the counter, Amelia saved it to give back to her the next evening. To thank her, Edie gave Amelia a lipstick charm, with a red enamel lipstick that swiveled up and down in its tube. When Amelia told Edie she was getting married, Edie bought her a book charm, with a "cover" on which was engraved FUTURE PLANS, a charm of a couple kissing, and a cluster charm with dangling pan, knife, fork, and spoon. The last of her gifts to Amelia was a folding picture frame that Dare had made. Covered in brocade fabric, it contained an oval-shaped photograph of Edie on one side, and Dare on the other, a copy of the photograph they had sat for to commemorate their Hollywood makeovers.

In the summer of 1939, Eva Tuttle, one of Dare's Laurel classmates, came from Cleveland to New York for the World's Fair. She contacted Dare, who arranged for her to stay in a room at the AWA, and they visited the fair together. Dare showed Eva the offices of the John Robert Powers modeling agency, where she was registered, and took her to eat at the Automat. To Eva, Dare seemed quite alone in the big city. But Eva admired how dazzlingly beautiful her former classmate had become. She wondered why Dare had no suitors. While Eva was admittedly boy crazy, she found her friend disinterested in the opposite sex. Except maybe one "boy."

Dare had found Florence Wright listed in the Manhattan phone book, at 410 West 24th Street, but had no way of knowing that her brother was living there too, a straight shot down Ninth Avenue from the AWA, or that a twenty-two-year separation could be bridged by a bus ride of thirty-three blocks.

Blaine had been living with Florence since Ivan's death, save for a semester spent at Hamilton College in 1930; finding college life too regimented, he had dropped out and returned to live with his stepmother. Perhaps because he was loath to leave the warm nest she provided, or because his stepmother was loath to push him out, he was still there a decade later, struggling to become a writer, with forays into acting and modeling work to bring in spending money, jobs he found even more sporadically than did his sister.

Since boyhood, Blaine had dreamed of becoming a writer. His most cherished possession was Ivan's typewriter, which he carried with him everywhere. His friends teased him that he was always banging away on it, even on camping trips, but he never shared with them the impressive short stories that came of all his typing.

The first piece he submitted for publication was turned down everywhere, a rejection that hit especially hard. His stories—which invariably featured divorced couples or fathers and sons—were attempts to face his dilemmas head on. "I read . . . with much appreciation of the manner in which it was done," *Redbook*'s editor wrote. "In our short stories, however, we are trying to get away from the tragic marital separation, which is the subject of so many of them." Blaine turned his hand to more marketable adventure stories, which were published in various pulp fiction magazines, but his output was inconsistent and the income negligible. In the spring of 1939, scanning newspaper help-wanted ads in search of a direction that still eluded him at the age of twenty-seven, the word *family* caught his eye. And so it was that he spent that summer—and the next—as an au pair for the Vaillant family at their summer home in New Hampshire. George Vaillant was a curator at the Museum of Natural History, while his wife, Susannah, was a loving mother to their three children. Had Blaine himself placed an ad seeking the perfect surrogate family, the Vaillants would have been the ideal respondents.

In the fall of 1940, Blaine, still a Canadian citizen, enlisted in the Royal Canadian Air Force. He was assigned to begin pilot training at a flight school near Montreal. Knowing that Ivan's only surviving brother, Austin, was an engineer there, Florence suggested Blaine look him up. That Christmas, Austin invited Blaine, on holiday leave, and Florence to join his family's celebration. Austin, who had not seen Florence or Blaine since Ivan's death, was shocked to learn that Blaine had had no contact with his mother and sister in the intervening years. Florence explained that they had respected Edie's wish that the children remain separated. Florence herself had no objection to their meeting. Austin decided to contact Edie. If Edie still resisted, he promised he would try to persuade her to change her mind.

Edie had always maintained that Ivan and Florence had handed down the decree that the siblings never meet and, as with all her stories, she had come to believe that it was true. Few of her friends or patrons even knew there was a son, but with the revelation that Florence wouldn't stand in the way, she had lost her only defense. Reluctantly, she gave Austin the telephone number at the

Hotel Bristol at 129 West 48th Street, where Dare had recently moved when the AWA was commandeered by the U.S. Navy as a bachelor officers' quarters. Austin's next phone call was to Dare. He told her that he and Blaine were coming to New York to meet her on her brother's next leave.

Austin described the reunion in Central Park of the tall, dark, and handsome Blaine and his model-chic golden-haired sister as "highly charged." Dare cried with joy when she laid eyes on her brother, and with relief. (She later said she had been afraid he would not like her.) That evening, Dare took Blaine to meet Genie Rawls and her new husband, Donald Seawell. When Donald answered the door, a beaming Dare standing beside the uniformed Blaine announced, "I'd like you to meet my new brother."

Together again at twenty-nine and twenty-seven, after a separation of nearly twenty-five years, neither Blaine nor Dare seemed to know quite how to view their relationship or what to make of the intensity of their feelings for one another. Austin told his son they fell in love and discussed the possibility of marriage with him; they thought they might conceal their actual relationship. Even before Blaine's return to Canada, though, the fantasy of romantic possibilities had dissipated. Instead, Blaine assumed the role of protective big brother. "Little Sister" was the affectionate term with which he addressed Dare from then on.

But if they were soulmates, with everything in common, there was one fundamental point on which they never could agree. During their long separation, they had each told themselves very different stories about their mother. Blaine considered Edie a selfish witch, who dumped him because he was excess baggage, and blamed her, not Ivan, for all that had gone wrong. If Dare had once explored related feelings, as she had in "The Little Green Door," they had since been banished from her conscious mind. Dare could not join her brother in his desire to burn the witch in her own oven, nor did she foresee that her new allegiance to Blaine would be perceived by Edie as tantamount to the same thing. Dare tried to ignore his rants against Edie, however much they hurt her, as earlier she had tried to ignore Edie's rants against Ivan.

Observing how thoroughly Edie controlled his sister, Blaine sought to undermine his mother's power. Hearing that Dare couldn't afford to pay her Actors' Equity dues and that Edie wouldn't pay them, he gave Dare the money. And bowled over by how beautiful his sister had become—he would always take immense pride and pleasure in her appearance—he also noticed how unaware she seemed of her desirability. He saw how carefully Edie had stacked the prohibitions, somehow programming Dare into believing that men were dangerous or that none were good enough. Blaine became determined to deprogram his sister.

During their reunion visit, Dare asked Blaine to pose for a pencil drawing. As she viewed Edie's portraits of her as expressions of her mother's love, so too her desire to draw Blaine would demonstrate her love for him, and certainly it was a way to keep him with her when he went back to Canada. After Blaine's departure, as if to return him to his mother as well, she sent on to Edie her exquisite pencil portrait of Blaine in uniform. She was unable to recognize how threatened and jealous the very mention of Blaine made Edie feel. Ignoring the portrait's subject, Edie commented only on Dare's impressive drawing skill, suggested that this form of portraiture might be a way for Dare to support herself, and arranged a series of commissions for pencil portraits of her Cleveland patrons' children that Dare could do in New York from photographs.

In denial of the evident tensions between her mother and her brother, Dare's dream of reuniting her family remained undiminished. While the war raged on, keeping Blaine at a safe remove, Edie did seem a little softened to the prospect of her son's return to their lives. She was clearly visibly flattered when Christmas 1941, which Dare and Edie spent together in Cleveland, brought two phone calls and a dozen red roses. Missing the fact that it was not to her but to her daughter that Blaine's attentions were directed, Edie began to revise her view of her son.

Blaine thrived in the RCAF, at least in the noncombat training stages. Upon completion of pilot training, he was promoted to the rank of flying officer and became an advanced training instructor on single-engine aircraft. In May 1942, he transferred to the U.S. Air Force as a first lieutenant assigned to the Eighth Air Force's 56th Fighter Group.

He made close friends in the Royal Canadian Air Force, chief among them one of his flight instructors, Philip Victor Glas Sandeman, a British RAF pilot of the sherry and port importing family, who had arrived in Canada a year earlier to help train pilots for the RCAF. "Sandy," as Blaine called him, was, at twenty, nine years Blaine's junior. In December of 1942, when the two men learned they would be sent to England in the new year, Blaine invited Philip to accompany him to spend their two-week holiday leave in New York. They could stay with Florence—and Blaine told Philip there was a woman he wanted him to meet.

Dare had already planned to spend the holidays in Cleveland with Edie. Learning that Blaine would be in New York, she decided to change her ticket to make it back to New York the day after Christmas. On her return, the Seawells invited her to bring Blaine to a cocktail party at their apartment; Blaine arrived with the charming and dashing blond English airman. The entire gathering was very impressed by Blaine's friend, none seemingly more so than Dare. Blaine and Dare spent the next nine days showing Philip around New York. Dazzled by the sister of the colleague he so admired, Philip dashed off letters to his family and friends declaring he had fallen in love at first sight. His recently widowed mother, Marie, and brother, Brian, were aghast. American girls, they cautioned him, were fast. Who knew what she might be up to?

The Sandemans had nothing to fear. Dare could not have been further from their notion of American girls. Suitors had swarmed around her ever since she arrived in New York. Their advances were, in all cases, rebuffed. Philip was only given consideration because he was safe, an extension of her adored brother. Those who knew of Dare's intense if impossible love for Blaine surmised that Philip was Blaine's gift to Dare, a hand-picked substitute.

During their visit, Dare did a pencil portrait of Philip in uniform, and the three took dozens of photographs of one another with a camera Blaine bought for the occasion and left behind as a gift to her. With no guarantee of when—or if—she would ever see them again, these images took on a special meaning for Dare. In photography she had found a means to hold loved ones steady and preserve them from loss.

On January 5, 1943, the sixteenth anniversary of Ivan's death, Blaine and Philip sailed away to war. Dare corresponded with both, and with Edie about them. Edie was wary. "I really can't tell about Dare with Sandy," Edie wrote Allie. "I know she appreciates him as a wonderful and good person, and fascinating, but whether he holds the spark for her I believe she herself does not know." As if to reassure herself, she closed: "He won't be getting a leave, nor Blaine, until after the invasion."

With Blaine and now Philip in her life, Dare seemed to regain a sense of purpose missing since her graduation from Laurel. Fairy tales and her dolls had been the focus of the stories she told herself in childhood; now, in her late twenties, she turned the focus onto herself. These stories were narrated not with words but through images, by means of her new camera and its self-timer. The resulting self-portraits, in which she tried on not only clothes but also personas, were first steps on the path to explore a self of her own, away from the role prescribed by Edie of good and precious daughter or that of beloved sister—and even as object of romantic love. The choice of medium alone represented a break from Edie. And these portraits could be created in privacy, out from under her mother's watchful eye.

The photograph itself was the last step in an elaborate process. The first was the creation of a desired tableau. The stage set was her Bristol Hotel room, which she had decorated in her favorite red-

and-white color scheme. She had used striped taffeta to make her draperies, bedspread and bolsters, armchair cushion, and even a pleated skirt to enclose the base of her standard-issue hotel-room desk. So disguised, the desk became a dressing table. On either side of an oval mirror she had displayed her talismans: a pile of treasured books including *Tales from the Secret Kingdom* (Blaine's childhood gift to her), a vase of red roses sent by Blaine, a bottle of Sandeman's sherry, and, on opposite ends, a photograph of Blaine and her drawing of Philip.

In one series of photographs, taken with the Kodacolor film that had just come on the market the previous year, Dare is seated at the transformed desk wearing a white satin confection, a cross between a wedding dress and an elaborate undergarment. Her blond hair is pinned up in front and set in cascading waves down her back. Her lips and fingernails are painted bright red. She holds a letter from Philip, but her glance is directed over her bare shoulder at the camera set up behind her. The red roses, the bottle of Sandeman's, and the striped curtains are doubled in the mirror's reflection.

These staged photographs have the quality of movie stills, as if depicting a moment in a larger though unexplained narrative. This, too, was storytelling. If the precise meaning is not clear, the images are still highly suggestive. In each, Dare is caught or trapped: between Philip and Blaine, within the bars of the chair's back, and by the vertical prison-bar stripes surrounding her. The colors—red representing passion and desire; white, purity and innocence—also imply conflict. And the déshabillé of her outfit suggests a mature and therefore sexual woman, or at least one investigating the prospect.

This was a time of waiting: for the war to be over, for Blaine's return and his reunion with Edie, and for whatever would transpire with Philip. There was nothing to do but prepare. In the meantime, Dare shuttled back and forth between Cleveland and New York. In New York, she gravitated to the Seawell family, where she became a regular fixture at parties at their Upper East Side apartment. Other guests included Genie's acting colleagues, among them Tallulah

Dare's future fiancé, RAF Flight Lieutenant Philip Sandeman, 1943.

Dare in her room at the Hotel Bristol, seated at her shrine to Philip and Blaine, New York City, 1944.

Bankhead, whom Genie had befriended when they co-starred in *The Little Foxes*. Tallulah had served as matron of honor at the Seawells' 1941 wedding and was now a client of Donald's.

The Seawells considered Dare a member of the family. Over time, Dare's friendship with Genie's husband, whom she placed in the father-protector role, became as close as her friendship with Genie. Women who didn't know Dare might have viewed her as a potential threat. She was beautiful, glamorous, and, on the surface, alluringly sexual. But Genie understood that, despite her low-cut homemade gowns, Dare was a little girl playing dress-up, not a predatory adventuress. No one who knew her at all well was fooled by her exterior.

Feeling increasingly displaced by Dare's preoccupation with Blaine and, now, Philip, Edie sought to restore herself to center stage in her daughter's life. She had come to view Blaine as Ivan's agent and could not overcome her fear that he, like Ivan, would seek to destroy her, as well as win away devoted Dare's attentions. And in Philip, a potential love interest, Edie perceived a threat in some ways even greater than that posed by Blaine.

Edie began sending Dare daily letters, calling constantly, and visiting New York more often. Dare, unaware of what lay behind this outpouring of attention, delighted in it. On Edie's visits to New York, she took her along to the Seawells, orchestrated picnics in Central Park, and accompanied her mother to the Metropolitan Museum of Art, where they took in the old masters while Edie fantasized aloud that her work would hang there someday too.

In Dare's hotel room they played dress-up, taking turns with the outfits and the camera to photograph each other. But Edie, whose creativity, like her daughter's, was practically boundless, could never seem to master the focusing of a camera. Dare set up each shot of herself so that her mother would have only to click the shutter.

As summer approached, Edie held out a rosy red apple, proposing that she and Dare go away together. Having heard that the

Seawells would not be using Mayport, the estate that Genie had inherited a mile from Bozman, Maryland, on the Eastern Shore, Edie had Dare ask Donald if they could borrow the house.

They were welcome but Donald cautioned that it had been unoccupied throughout the war years; it might be in disarray and the grounds would be untended. Edie was undaunted and undeterred, even upon learning that a propeller on the roof generated enough electricity for just one lamp.

Indeed, they found the sea myrtle grown up to the front door and the house in exteme disrepair. After sunset, they huddled together in the darkness, terrified by strange noises, which turned out to be the roof propeller, "screeching like a banshee," and animals unused to the presence of humans. Unsettled, Edie wanted to leave. Dare comforted her, assuring her that the beautiful sunny days would more than make up for the scary nights and the primitive conditions.

They did stay, for the entire summer. In this deserted house in its own overgrown forest but just a few hundred feet from the estate's two miles of waterfront, they found the perfect backdrop for their favorite fantasy: wrecked but not mussed—Edie hated being mussed—on a desert island. As when they had first landed in Cleveland, they thrived by relying on their own considerable resources, the chance to utilize all their ingenuity and industry. Although they would come to prefer actual islands, all that was really required was a place at a remove from the outside world where they could create one of their own.

They spent the days sunbathing—they both adored the physically transformative aspect of a suntan—rowing on Leadenham Creek, as this inlet of the Chesapeake Bay was called, and playing dress-up, indoors and out. With Dare's camera, they documented it all.

It was on this trip that the dress-up game took a new turn. As usual, they posed in a variety of outfits, both in their everyday clothes, exotic enough, and in gowns with balloon sleeves and bustles that

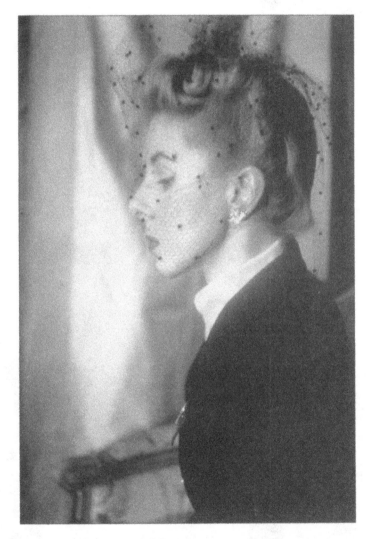

Hide-and-seek:
Dare in one of her favorite poses, behind a veil.

One of the first nude shots: Dare, in a rowboat on Chesapeake Bay on a visit to Mayport, the Seawells' home on the eastern shore of Maryland, 1945.

have the look of period costumes. But now Edie suggested they photograph Dare not just in the complete outfit but in the act of putting it on or taking it off or, alternatively, without any garments at all. Edie clicked the shutter on Dare wearing only the high-heeled black pumps she had earlier paired with a flouncy skirt and top, or in the skirt with no top. She photographed Dare stretched across the inside of the rowboat nude or sitting on the dock wearing nothing but a straw hat. Dare, ever compliant, willingly played the exhibitionist to Edie's voyeur, a compliance that had everything to do with her desire to please her mother. Edie had bigger aims. Consciously or not, as if Dare's body were a territory yet to be claimed, Edie had put down her flag.

That August brought the news that Blaine was on his way home from the war. Philip, already settling into civilian life, would soon be free to launch his courtship. While Dare rejoiced, for Edie it was as if a dark cloud descended. Edie wrote to her cousin Allie that the Mayport idyll had been "wonderful, but any time with Dare—wherever—is always wonderful. Wasn't I lucky to get her instead of Blaine." The meaning of this last sentence cut two ways. But there was no ambiguity in her intention.

CHAPTER FOUR

Making Family

*Children never forget injustice. They forgive heaps of things
grown-up people mind; but that sin is the unpardonable sin.*
—VIRGINIA WOOLF, *The Voyage Out*

After five years and two months in the military,
the much-decorated Major Blaine Wright returned
to New York in October 1945, as unsure of what to
do with his life as he had been before the war. In
military life, he had found a family of sorts and a
role to fit into, but now that it was over, all he took
with him was a variation of his uniform: khaki pants
and a white shirt under his flight jacket.

Although he had succeeded in the air force,
he was in no way a warrior. He would always be
haunted by the lives lost, by guilt at having survived,
and by what he saw as gratuitously violent behavior.
Returning from missions, his fellow pilots would
machine gun "targets of opportunity," killing horses
and cows for sheer sport. Blaine was horrified; he
liked to rescue, not kill.

The wartime accomplishment of which he was proudest was having saved the life of a newborn baby girl. Despite disastrous weather conditions, he flew the Rh-negative blood she needed from Colchester, England, to the Isle of Man. The Colchester Hospital blood transfusion officer who waited with him on the tarmac blanketed in fog later wrote Blaine's colonel that Blaine had "expressed very forcibly that it was a real pleasure to him, since he had come to this country to kill, to have a chance to co-operate with us to save a life." Otherwise, if he had excelled in the air force it was not because he was ever on board emotionally or philosophically. It was because he discovered his talent for and love of flying. He mastered the technical requirements quickly and relished the sense of freedom it gave him.

On his return, Blaine, thirty-three, gravitated toward those who had offered him sanctuary before the war: Florence, the Vaillants, and the newest point on his emotional compass, his sister, Dare. He wanted them all to know and love one another as well. He had come to care deeply for the Vaillant children during the two summers spent with their family. He had also grown close to their mother, Susannah, and was always transfixed by her maternal attentions.

Blaine and Suzie Vaillant had corresponded throughout the war years. But she waited until his return to tell him about her husband's suicide the previous May. Blaine left immediately for Washington, D.C., where she and the children were staying with relatives. Joanna, the eldest, recalled how happy it made the shaken family when Blaine walked through the door. Her brother Henry recalled, "Blaine stepped into the breach after my father died. It was a very safe place for him."

And there were other families to check on. He had warm feelings for Florence's sister, Grace Hann, and her family; he had spent his boyhood summers at their home in the upstate New York town of Walton. While visiting the Hanns, Blaine paid a call on the widow who owned Butternut Island, a nearby land outcropping in the Delaware River. Blaine had cherished memories of the camping trips and cookouts there each summer and proposed becoming the island's caretaker. She said he could just have it if he could manage the taxes. Blaine accepted the offer on the spot and decided he would make Butternut Island his home. He could fix up the island's only remaining dwelling, a cabin that had been part of "Idlewild," a boys' camp once based there, fish, get back to his writing, and ponder his next move. And as it was only a three-hour drive from New York City, his friends and sister could easily come up on weekends. He rechristened his new home "The Isle of Pot." Visitors could say they were "going to Pot."

If Dare was overjoyed to have Blaine back from the war and to be included in his circle, she was impatient to bring her real family together again. To her suggestion of a reunion with Edie in New York or Cleveland, however, Blaine, as wary of his mother as she was of him, threw up obstacles. If they got together, he insisted, it would have to be on his own turf—and terms. He told Dare they should wait until summer, when he would have had time to fix up his cabin and make improvements to his island. Knowing that Dare wanted things nailed down, he agreed to send a formal invitation to Edie, a letter he closed by saying, "We will meet as two people with no background and see if we like each other."

These days, Dare was modeling sporadically—and halfheartedly. She was far more enthusiastic about her new interest in photography. She was teaching herself to process and develop film in the darkroom she constructed in her hotel bathroom, the equipment set on removable planks over the bathtub. She also sewed, not only for her own benefit but for friends, filling orders from those who admired the silk scarves and leather handbags she had made for herself and Edie. And as Dare had become accustomed to making gifts for Edie's patrons, she continued this pattern with Blaine's friends. She sewed Suzie Vaillant an elaborate quilted taffeta housecoat trimmed with velvet, a blanket coat, and a New Look skirt, and photographed her in them.

A dress-up session in Edie's room at the Hotel Cleveland, 1946.

Blaine had invited Edie and Dare to Walton for August. Philip had written that he would visit in July. With a full slate of house guests scheduled, Blaine wanted Dare to see his new home and share this place of childhood happiness. While Dare did not partake in Blaine's enthusiasm for the opening of the trout season, April 1 was an important day on his calendar. On March 31, Dare took the bus to Walton and Blaine ferried her to Pot across a narrow patch of the Delaware River in his Willys Jeep.

As there was still snow on the ground, he was forced to postpone his sister's fishing education. Housebound, Dare immersed herself in domestic activities, attempting to transform her brother's rustic dwelling into something homier. She cleaned, rearranged what furniture there was, and measured for curtains and bedspreads. These she began on her return to the city, along with a new wardrobe for herself for the summer ahead.

In July, Philip arrived in New York to meet Dare and head up to Blaine's island. For two weeks, the trio swam and fished; in the evenings, after dining on the day's catch cooked on an open fire, they played baseball. They took turns photographing one another in all their activities. In the pictures Blaine took of Philip and Dare, they appear lit from within. Philip's attraction to Dare is palpable. But if Dare's attire was sexually suggestive, whether a Little Bo Peep dress that pushed up her breasts or tight-fitting striped pedal pushers that showcased her derriere, her behavior toward Philip was more sisterly. She clearly viewed Philip as another brother, a playmate.

Blaine made no secret of his wish that Philip and Dare marry. Not only would it mean a safe guardianship for his sister, it would secure Philip as a brother for himself. No one seemed bothered that, at twenty-five, Philip was seven years Dare's junior. With Blaine's encouragement, Philip asked Dare to marry him. Dare accepted, but she seemed to view the proposal as abstractly as she had the possibility of marrying Blaine, as if it were a sort of game. They commemorated

Dare and Blaine together again, postwar.

Dare with Philip during his visit to Pot on the day of their engagement, July 1946.

their engagement by posing in bathing suits, perched on a rock in the river and holding hands. If Philip wondered what to make of Dare's reticence, the way she pulled away from his physical advances, he was respectful and did not press her. Perhaps he told himself that physical intimacy would come after they were married. In any case, he had to go back to England; the holiday was over.

It would be some time before Dare would break the news of her engagement to Edie. She did tell friends—including a steady stream of would-be suitors—that Philip was in her life, but in vague terms. She gave Roy Wilder, Jr., a writer at the *New York Herald Tribune*, introduced to her by Genie Rawls, no reason to think that Philip would be an impediment to launching his own courtship. To Wilder's annoyance, when Blaine was in the city, Dare invited him along on their dates. When he was not, she asked Wilder up to her room at the Hotel Bristol, where she showed him the darkroom in her bathroom or discussed the relative merits of breaking into the piggy bank where she kept her savings. Roy was smitten, even if he found her odd and exceptionally shy. Although she listened with interest to whatever he had to say, she barely spoke herself. Still, he came to care genuinely for her. Deciding that the reason she ate so sparingly—usually nothing more than a can of soup heated on her hotel room hot plate—was to economize, he took her out for roast beef dinners. And when she had the flu, he watched over her like a worried father.

In August, the much-anticipated visit took place. Edie came to New York from Cleveland and Blaine from Walton to take his mother and sister up to his island. This reunion, too, was emotionally charged, but it was not joyful. Blaine was put off from the moment he laid eyes on his mother, who was dressed as if she were off to the Riviera—down to her high heels—rather than a cabin in the woods where bats flew through the bedroom at night and the toilet was located in an outhouse.

Edie's expectations of what would transpire on this visit were as off-base as her getups. Her imperious manner alienated her son even further. Blaine decided he did not like his long-lost mother and proceeded to attack her verbally, unleashing the rage built up during all the years of their separation. Edie wrote Daisy Whiteside in an uncharacteristically shaky hand: "He thinks I am all emotion and talent and not very intellectual. That I haven't worked hard at all but had an easy time and that the corners of my mouth turn down because I have held spite against Ivan all these years and therefore made no openings for happiness for myself and now expect him to make up to me for what Ivan didn't give."

Dare suffered as her mother and brother feuded. Edie recognized this in her letter to Daisy. "Poor kid—she had a rotten time between us." Try as Dare might, there was apparently no way to make peace between mother and son. She tried everything to "unite" them, even her camera. But the photographic record reveals they were no more eager to pose together than they were to try to get along. Dare captured what would be the first photograph of Edie and Blaine together since 1917 when Blaine did consent to take Edie punting on the Delaware River. In that shot, Edie sits, posed dramatically with one hand on the rim of the boat, the other on her knee, looking pensive and sad. Blaine stands, peering down at the water, as he propels the boat with a pole. Dare caught only one other shot of them together, sitting on either side of what looks like a conflagration but is actually a particularly smoky campfire. Again, Blaine's head is lowered and turned away, his eyes closed to shield them from the smoke that all but obscures the pair.

If Dare could not arrange them into a happy family, she could arrange a felicitous room, and she had worked hard to fix up the bedroom she shared with Edie. She had dressed up the two pushed-together camp beds in which they slept with a satin scallop-edged bedspread she had made herself and cotton sheets she had embroidered. As there was no closet, she hung their clothing, straw hats, and baskets on hooks. On the dresser, she set up their toiletries, books, and a bouquet of flowers into an artful still life. She hung a creel, the wicker basket carried by trout fishermen to hold fishing supplies and fish, over the head of the bed and placed their folded nightgowns upon the two pillows.

Edie was utterly unimpressed by Blaine's crude home and his island, never mind that the conditions were similar to those she had endured, and happily so, for the entire summer with Dare at Mayport. Edie's island fantasy did not include a third person, particularly not her son. In any case, she did not share his affection for the natural world and belittled his spartan lifestyle. And it irked her to see that her son seemed without ambition or any drive to improve his circumstances. The material world meant nothing to Blaine. His one armchair was held together with duct tape; his only cherished possessions were his typewriter, his fishing equipment, and his books.

Edie was, however, quite impressed by Blaine's appearance, his handsome features and Adonis-like physique. What was beneath was another matter. When Dorothy Brandt, a local woman who had known Ivan since he married Florence and Blaine since boyhood, paid a visit, Edie quizzed her about Ivan. She reported to Daisy: "The old lady in Walton said his father was so strict with him—his every move—that he probably reacted by doing nothing after his death. Yet he idealizes his father no end now." Ivan was said to be a stern and sometimes violent disciplinarian, overcompensating perhaps for his own inability to exert control over his own life and his epic drinking. Edie blamed Ivan for the fact that her son was so troubled and would never acknowledge any responsibility for the damage done.

Blaine was not, in fact, "doing nothing." He had invented a fishing lure whose hydrodynamic curvature and etched markings created the illusion of a plump bait fish in the water. To some he claimed the Phoebe was named for an English girl he had loved who was killed in the blitz; he told others it was named for the flycatchers—phoebes—who made nests of moss, mud, and leaves under the eaves of his front porch. Edie could not know that sales of the lure would support Blaine for the rest of his life. She considered the Phoebe a worthless achievement.

Blaine told his mother nothing of his real ambition. For the decade following the war, he continued to dream of writing a great novel. But visitors to Blaine's cabin took note of the typewriter gathering dust, all but obscured beneath a pile of Dare's photographs. Blaine's storytelling had unfortunately stalled out with his tales of Captain Bitters Angostura, who kidnapped a princess, and his greatest enemy, the pirate Rossi Martini, who was swallowed by a whale, stories with which he entertained the Vaillant children, assuming a different voice for every character. For his characters' names, he used the makings of old-fashioneds and martinis, ingredients with which he was increasingly familiar. After Edie's visit, he began to drink heavily. From that point on, he would always speak of hating his mother "like poison."

However shaken Edie was by the time spent with Blaine, she was far too pragmatic—and vain—to brook pain through self-destruction. Instead, she attempted to regain her emotional balance by tearing down her son, blaming him for the failure of their relationship. To friends, she painted a picture of Blaine as "a wayfarer and a loner," to whom she had tried very hard to be close. To Daisy, she confided something more of the truth. "He is quite handsome and has very polished manners and people fall for him. . . . I suppose I expected something I shouldn't have because I felt he had found himself in his fine war record and forgot that all my previous contacts were extremely unpleasant." She wrote that his idea that they wipe the slate clean and meet as though for the first time was "foolish, after all!! I think he really resents the fact that I didn't raise him too. . . . Well, OK, I am willing to go along as usual—Dare is all I need."

Edie still did not know that Philip and Dare had not only discussed marriage but were, however informally, engaged. When Dare finally did tell her mother, Edie tried to conceal this new upset. Perhaps she could see just how abstractly her daughter viewed the prospect. Still, even Edie could not find fault with the abundantly good enough and very handsome Philip, who was from a fine family and a wealthy one. And if the marriage did come to pass, and Philip spirited her daughter away to England, Edie decided there was no reason not to join them there herself.

But if she were to move to England, she would need to build her reputation as an artist there. During the war, she had become a devotee of Winston Churchill. She listened raptly to his radio speeches and considered him "a good combination—half American and half English," just like herself. Reading that he continued to serve as Chancellor of the University of Bristol in the postwar period, and having saved a reproduction of the famous 1941 Yousuf Karsh "Bulldog" photograph of him, she decided to make a painting of it. If the university could not be convinced to buy it, she would offer it as a donation.

However well she concealed it, Edie was greatly shaken by recent events, first the reunion with Blaine and now Dare's possible impending marriage. She fastened the blame on Blaine, writing to Allie: "Everything seems to have gone haywire since my association with Blaine this summer. I guess he is as bad for me as Ivan was." Seeing how upset her mother was, Dare begged her brother to apologize to Edie for treating her badly. In deference to his sister, Blaine wrote to Edie, saying he would act differently if given another chance. Edie was unmoved. Her cruel streak had been unleashed. She never revisited Walton, and whenever they saw each other in the future it was only because Dare trapped them into doing so, and it involved— invariably—an ugly scene.

Dare's dream of re-creating a united family had been dashed by the animosity between her mother and her brother. But she would not choose between them. Instead, she established a pattern she would maintain for the rest of Edie's life, enduring their sparring on the rare occasions when they were together and spending time alone with each of them, even if it provoked the other's wrath. Edie behaved like a jealous lover when Dare went off with Blaine to his island or spent time with him in New York. The rivalry between Blaine and Edie meant an enduring sadness for Dare, but it did continue to bring Edie closer to her. Now that Edie was forced to compete for her daughter's love, she became more consistent in her attentions—and more and more possessive. This gave Dare a power over her mother she had never before exerted. But even with Edie so completely centered on her, Dare worked as hard as ever to please and appease her mother, as if the threat of losing her was as real as it had felt in her younger years.

Edie, too, was working hard, and scheming for ways to divide her children. As she looked ahead to the next summer, she knew she would need an alternative to Pot with which to entice Dare. Edie and Dare had first heard of the island of Ocracoke, one of a narrow chain of islands on North Carolina's Outer Banks, from Donald Seawell and Roy Wilder, both native North Carolinians. They described it as an isolated and romantic place, almost lost in time. There was one telephone on the island, no cars, not even any paved roads, just a network of sand paths under a canopy of willows dripping with Spanish moss. Down one of these paths, the pirate Blackbeard's house was still standing.

As the Seawells had resumed using Mayport, Edie decided to stake out Ocracoke as her Pot. Seawell and Wilder recommended they stay at the Wahab Village Hotel. As the monthly room rate was a better bargain, Edie decided they would spend the month of August 1947 there. Having placated Edie with the promise of a month on Ocracoke, Dare told Blaine she would spend July with him in Walton. When Philip wrote to invite her to England, Dare put him off. Her summer was overbooked; she suggested she come in the fall instead.

Edie and Dare adored Ocracoke, finding there their Shangri-La, a magical sanctuary, remote and outside time. The peaceable island existed without government or police, watched over by a lone peppermint-stick lighthouse. Only nature, hurricanes, and sudden gales threatened the island's tranquillity. The wild ponies that ran free, said to be descendants of those that swam ashore from shipwrecked Spanish boats, were a reminder that the waters surrounding Ocracoke had been and still were treacherous. Its shoals were known as the Graveyard of the Atlantic, for all the wrecked ships buried there. But the waters also formed the ultimate barrier, making the 15 miles of unspoiled beach feel all the more protected.

Edie and Dare were to return almost every summer. It was not surprising that Dare loved Ocracoke; it was a place where her mother's undivided attention was guaranteed. Edie's affection for Ocracoke was more surprising. She seemed to find this sparsely inhabited island, where there was no one to impress but islanders whose life was remarkable only for its simplicity, a refuge and a relief. In Cleveland, she complained endlessly of physical exhaustion, plagued by feelings of being "pushed" and "pressured." Now sixty-seven, she indulged herself for the first time in what she called "chaise longue" days, when, too tired to lift even a paintbrush, she would lie about nibbling candied rose leaves. More than ever, the exposure to the affluence and domestic security of her portrait subjects was stirring up envy and resentment. The only respite was to be away from that world, with Dare, the one person with whom she could enjoy a sense of relaxation and intimacy. Ocracoke became the place where Edie could drop her masks.

That first summer, they established the routine they would maintain on all future visits. In the mornings, Dare would descend to the hotel dining room to carry up breakfast to Edie. Midmorning, to give them time to complete their elaborate toilette, they were picked up by Jake Alligood, a fishing guide and taxi service operator whose entire fleet those first summers consisted of one old army jeep left

The first of many summer visits to Ocracoke, August 1947.

over from the war. Jake would drive them to an area locals call the "break of the dunes," three miles down the beach, where there was no chance that anyone might happen upon them. There, day after day, they would sunbathe nude, swim, eat the boxed lunch made up for them by the hotel, photograph each other, walk, and read. Blaine would have been amused by one photograph in which Edie reads a detective novel called *A Pinch of Poison*.

At 5 p.m., Edie would wave a white handkerchief to signal to Jake, trundling down the beach in his jeep, that they were dressed and ready. Dinner was served early, family style, in the hotel dining room. While the other guests would play cards in the evenings or talk on the front porch, Edie and Dare would head up to their corner room on the second floor. It was the room they requested each summer. It had one double bed.

Edie and Dare, especially Dare in her revealing outfits, caused quite a stir among the male population on Ocracoke. But Dare had eyes only for one Ocracoker, the grandson of the hotel's owners. That first summer, Jim Wynn was just shy of his fourth birthday. Dare took dozens of photographs of this spirited child. Unthreatened by her daughter's attachment to *this* little boy, Edie decided she also adored Jimmy.

Jim's mother, Lanie Boyette Wynn, was puzzled by the Wright women's devotion to her son, but she wasn't at all surprised that Jim would be taken with them. They lavished upon him just the sort of attention a boy his age would want. They took him up to their room, where they read to him from his picture books or told him stories. The biggest lure was Bongo, Dare's monkey hand puppet, a gift from Blaine that she took with her everywhere. Whenever Jim saw them, he would light up and ask, in his Ocracoke drawl, "Whar's the monkey?"

Before Dare's departure for Ocracoke, Roy Wilder had joked that he himself was planning to retreat to Ocracoke, to live on the beach and write a novel. When winter came, he told her, he would

Edie relaxing on Ocracoke, August 1947.

warm himself by driftwood fires; would she gather driftwood for his arrival? When she returned to New York, Dare presented Wilder with a large scroll of rolled parchment, tied with ribbon. She had drawn a pirate map, complete with **X**'s to mark buried treasure, in this case piles of driftwood. On it, she wrote: "This map to show where driftwood is buried—sufficient to see a man through one winter. Standing on big dune on the 28th day of August walk two miles in direction of your shadow past lake (possibly a mirage), take 20 paces north. You will see three dunes. Dig halfway between eastmost dune and wrecked ship. A second store lies north of the gull's nests on a line between Beacon Island and lighthouse."

Roy didn't know how to read Dare's behavior. Despite her attentions, she never seemed to warm up to him and always kept at a distance. Although she did let him kiss her, it didn't go further than that. And when they kissed, her body would go rigid and she would pull away. "You wondered what had happened to her," he recalled. The Seawells suggested the issue might be Philip. Wilder accepted that explanation, telling friends, "I'm getting competition from some wine peddler in England." (Wilder, like everyone else in Dare's life, had been led to believe that Philip was heir to the Sandeman sherry and port importing fortune. In fact, his branch of the family had broken with the firm. Philip's father, Victor Staunton Sandeman, was a career army man.)

Although the chief topic of Dare's correspondence with Philip was their impending marriage, Dare gave no one the impression that it was a reality. Edie, who worried endlessly about their finances, nagged Dare, whose interest in a modeling career was flagging, to consider alternatives. Dare insisted she would much rather be a photographer than a model. Edie suggested they make a portfolio of some of Dare's work, throwing in some of her modeling tearsheets. Dare hated what she called "selling herself," but Edie had no such qualms. It was Edie who, on a visit to New York, paid a call on *Town & Country* magazine to show off Dare's portfolio. Typically, she talked more about herself than Dare. When she learned that the magazine was planning a spread in which "real" women, not models, would be photographed in clothes available in stores, women chosen not only for their stylishness but also for being daughters or wives of distinguished men, she convinced them that Dare was the daughter of a well-known woman. After all, she told them, she had just painted Winston Churchill. Duly impressed, *Town & Country* included a photograph of the "daughter of Edith Stevenson Wright, whose portrait of Winston Churchill is to be hung in the University of Bristol, England" in the article, whose other subjects included European aristocrats, Hollywood wives, and East Coast socialites. If Edie considered this a victory, it was hers alone. Dare had gotten no closer to realizing her career as a photographer.

In October 1947, Dare winged her way to England to visit Philip with an exquisite new wardrobe in her suitcase—whipped up in yet another sewing marathon—and Bongo, the monkey puppet, in her handbag.

Consumed with foreboding, Edie fretted over her impending abandonment. She seemed to find comfort in shifting her thoughts to Jimmy Wynn. Just after Dare left for England, Edie went out to buy him a monkey puppet of his own, as well as a phosphorescent lamb nightlight that had caught her eye. She enclosed this note:

> Darling Jimmie [*sic*]:
> This is Bongo's twin and he is to be your monkey now. He likes the little lamb because when Bongo is going to sleep, the lamb makes a little light for him. When you want him to light up just hold him close to a lightbulb until he gets warm—Then he will shine in the dark. I am homesick for Ocracoke. Give my love to your Mama and everyone. Hoping to see you next summer.
> Lovingly, Dare's "Mama."

In their two encounters so far, both brief and both in the safe company of Blaine, Philip and Dare had played together like children. For the rest of the time they had known each other, there had been a war and an ocean between them. They shared an exceptional attractiveness and a tendency to play hide-and-seek with the world; it was as if they used their surface attractiveness to deflect others from getting too close. But in critical ways they were different. Impulsive, reckless, and somewhat immature, Philip was the much-loved product of a happy marriage and a privileged childhood. Dare was more fearful, cautious, and stunted emotionally. Whatever Dare's expectations for this trip, she was in no way prepared for the fact that the childlike and therefore "safe" twenty-year-old she had met in 1942 had, in the intervening years, become a real man. When the war ended in England, Philip, then twenty-four, had gone to work for Vincent Korda, the Hungarian movie producer, who with his brother, Alexander, ran London Films at the studios outside London known as Hollywood on the Thames. Philip—who, like Dare, had shown acting promise at preparatory school—hoped this job might be a way to launch a film career. In fact, according to Vincent's son Michael's family memoir *Charmed Lives*, Philip did little more than answer questions about English customs for his Hungarian boss and babysit Michael and his aptly named dog, Nuisance.

Philip was still working at London Films when Dare arrived in London. The trip had been carefully planned in advance. Philip was to meet Dare at the airport and take her to the Savoy Hotel, where she would stay during the London leg of the trip. Philip would take Dare on a tour of a house he had picked out for them. After that, they would travel to the island of Jersey, where Philip's mother lived. Assuming Marie Sandeman approved the match, the official announcement of their engagement would be made. Dare would begin preparations for the wedding on her return to New York, where the ceremony would take place the following spring.

The unraveling began at the airport. Philip wasn't there. Eventually,

Dare made her way to the Savoy on her own. After what she described to Donald Seawell as "four awful days," Philip finally did appear. Acting as if nothing had happened, he took her to see what was to be their home in Slough, outside London. There, following Edie's directive, Dare took measurements of the house, as well as photographs of its exterior and interior, so Edie could begin decorating plans from Cleveland.

Philip also took Dare to meet the couple with whom he had been living since his return from America. The husband was his colleague at London Films; Philip and the man's wife had become sexually involved. Initially, Philip seemed to view this as an acceptable way to tide himself over, and he continued to tell friends that he and Dare were going to be married. But his mistress had grown controlling and possessive, and despite her own married status she did not want to lose Philip.

Philip's colleague's wife greeted this rival for his affection with contempt on sight. It was still hard times in England, and she thought it bad form for Dare to appear in what she assumed were couture clothes. After she had gotten over Dare's appearance, however, she was no doubt relieved to see that this fashion plate was far less sophisticated than her clothing suggested. She thought Dare quite childlike, almost like a doll. When Dare told them the "Bare Wright" name-tape story, she couldn't believe that Dare would even remember this incident, let alone recount it.

The visit, which her hostess felt was inappropriately long, became an extended game of "get the guest," with Philip's paramour as ringleader and Philip too intimidated or confused to intervene. When Dare expressed interest in seeing Dover Castle, the other woman jumped at the idea. Conveniently, her father, a World War II general, was still stationed there; Dare could stay with him. Once the unsuspecting Dare had been removed, temporarily at least, she launched her campaign to set Philip against marrying Dare.

Dare had felt out of her depth with this unkind woman and

Philip's strange behavior. Happily, on her return from Dover, Philip did take her away—to Jersey, to meet Marie Sandeman and his brother, Brian. Her reception there could not have been warmer. Marie, entranced, gave her son a diamond engagement ring for his fiancée and presented Dare with a diamond brooch as a gift from herself. A few days later, on October 14, 1947, Marie placed the news of Philip and Dare's engagement in the "Forthcoming Marriages" column of the London *Times*.

Back home, Dare told both her mother and Donald Seawell about Philip's behavior and expressed doubts about the marriage, but Edie forged ahead. If Marie Sandeman had placed the engagement notice in the newspaper, the wedding was on, regardless of Dare's reservations. Edie ordered a wedding dress from the House of Worth in Paris, and began filling Dare's hope chest with trousseau lingerie she was sewing. Genie was enlisted to serve as matron of honor and Donald to give Dare away. Edie also began furnishing the Slough house, ordering carpeting and an icebox, washing machine, and stove, because, as she wrote to her Aunt Daisy, "heavy-duty items are so scarce in England."

Publicly, Edie acted thrilled at Dare's good fortune. It was only to the now five-year-old Jim Wynn that Edie confided how bereft she felt at the prospect of this marriage.

> Dearest Jimmie [*sic*]:
> It was lovely to get your letter speaking of all the fun this summer and knowing you remember all the things we do. I was also glad to learn that Bongo II arrived in good shape and is having such a happy time with you. I hope the little lamb still shines for you both. Dare is going to marry the Englishman and leave her Mama—just as you will some day. . . . My love to the finest little lad I've known. Yours, "Dare's Mother."

In fact, Dare was less and less certain she was going to marry the Englishman. She had figured out that Philip was involved with his colleague's wife, and she did not want to leave "her Mama" any more than her mother wanted to be left. It took three months for Edie to entice Dare to work with her on the photograph for the engagement announcement in the Cleveland newspapers. And when they finally did shoot the photos, Dare appeared trapped and frightened. She tried a variety of outfits, hairstyles, and poses, including lying back with her head on a satin pillow, evoking a sacrificial offering. Dare also photographed Edie, in the same dresses and in the same necklace—a choker they made with a star charm hung from a black grosgrain ribbon—admiring herself in a heart-shaped Venetian mirror, wielding a golden tube of lipstick in her right hand and holding a bottle of perfume in her left. There could be no other caption for this photograph than "Mirror, mirror on the wall, who's the fairest of them all?"

The announcement that ran in the *Cleveland News* in February 1948, under the rubric "Girl About Town," was headlined ARTIST'S DAUGHTER TO WED ONETIME FLYER FOR RAF. Instead of a smiling bride-to-be head shot, the newspaper chose the shot of an unsmiling Dare, her head resting on a pillow, and ran it larger than any other photo on the page. Edie had scripted the announcement: After a reference to the "well-known portrait painter in Cleveland" mother, it mentions Laurel, Dare's attendance at the American Academy of Drama [*sic*] in New York, and her stage debut in *Pride and Prejudice*, by now a dozen years in the past.

> In addition to her theatrical career she has been a Powers model and has gained quite a reputation as a portrait artist, following in her mother's footsteps. She has done pencil sketches of a number of well-known theatrical stars, including Tallulah Bankhead. . . . [The wedding] will be held on April 14 at St. Thomas Church in New

York and the bridegroom will fly over the week before the ceremony and will take his bride back to England on the *Queen Mary*.

The wedding never took place. There were many interpretations of what happened. Edie's story, made up out of whole cloth, was that Philip had asked Dare to convert to Catholicism and Dare's refusal had ended the relationship. Philip's family understood Philip's dalliance with his colleague's wife to be the reason for the breakup. "It was something very sad," said Brian Sandeman. "A married woman—we knew her as The Witch—got her talons into Philip." In Brian's view, she had worked a spell on Philip, who, he and his mother agreed, was "obviously in love with Dare." Philip himself told close friends that Dare had learned of his involvement and consequently broke off the engagement. Philip returned the wedding present sent by Lavinia Emmet Fleming, a childhood friend, with a letter saying, "Sadly I've done the stupidest thing in the world and Dare has thrown me over." Lavinia believed that "Philip was desperately unhappy when Dare broke with him."

Others speculated that it was Philip who had broken with Dare over his concern that she was not prepared to have a real—sexual—relationship. A telegram that Philip sent to Blaine said he needed to have a "normal" relationship with a woman.

Both Dare and Philip seem to have grown ambivalent for their own reasons. Perhaps Philip feared that Dare would always remain, in essence, a child, and his dalliance with another woman and his thoughtless behavior during Dare's visit reflected a growing awareness that he would not be able to go through with the marriage. If Dare had been able to enter into a sexual relationship with Philip he might never have had one with his colleague's wife. But because he had, it gave him an out. Or was it that Philip's affair provided the ambivalent Dare with an out?

Philip did come to New York, asking Blaine to accompany him

to Dare's apartment so the relationship could be ended face-to-face. According to Donald Seawell, who was among those who believed Philip ended it, "She took the news well, without any trace of anger. She remained composed and simply accepted it, without putting up a protest or argument of any kind."

Blaine, on the other hand, did not take the news well. He was furious—at Dare. By providing Philip, Blaine had tried to offer Dare an escape route from their mother. Now he despaired of Dare ever taking that path. Before long, however, he had eased up on her and transferred his anger to Edie. After all, Dare was not to blame for the emotional damage Blaine believed Edie had wrought. Edie told friends that Blaine had begun "bombing" her with late-night phone calls. She defended herself against Blaine's attacks by denying that it was over between Philip and Dare. Did he know that Dare had tried to return Marie Sandeman's jewelry and she would not take it back? This must mean Marie thought there was still hope. Whether Edie's idea or her own, Dare sent Marie an album of photographs of herself with Philip as well as photographs of Edie's portrait of her in a low-cut white princess gown, inscribing the album "To Marie Sandeman with great affection, Dare."

While Blaine attacked Edie and friends marveled at Dare's equanimity in the face of losing Philip, Dare herself must have felt some sense of relief. The Philip episode had brought her closer than she wanted to the world of the grown-ups, where sexuality was not only accepted but expected. Dare seemed determined to avoid that world. It was the only way to stay in the family—or what was left of it.

Blaine, in a conciliatory mood and no longer angry, proposed a road trip to Florida and invited Susannah Vaillant to join them. They drove Sue's 1948 Oldsmobile to the Florida Keys, Dare photographing every moment of the trip. They slept most nights in campsites after dinners of fresh-caught fish cooked on an open fire. And they spent a great deal of time sitting by the side of the road as

Dare and Blaine on the trip they took with Susannah Vaillant to Florida, 1948.

Blaine tried to remedy various kinds of car trouble. Back home, Dare developed all the film, gluing the prints onto board, and penciling in clever captions. She called it "The Florida Book."

Dare continued to model and, in her spare time, to play dress-up and pursue her interest in photography. With money saved, she made steady improvements to the bathroom darkroom, where she spent more and more time, experimenting with processing and printing. She had successfully found a safe place to hide but no solution to her conflicting desire to be seen.

CHAPTER FIVE

After Philip

Children have no fear of their dolls coming to life, they may
even desire it. —SIGMUND FREUD, *"The Uncanny"*

Edie had assumed that, after their marriage, Philip's family's wealth would support Dare in style and, she hoped, herself too. Now that the marriage was off, Edie was once again concerned about her daughter's financial future. She paid a second visit to *Town & Country* with Dare's portfolio but, as on her earlier visit, she spent more time extolling her own talents than her daughter's. And, as had happened in 1947, an assignment was cooked up with Dare as model rather than photographer. This time, the magazine thought it an interesting proposition to have Edie behind the camera. The only hitch, of course, was that Edie did not know how to take a good picture.

Although Edie would take the credits on "Silks Resurgent," this spread was actually Dare's debut as a fashion photographer. Dare did all the work on both sides of the camera. Edie's contribution was to click the shutter and revel in the chance to get paid to play dress-up with her daughter. On the contact sheets Dare saved from this project, the first twenty-four shots follow the assignment. Dare models four silk dresses provided by the magazine; she wears her hair pulled back into a tight chignon and sports the same unsmiling, trapped look she had in the *Cleveland News* engagement photo. The next six shift to Edie, in the asymmetrically necklined gown Dare had worn in her engagement photos. Then back to Dare, who has changed into a low-cut gown, the bodice held up by thin straps, also her own and not part of the assignment. In several subsequent frames, one and then the other strap falls, as though she is on her way to a striptease. Next, she has changed into a leopard-print jacket and skirt, with a clingy leotard-like top, and let down her very blond hair. After a few shots in the leopard outfit, she reappears in the silk *Town & Country* dresses, her hair pulled back again.

Finally, there are a dozen shots of Dare in a transparent white nightgown posing in and around the bed, her naked body visible beneath the gown. In three shots, Dare buries her face in a floor-length tulle bridal veil hemmed with seed pearls, and in one she has placed the veil on her head as if playing the bride, a believable one, but for the see-through gown. This was the veil her mother had worn at her own wedding, the veil Dare planned to wear as Philip's bride.

It was Dare who delivered the "Silks Resurgent" photos to *Town & Country*. She did not tell the editor that she had acted as the photographer, but she did mention her desire to become one. Just after the March 1949 issue of *Town & Country* appeared, Dorothy Tivis, the head of Figureheads, a new but successful modeling agency, received a call from the "Silks Resurgent" editor, who wondered whether Dorothy would see a model who was hoping to become a photographer.

Dorothy, a six-foot-tall natural beauty, had moved to New York in 1942 from Fargo, North Dakota. Three years later, as she was riding the Third Avenue El to her job as a writer on the foreign desk of United Press International, she was "discovered" by a *Vogue* editor. Irving Penn did Dorothy's test shots, and she was soon gracing the cover and inside pages of *Vogue*. In 1948, while continuing to model, Dorothy had started her own agency. At their first meeting, Dorothy signed Dare on as a model. Equally impressed by her photography skills, she also hired her as a sort of in-house photographer.

The first assignment Dorothy gave Dare was to make up her own modeling cards. Edie and Dare carried out this project enthusiastically. They collected dress-up photographs from the Mayport and Ocracoke trips, which Dare reprinted, and took many more photographs in Edie's studio of Dare in a full repertoire of apparel—from bathing suit to evening gown—all of their own creation.

But someone else would be making use of Dare's stunning looks even before she had the chance to be launched by Dorothy's agency. Dare had been introduced to Bayard Hale, a Harvard-educated advertising man, in the mid-1940s. Despite his real-world credentials, Bayard too had something of a problem with growing up and still lived with his mother. Bayard found Dare as gentle and fey as he was, even if she offered him no more than the chance to pal around together, often in the company of their mothers. In early 1948, Hale introduced Dare to his oldest friend, Fenimore Cooper Marsh, president of the Baker Castor Oil Company, and and his wife, Mary Veit Marsh. The Marshes were soon including Dare at cocktail parties in their Park Avenue apartment or weekend luncheons at their country home north of the city. After lunch, Dare and Mary liked to play badminton while the men talked.

Mary, who had married Marsh in 1940, was unhappy with her husband and was looking for a way out, but only if she could secure a good financial settlement and custody of their twin daughters. A charge of adultery was one surefire way. But Cooper Marsh, who was indeed wealthy—he had inherited some $5 million in securities at the death of his father in 1948 and ran a profitable company—was not a philanderer. Watching a friendship develop between her husband and Dare—Marsh was an amateur photographer who loved discussing his hobby with the more knowledgeable Dare—Mary hatched a plan. She encouraged her husband to give Dare a tripod he wasn't using and to help Dare with the darkroom under perpetual construction in her bathroom at the Hotel Bristol. Marsh began visiting Dare at the Bristol, unconcerned because Mary seemed to have no objection to what she had to have known was a platonic relationship.

In March 1949, Mary Marsh put her plan into play. She hired a private detective to trail her husband, knowing the detective would pick up on his frequent visits to Dare's hotel room. On May 26, a sting operation was carried out. The detective, Richard Shorten, Mary's two brothers, Mary herself, and Ruth Mason, a psychic who had worked for Harry Houdini, would descend on the hotel and discover Dare and Marsh, if not "in the act," in a situation that a jury might construe along those lines.

After the "raid," which came off beautifully, especially as the raiders claimed Dare was wearing a negligee, "socially prominent Mary Amelia Veit Marsh," as the newspapers referred to her, moved out of the couple's Park Avenue apartment and into a hotel with her children. She filed for divorce, naming Dare as co-respondent and asking for a steep weekly alimony while the case was resolved. Hearings began in New York Supreme Court on July 7 and were covered by the tabloids in lurid detail over the course of their two-week duration: RAIDING WIFE SEEKS TO DITCH CASTOR OIL KING, JUST CAMERA PALS, SNAPS CASTOR OILER, SURPRISE IN HIS DARKROOM NETS WIFE $3,000 A WEEK. The July 9 report in the *Daily News* began:

> A battle over Dare Wright's attire—or lack of it—the night of the raid on her hotel room developed yesterday as castor oil tycoon Fenimore Cooper Marsh denied that he had been intimate with her, insisting they merely shared "a common interest in photography."

In her affidavit, Dare declared that she was "flabbergasted, but fully clothed." Mary maintained Dare was wearing a diaphanous flowing gown. Dare countered that "I was clad in a yellow silk shirtwaist and a quilted cotton skirt of red and yellow colors," which she maintained was suitable for street wear as well as home.

Knowing that her profession as model might not sound wholesome enough, Dare told the court she was a professional photographer specializing in children's portraits, although beyond the pictures she had taken of Jim Wynn and the Seawells' daughter, Brook, she had little experience in photographing children. She claimed that Marsh had assisted in the construction of her darkroom. Marsh, in turn, said Dare had insisted on buying the tripod he offered to give to her. Dare pointed out that she was actually friends with Mary. She spoke of their lunches and said they had played a great deal of badminton together.

Dare—always "comely female photographer" and "pert blond model" in the articles—was being used. She knew Mary knew there was nothing untoward going on. She turned to Donald Seawell for help, and he and his partner Nahum Bernstein prepared a foolproof defense, although they hoped ultimately to spare Dare the embarrassment of using it.

The trial began on December 8, 1949, and again the tabloids reveled. PEEPER SAYS HIS EYES POPPED, TELLS OF CANDID PEEP AT PAIR IN DARKROOM. Detective Shorten testified with unchecked glee to his first discovery, observed through a crack in the room's transom: lights going on and off at intervals, accompanied by the sounds of laughter and giggling. It was, the detective suggested, proof positive of illicit activity. In fact, Dare and Marsh were developing photographs.

On the night of the "raid," Shorten told the court he and his team pounded on the door for admittance. When Dare opened the door, he said, they saw Marsh "in the process of dressing." In fact, Marsh had earlier taken off his necktie because the evening was a warm one and he was putting it back on. At 10 P.M., Mrs. Marsh herself arrived. She testified that Dare was wearing a yellow negligee and bedroom slippers. Was it diaphanous? Dare's lawyer asked of Shorten. The detective wasn't familiar with the word. Was it transparent, then? No, Shorten replied. Mercifully, Mary withdrew her case two days after the trial began, when Marsh agreed to pay her $28,000 in annual alimony. MARSH DIVORCE TRIANGLE SQUARED exulted the next day's headline. It was also agreed that Mrs. Marsh would sign a statement of apology, clearing Dare of any allegations of misconduct. Under the headline CLEAR PHOTOGRAPHER AS DIVORCE SUIT IS SETTLED, the final article about the case, which ran on December 10 in the *Daily Mirror*, revealed Seawell and Bernstein's ultimate defense. "Miss Wright's attorney said after the settlement that he had subpoenaed two gynecologists who were prepared to testify his client was a virgin."

The Marsh incident had been an ordeal, but Dare walked away from it as though it had not happened—or had happened to someone else. She never lost her composure or betrayed any sign of emotion. Dorothy Tivis, who stayed by Dare's side throughout the case, became an important friend in this period, although one who kept the requisite distance. "Dare was never very vocal about her feelings or her private life," Dorothy said. "I didn't pry."

One afternoon, finding herself near the Hotel Bristol, Dorothy went in and called up to Dare's room from the lobby. A few minutes later, Dare walked into the lobby accompanied by a "gorgeous man." Just as she was feeling a twinge of envy at Dare's handsome beau, Dare introduced the stranger as her brother. The three of them began spending time together and Dorothy fell in love with Blaine, even if Blaine and Dare's mutual adoration often left Dorothy feeling like a third wheel. She also met the "strong-willed, dominant woman who ran Dare's life" and was struck by how differently the siblings viewed their mother. Blaine, she learned, detested his mother, and not just for her treatment of him. "Blaine once said to me, 'If I could tell you the wreckage she has wrought, and my sister is part of it.'" Dorothy recalled shouting matches when she would arrive with Blaine at the Bristol to find Edie there. "Blaine would see Dare all dressed up like a fairy princess and scream at his mother, 'My sister's not a doll!'"

Dorothy soon joined the "going to Pot" circuit, where, each weekend, Blaine's island became the scene of free-flowing house parties. Other guests might include outdoors writers whom Blaine knew through the Phoebe lure or Suzie Vaillant and her children. While Blaine's female visitors might seem far too glamorous for his accommodations, roughing it didn't seem to bother anyone. When it was too cold to swim in the river, they would heat water on the stove and wash in the kitchen in a big basin. They used the outhouse and, when all available beds were occupied, slept on the floor.

If Dorothy had no objection to the physical discomforts on Pot, she was put off by Dare and Blaine's endless game playing. They would shoot Necco wafers off the porch for hours, or Blaine would entertain his sister by telling stories acted out by his monkey hand puppet, or Dare would hop onto Blaine's lap, muss his eyebrows, and teasingly address him as Victor.

Sometimes, their interactions were more intense. One witnessed by fourteen-year-old Henry Vaillant became the basis for a school essay on an unforgettable character. In the summer of 1949, while Blaine, Dare, Henry, and some others walked through a field in Walton, Dare discovered she had lost an earring. "First," recalled Henry, "Blaine scolded the bejesus out of her for wearing it in the country to begin with. Then he went and got a pair of scissors." Blaine spent the next eight hours on his hands and knees cutting the high grass blade by blade. Despite Dare's entreaties to stop, amid assurances that the earring didn't matter, Blaine continued. When he had cut a patch roughly a hundred feet square, he did stop—but only because he had located the earring. "His fingers were bleeding like crazy," Henry said, "but he kept on until he found it. It was so

On the back steps of Blaine's cabin on Pot, top row, *left to right*, Dorothy Tivis and David Goodnow, second row, Blaine, Dare, Hermann Kessler, 1950s.

unnecessary. In the essay, I called this an example of self-destructive perfectionism." Or an example of the lengths to which Blaine would go to try to make things right for his sister.

While Dare had made little headway in her career as a photographer, she was more in demand than ever as a model. Increasingly high-profile jobs were coming her way, thanks to Dorothy's management. At the start of 1950, just after the resolution of the Marsh case, Dare was featured in the Maidenform bra "I dreamed . . ." advertising campaign, which had been launched the previous year. Dare's ad, which appeared in women's magazines in 1950 and 1951, identified her as "Sally Starr," a movie actress. The copy ran: "I dreamed I had a screen test in my Maidenform bra. Lights! Camera! Action! I never felt so like a star . . . and all because my Maidenform bra plays my best supporting role!" Dare, shown in five different poses, wears a black hat with a floor-length net train, full-length sheer black gloves, high heels, a full skirt, and the bra, the "3-way Maidenette-Declatay."

Dare was also shot for an October 1950 *Esquire* magazine feature, "All American Model," in which four models were singled out for their ideal features: face, legs, bust, or back. Dare was represented by a full-page nude shot of her back, from her head down to her buttocks. That same month she was photographed for a future cover of *Cosmopolitan*.

But then word came to the Figureheads office that *Good Housekeeping* magazine was hiring photographers. Dare submitted her portfolio, met with one of the art editors and Margaret Cousins, the managing editor, and was hired to shoot illustrations for an editorial section called the Baby Center, which ran monthly articles on child care. She was later reassigned to the Beauty Clinic section, where her first photo credit, for a story advocating pin-curl rather than chemical permanents, misidentified her—shades of the name-tape incident—as "Bare Wright." Over the next six years she would complete dozens of assignments for Good House, as the staff called it, and see 122 photographs published, illustrating mostly how-to articles on everything from car care to skin care.

With the promise of steady work at *Good Housekeeping*, Dare needed a more professional darkroom than she had been able to create in a hotel bathroom, and a real studio in which to hold her shoots. With savings from modeling jobs, Dare decided she could afford to rent her first New York apartment. She found one in a subdivided four-story townhouse at 29 West 58th Street, a few doors west of the side entrance of the Plaza Hotel, that had once been the home of Nancy Carroll, a popular cherubic-faced movie star of the twenties and thirties, whose nickname was Babyface. Dare's second-floor apartment had been Carroll's ballroom. The floor was dropped—one descended a couple of steps on entering—and the ceilings were high. It also boasted a working fireplace.

Dare sectioned off the room with floor-to-ceiling bookshelves that she built herself. She also made draperies and some of the furnishings and did most of the upholstery work herself. As in Edie's first apartment in Cleveland, she painted the wood floors black with stenciled white squares, and then echoed this motif on the concrete on the north-facing "terrace," which she reclaimed from the roof of an adjoining building. The only way to get onto the terrace was by climbing out the window, so she built a set of steps for this purpose. And she dressed up the terrace, suspending a striped awning she sewed and rigged herself off the side of the building. "She did things with nothing," marveled Wanda Ramsey, who met Dare through the Seawells and whose husband Robert, a set designer, was particularly impressed with Dare's inventiveness. "It *was* a stage set," said Dorothy.

Dare's first *Good Housekeeping* assignment, for an article on "Psychosomatic Ailments in Childhood," was shot in her new apartment in May 1950. The image, evoking a mother trying to coax her baby back to sleep in the middle of the night, featured Wanda Ramsey's sister Iza Warner and her infant daughter Daphne. Dare dressed Iza in one of her own flowing white nightgowns.

That same year, Edie too arranged a live-in studio for herself. Since 1926, she had worked out of a succession of Hanna Building office suites, but none were suitable or big enough to live in as well. Edie had long had her eye on the building's penthouse, as it was called, on the ninth floor of the Hanna Building annex. For most of her tenancy it had been used for the purpose for which it was built—a love nest. Knowing it was now empty, Edie asked if she might take it over. In 1950, Dan Junior agreed. This thousand-square-foot apartment, with a foyer, a large central room perfectly suited for a painting studio, a sectioned-off bedroom, high ceilings, and north-facing windows, was, in Edie's view, the perfect home and studio. While the word *penthouse* calls to mind a swank Art Deco aerie out of a 1930s movie, aside from its north light and its hidden location, the virtues of Edie's new apartment were few. But in Edie's hands it was quickly transformed, and as soon as it was she invited curious newspaper reporters in for a look—a close look, right down to her bed's white satin sheets. They came away impressed, marveling at this unlikely dwelling at the top of an office building, its walls covered with art and with what one described as a "lavish boudoir all cream and gold with a taffeta-canopied bed."

As Edie consolidated possessions from her former studio and her room at the Hotel Cleveland, she sent several trunks of Dare's belongings that she had been storing to New York. In one trunk, to Dare's delight, was her childhood's very survival kit: her books and her doll Edith. The return of this long-ago companion called up powerful feelings. Unlike Dare's animate friends who caused complications, Edith was an ideal friend. She could make no confusing demands or force Dare beyond her limited interpersonal abilities. Without self-consciousness, Dare played with Edith—and photographed her. When Iza Warner brought her daughter, Daphne, back to Dare's apartment to be photographed for an article on Christmas toys, Dare took photographs of Daphne sitting on her bed beside her own "new" child, Edith.

In May 1951, Dare's face, sultry this time, stared out from the cover of *Cosmopolitan*. The photograph is a tight head shot of Dare's heavily made-up face partially concealed by a "whimsy," a black net veil gathered at the top with a bunch of silk flowers. It was Dare's last appearance as a model.

In the period that Dare was moving from modeling to photography, Philip Sandeman, too, had been making career changes. In 1950, he left the Kordas to work in an insurance group affiliated with Lloyd's of London. He also joined the Royal Auxiliary Air Force, training pilots for the Korean War. He told his family he had other changes in mind as well, leading Marie Sandeman and Brian to wonder whether he might attempt to rekindle his relationship with Dare, whom they both still considered Philip's true love. Although Philip and Dare were not in contact, Marie and Dare continued to exchange letters and occasional phone calls.

On the evening of June 19, 1951, Dare received a phone call from Marie. Philip was dead. His Meteor plane had collided with another plane over the Biggin Hill RAF station in Kent. Three planes had taken off simultaneously, one piloted by Philip, one by his student, and the third by his flight sergeant. The student's plane failed to climb at the end of the runway and crashed into a house about 100 yards beyond. The flight sergeant, his eyes on the blaze below, did not see Philip's plane until it was too late.

Dorothy's phone rang at 3 A.M. It was Dare, sobbing so hard Dorothy could not even make out what she was saying. When she arrived at Dare's apartment, Dare could only point to the pencil drawing hung at eye level to the left of a mirrored wall over the mantelpiece. It was the sketch of Philip in uniform that Dare had made during the week of their first meeting. Dorothy had never even noticed it. Just as she had never heard of Blaine before she met him in the Bristol lobby, she had never known of Philip's existence. As Dorothy tried to comfort her distraught friend, Dare confided the story of Philip or, rather, *a* story of Philip, and why they had

COSMOPOLITAN

The modeling years: *below left and counterclockwise,* Dare's card for the Figureheads Modeling Agency, 1949; the Maidenform ad, 1950; the *Cosmopolitan* cover, May 1951.

not married, falling back on Edie's old fiction of her refusal to convert to Catholicism.

After that night, the story of Philip never altered. Her fiancé, an RAF pilot and heir to the Sandeman family port and sherry empire, her great love, her one true love, was shot down over the English Channel during World War II. After his death, she could never love another. She told this tragic and romantic story so convincingly that she must, in some way, have come to believe it herself. Death had frozen Philip in time. In many ways, he had become more real to her than when he had been alive. Now he provided the oft-cited and perfect alibi, one she would hold up to each of the long chain of men who would meet and fall in love with her.

A few weeks after Philip's death, Edie and Dare went off to Ocracoke, where Dare could take solace in its wilderness of sand and sea and in her mother's arms.

Back in New York that fall, Dare, who had begun wearing her long blond hair in a high ponytail with short bangs, turned her attentions to the other Edith. As she went about Edith's refurbishment—transformation might be the better word—she gave her doll the exact same look. She detached Edith's curly mohair wig and fashioned her a new one from her own false chignon. She even pierced her doll's ears with gold hoops, miniature replicas of the earrings she herself was never without. The clothes that Dare made to replace Edith's original outfit (an orange organdy dress, felt bonnet, and felt slippers), however, were still a little girl's: white ruffled cotton panties and a white eyelet cotton petticoat worn under a pink-and-white gingham dress, over which was tied a white cotton apron.

In Edith's original incarnation, she looked like a baby. Now she looked like a sort of effigy of her owner—and, for a doll, oddly sexy. Her face appeared made up, and her petticoat and dress did not completely conceal her ruffled underpants. Clearly this was intentional: Dare's sewing skills were more than up to the task of measuring a dress that would have better obscured Edith's underwear.

Dare also chose not to hide the stitch marks of Edith's wig, but left them visible. Whereas her own mother's love was predicated on perfection, Dare could love Edith in the way she herself had always wanted so desperately: unconditionally, however imperfect.

Once Edith's look was established, Dare also constructed a personality for her doll, assigning to Edith many traits she may have wished were her own, traits that for myriad reasons Dare had had to suppress. Through Edith, Dare could begin to explore a lost side of herself, a self who transgressed, who could risk being mischievous and disobedient, adventurous and independent.

With her look and persona in place, Edith was ready for her debut. "I started her sitting for the camera," Dare later told an interviewer, shades of her own mother starting Dare sitting for portraits. But unlike Dare in her early years, Edith would not be left to languish alone. Dare held a cocktail party to introduce her long-lost companion to her friends. No one present quite understood just what this doll meant to Dare or could have predicted that, in Edith, their hostess would find a springboard for a new career, not to mention a guiding purpose.

CHAPTER SIX

Behind the Little Green Door

With naked neck she goes, and shoulders bare;
And with a fillet binds her flowing hair.
By many suitors sought, she mocks their pains.
And still her vow'd virginity maintains . . .
　　　　—OVID, *Metamorphoses: The Transformation*
　　　　　　　of Daphne into a Laurel

By 1951, when Edith came into her life again, the distance between Edie and Dare had been bridged so completely that they had all but merged in their own magic circle. Edie's letters to others arrived signed "Edie-Dare" or "Love from us both," even when they were not together. But in truth they were almost always together. Dare made frequent visits to Cleveland, and for at least one week a month Edie would fly to New York to stay with Dare. Despite their very different figures and an almost five-inch difference in height, they shared many of the same clothes. They shared one another's makeup and accessories. And they shared the same bed. As Edie told Brook Seawell, "I reach over and pat her little bottom in the night." They seemed to have no idea how odd others found this arrangement.

As in her *Laurel Leaves* story, Dare, it seemed, had entered the little green door and the old woman who lived there had cast a spell over her to ensure she would stay a child—and a good one— forever. In return, she would never be abandoned. And it was starting to appear as if they would live in that tall palace tower for the rest of their lives.

They were in many ways perfectly complementary. Dare, avoidant, withdrawn, and shy, could rely on her mother's dominant personality; Edie's insistence on playing impresario for both women's lives released Dare from having to take any real responsibility for her own. While Edie did take pride in Dare's accomplishments, she took the greater pleasure in her beauty. For Edie, Dare became a sort of trophy wife, compliant, supportive, and happy to remain in the background.

Friends and acquaintances were shared as well. In New York, it was taken for granted that an invitation to Dare included Edie, and in Cleveland it was assumed that Dare would accompany her mother wherever she went. On those rare occasions that Dare accepted an invitation on her own, Edie would make no secret of her displeasure—or she would pretend to be too tired to go anyway.

The Seawells had always served as Dare's social linchpin. Gayelord Hauser, a nutrition guru to the rich and famous, was Edie's counterpart, her protector and admirer of longest standing. The Wrights had met Hauser on the beach in Cannes in 1930. With his well-trained eye for beauty, he had picked out the glamorous mother and the striking teenager and introduced himself.

As a young man, Hauser, like Ivan, had suffered from tuberculosis of the hip. When medical treatments failed, he made dietary changes. He found his condition improved when he kept to a diet of "wonder foods": raw vegetables, brewer's yeast, skim milk, yogurt, wheat germ, and blackstrap molasses. He became a health food convert and a proselytizer. In the 1920s, he opened a diet clinic in Chicago and one of the country's first health food stores, later buying a Milwaukee company that produced many of the nutritional supplements sold at the clinic. By the time he met Edie and Dare, he was living in Los Angeles, while wealthy women in this country and abroad followed the craze he created for "vegetable juice cocktails" prepared with the Hauser juice extractor.

The Wrights and Hauser renewed their acquaintance in California in 1937. Edie was drawn to the man far more than to his dictates. While obsessed with the exterior of her body—and Dare's—Edie gave little thought to what she put in it. They maintained their remarkable figures by eating very little, helped along by a common disinterest in food. But even if, to his feigned annoyance, they eschewed his nutritional dictates, Hauser and the Wrights would remain lifelong friends.

Hauser's message was reaching a mass market through a series of books with titles such as *Eat and Grow Beautiful*. Modern Products in Milwaukee was a burgeoning business, specializing in Swiss Kriss (an herbal laxative), Hauser broth, and herbal seasonings, all still sold today. There had been dust-ups with the medical establishment; his qualifications and his claims had been questioned. But his followers never wavered. Handsome, trim, and fit, Hauser was a perfect advertisement for the benefits of the diet he preached. And press attention was constant, especially after the late 1930s, when his friendship with Greta Garbo began. She became his most famous follower and used him as a sort of personal adviser. For a time it was rumored that they were lovers. They made an exquisite couple, if only the appearance of one.

In 1950, Farrar, Straus and Giroux published Hauser's *Look Younger, Live Longer*, which shot to the top of the bestseller list and by 1952 had sold more than 450,000 hardcover copies. By the end of 1951, ABC-TV gave Hauser his own twice-weekly daytime television show, on which he dispensed beauty tips and nutritional advice, and chatted with guests who could plug their latest projects while drinking orange juice to please the show's sponsor, Minute Maid.

With homes by then in Los Angeles, New York, and Taormina,

Sicily, Hauser and his companion, Frey Brown, used their New York townhouse at 238 East 62nd Street as their base during this period. Edie and Dare were frequent guests at gatherings there, including one staged event, when *American Weekly* came to photograph a Hauser dinner party. In a photograph accompanying the article, captioned "Hauser prepares to serve non-fattening yogurt pie to his guests at one of his famous dinners," Edie is seated to his left and Dare to his right. The Wrights were also invited to appear on his television show.

In 1952, Gayelord had commissioned Edie to paint his portrait. At the unveiling held at Dare's apartment, Gayelord was so pleased he decided the portrait should adorn the jacket of his next book and commissioned Edie to paint Frey as well. He told her he hoped she might do Garbo's portrait but warned that getting Garbo to go along might require some strategizing. But he had a plan. He decided they should stage a second "unveiling" of his portrait at Dare's apartment for Garbo's benefit. He was almost certain that Garbo would be so impressed by the portrait she would agree to sit for her own. Edie was excited and optimistic. She wrote to Daisy shortly after the unveiling, "Garbo 'the divine' . . . came. . . . She gave the portrait the greatest attention and pronounced it very wonderful. . . . She looked at Dare and me—shook her head and said 'Mother and daughter—and so mooch talent.'" Edie reported that Garbo also wanted to see a picture of Blaine, and that Garbo pronounced him "beautiful too." Garbo's visit lasted an hour and a half, which was, according to Edie, unusual for her. During Garbo's stay, Gayelord mentioned Dare's "pirate pants" that he'd seen when he was sitting for his portrait. He thought Garbo would love them and had Dare show them to her. Edie recounted Garbo's reaction: "[Garbo] held them up and said 'Oh. They are so leetle.' I said, 'Would you like Dare to make a pair for you?' She said 'For me? O.K. Thank you, yes. You take my measures?' . . . Garbo has a fear complex—fear of everything. Someone asked me was I nervous about painting. I said 'yes, I was afraid to begin, afraid while painting, and afraid to show.'"

She looked at me and said: 'Are you really afraid?—Really?'. . . They are waiting and hoping she will say she'd like me to paint her."

Garbo told everyone she saw in this period how "intrigued" she was by the "lovely mother and daughter" and their respective talents, and that she hoped to be invited for a return visit. When this got back to Edie, she wrote Daisy that she was certain the portrait of Garbo was now "clinched."

Gayelord had become so portrait-obsessed that he invited Edie to unveil one on his television show. Edie chose a recent painting of Brook Seawell. Although Dare did little but stand there, she was a hit. In a letter to Daisy, Edie wrote that the show's director had called to say "he'd received letters and telegrams galore requesting that they have her all the time. That she is so fresh and unaffected and lovely. So they are talking of having Dare all the time starting in September on CBS [*sic*] TV. It would give her $300 a week for two shows of 15 minutes and two hours' rehearsal for each show." This never happened, although the Garbo portrait did. The sittings were held at Dare's apartment with Dare, Gayelord, and Anthony Palermo, a young Hauser protégé in attendance. The finished portrait, also signed—for some reason—by Dare, hung in Gayelord's guest house in Beverly Hills until his death in 1984. It was the only portrait for which Garbo ever posed.

That year Gayelord had arranged for Anthony and George Palermo, two sons of Italian friends, to come to live in America. The older brother, George, had just finished medical school in Rome; Gayelord arranged an internship for him at St. Michael's Hospital in Milwaukee, where Modern Products was based. Tony, nineteen, told Hauser he wanted to come also. Gayelord arranged for him to attend Marquette University and work at the Modern Products factory to support himself.

Tony, who preferred big cities, came to New York whenever he could. He first met the thirty-eight-year-old Dare at a party at Gayelord's apartment. Despite their age difference—considerable even when she told him she was twenty-six—Tony was smitten.

Finding her skittish, he assumed it had something to do with the Marsh scandal, which Gayelord had mentioned. For a time, he was pleased to see how perfectly Dare fit with his preference for women who "played hard to get." But as he continued his courtship, he soon realized he had no terms in his Lothario lexicon to describe what he had before him. There was clearly some disconnect. She would walk away when he tried to kiss her.

An additional obstacle was that Edie was always around. Tony called her Tag Along. He didn't mind the double dates with Blaine and Dorothy, but he did resent the constant presence of Dare's mother. In addition to Edie, there was another intrusive presence. He once showed up at 58th Street to find Dare playing with the doll. "You didn't say hello to Edith," Dare chided, as though Tony had rudely neglected to acknowledge a human presence. "It scared the hell out of me," he recalled. Wanting to please Dare, however, he did comply. "Oh, hello, Edith," he said in a singsong voice. Dare was without irony in her relation to her doll and would always remain so.

Hoping to reroute the proceedings, incapable of understanding how an almost forty-year-old woman could view a doll as a child would, Tony now offered Dare a kiss. "Dare turned white, hysterical," he recalled. "She became frozen." Grabbing Edith, Dare held up the doll between them as a shield.

Tony pursued Dare for two years but eventually gave up. While he respected her and thought her smart and clever, he found her tormented by what he called "inner dilemmas."

"It was like she came from another world," he said. "She and her mother were both children. Dare lived in a fantasy world playing with dolls. I think the mother ruined that girl. There was some Svengali type of thing going on. She was under her mother's spell."

Tony's enchantment had run its course. His parting advice to Dare was that she make something of her doll obsession. "Since you think Edith's real," he told her, "why don't you write about her? Make a story. Make a book."

Dare's apartment had always doubled as the set for her shoots. It was here that models reported each morning to be photographed engaging in real-life activities, grooming their hair, nails, and skin or painting at an easel. She would dress them in her own clothes accented with her own jewelry, using her belongings as props and posing them in her own bed or at her dressing table or on the terrace out back.

When Maggie Cousins, *Good Housekeeping*'s managing editor, came to 58th Street to be photographed for the editor's letter page, Cousins suggested using Dare's apartment in a feature on decorating on a budget. The photographs of Dare's apartment ran in the November 1952 issue with this introduction:

> If you simply like what you like, regardless of the country or period that inspired it, you can make your personal preferences your decorating point of departure. Here, the one-room apartment of a young photographer who has . . . completely ignored rules and, with her own very catholic taste as a guide, created a charming, individual home.

Pictured are a pile of three big cushions (on which Dare sat when Garbo visited), a kidney-shaped wood coffee table and end tables that Dare jigsawed herself, as well as the floor-to-ceiling bookshelves she built. There are the draperies of white quilted satin Dare also made and hung around the bay window, enclosing a dining alcove, where stools that slide under the trestle table are actually folding luggage racks nailed open with cushions placed on top. The jalousie blinds are painted dark green to match the dark-green sateen she used to upholster a loveseat.

Over a bigger couch, Dare hung a series of screens on which she drew various backgrounds. A scene from ancient Rome was usually on view unless she needed some other backdrop for a photo shoot,

Dare's apartment at 29 West 58th Street, photographed for a *Good Housekeeping* spread on "Decorating on a Budget," November 1952. Dare's drawing of Philip hangs to the left of the mantelpiece.

Outtake from a shoot for *Good Housekeeping*, 1953. The model wears Dare's clothes and accessories; the hat she's wearing will later appear in *The Lonely Doll*.

in which case another could be rolled down like a window shade. On either side of the screen hung white quilted-satin wall hangings, which matched the draperies. The sofa bed rolled under a storage cupboard. In the daytime, the half she left exposed was covered with pillows to provide another couch. At night, she moved the furniture aside in order to pull out the bed. From it, she could glance directly at her pencil drawing of Philip hanging to the left of the mantelpiece.

After the day's shoot, Dare's apartment became the setting for evening-long cocktail parties. "Everything was the cocktail party," said Dorothy. "Dinner was your problem. I was always starving with these people." Regulars included the Seawells, Gayelord and Frey, friends of both those couples, and Edie or Blaine when they were in town. Edie, who viewed Dare's apartment as an extension of her own home, would send over any of her Cleveland coterie—or their children—when they were in New York, even when she herself was not there. Edith, propped on a chair, was a fixture.

In the evenings, Dare also brought out her camera, but not to photograph the guests. Before their arrival, or after they left, with Edie's help or using a self-timer, she captured herself wearing the stunning evening gowns she made, her standard hostess attire. She appears at once a glamorous woman and a little girl playing dress-up.

On the weekends, Dare went to Pot, transforming herself from the urban sophisticate into Blaine's ideal, a nature girl, although, to his annoyance, one who persisted in maintaining a fully made-up face. Here she was thrown in with Blaine's set: friends who lived in the area and others who arrived for weekends, including Hermann Kessler, the art director of *Field and Stream*, and A. J. McClane, its fishing and later executive editor.

In the early spring of 1953, McClane brought along his friend Lee Wulff, a handsome and accomplished sports fisherman. A twice-divorced father of two at the time, Wulff soon found himself more interested in Blaine's sister than in the trout in the Delaware

Dare in an evening gown of her own creation, typical attire for the
cocktail parties she threw in her apartment in the 1950s.

River. Hearing of Dare's love for Ocracoke, Wulff suggested he fly her there in his own plane before June, when he would be heading up to his hunting and fishing camp in Newfoundland.

Dorothy and Blaine joined them for a long weekend of fishing and frolicking on the Ocracoke beach, activities that Dare photographed. As Lee was also a skilled lensman, he borrowed the camera to photograph Dare and the others. They stayed at the Wahab Village Hotel, Dorothy and Dare in one room, Blaine and Lee in another.

Blaine felt threatened by Wulff and became uncomfortable with the man's ardor for his sister. Surely Wulff outclassed Blaine at all his games. Not only was he known for inventing flies that revolutionized salmon fishing and the now-standard short wading vest for fly fishermen, he was a pilot, an accomplished hunter, photographer, and filmmaker, and an outdoors writer who would eventually publish eight books. He had even studied art in Paris after graduating from Stanford University. Blaine told several friends in Walton that Lee was not good enough for Dare. Maybe he was being protective of his sister, whom he feared might not be up to being the consort of such a man. And, too, he seemed as ambivalent as his mother at the prospect of a sexual union for her.

If Blaine tried to discourage Wulff, Edie, usually harder to please, was in favor of him. Wulff played up to her, having intuited the special technique required for catching Dare: Include her mother almost every step of the way. This allowed Edie to sustain the confused fantasy that always took hold when Dare was being courted: She believed she was being courted as well.

In the spring of 1953, Lee asked Dare to pose with him for the cover of *Flying Magazine*. The photo was shot at Hedges Lake, New York. Dare is standing in front of a 1952 Piper Pacer on Edo floats looking leggy in a pink Claire McCardell-like shorts playsuit she had made, and holding a fishing rod. Beside her, Lee is preparing to cast his rod. The cover photo is described on the magazine's

Blaine and Dorothy Tivis on the 1953 trip to Ocracoke with
Lee Wulff and Dare.

contents page: "A day in spring, a plane on floats, good fishing, a beautiful girl—what more could anyone ask?"

Wulff had custody of his two sons for the three months a year that he spent in Newfoundland. The rest of the time he lived near the Vermont border in Shushan, New York, with his mother, who had come east from California to help run the household. Edie wrote that his mother wished to return to California but was waiting for him to remarry. "He [Lee] is courting [Dare] madly. Says she is first girl he has known who is beautiful inside and out. He says his boys would adore her."

For July of 1953, Lee asked Edie and Dare—several times—to fly up with him to his fishing camp in Newfoundland. The invitations, Edie wrote Daisy, came in the form of "yard-long telegrams." Edie seems to have been willing to forfeit their trip to Ocracoke that summer, or to go to Newfoundland after Ocracoke, but the beloved herself said she had to be back in New York on August 15 for *Good Housekeeping* assignments, and she was not moved to go anywhere but Ocracoke with her mother for a full month before that.

On Ocracoke, Dare was safe from Wulff's advances, but back in New York that fall, they resumed. Dare did accept Wulff's invitation for a weekend at his home in Shushan, where she met Lee's sons, Allan, fifteen at the time, and Barry, twelve. They took long walks in the woods and made popcorn in the fireplace and Dare and the increasingly smitten Lee traded the camera back and forth. Wulff told friends he was impressed at how well Dare fit in.

Relying on Edie to help his cause, Wulff invited them both to Shushan for Memorial Day the following spring. Lee's son Allan remembered Edie as "a very snazzy, pretty lady" who was "promoting a relationship between Dare and Lee." Dare, whom he found "pixielike," struck him as "lukewarm" about the idea.

Lee continued his courtship that summer and fall. In December 1954, he asked Dare to marry him. She announced she was going to Cleveland for Christmas to be with her mother and somehow managed to slip away without giving him an answer. Invited to dinner at the Kesslers while Dare was in Cleveland, Lee spoke of how agonizing it was to have to wait. The Kesslers encouraged him to call Dare in Cleveland and handed him the telephone. Dare told him she didn't want to give an answer over the phone but she would when she returned to New York.

It had been a busy Christmas in Cleveland. Edie's portrait of Churchill had just been unveiled at the University of Bristol in England, with Sir Philip Morris, vice chancellor of the university, presiding. Morris was so impressed with Edie's work that he offered to arrange for her to come to England to paint a portrait of the Queen. "The people who want me to go wrote that if I did a likeness of her as fine as the Churchill that England would be at my feet," Edie wrote to Allie. In preparation, Edie made Dare pose for a "practice" drawing on an eight-foot-tall canvas. She planned to do a practice painting on Dare's next visit.

Dare had not only posed for the Queen drawing and deflected Lee Wulff's marriage offer during that visit, she had also undertaken the redesign of Edie's bathroom. "It was impossible," Edie wrote Allie. "Now it's too wonderful." An entire page of this letter describes Dare's handiwork, both in words and in a three-dimensional drawing. "Dead white walls, large black and white squares on floor. 'Deceive the eye' in raw umber (pale pale) on walls—shelves black and white-marble—towels of lipstick red-white-pale pink & umber."

By the end of the Cleveland visit, it was decided that Edie would handle the Wulff problem, sparing Dare from ever having to speak to him again. Edie called him herself and told him that she could not let Dare marry him—because he had been divorced. While Helen Kessler commiserated with Lee, she also understood, perhaps better than Lee, why Dare was unattainable. "Dare had had the courage to come to New York, away from her mother's influence, but her mother had let her go with a long leash attached. I don't think Dare was ever free of her. Dare dated a lot of well-known people but her mother was always in the way. I think Edie thought Dare was too good for anybody."

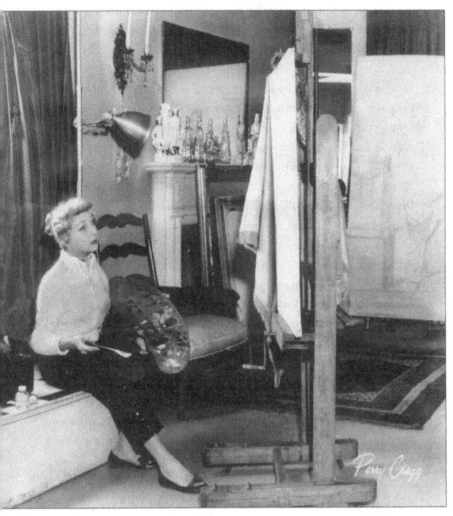

Edie in 1954 at work in the Hanna Building penthouse, where she would live until 1969.

Wulff, like Tony Palermo, was not the sort of man to linger trying. By the following year, he had met and married his third wife. After Edie ended the relationship, Dare retreated back to her apartment. But she always saved her photographs of Wulff.

Dare was making strides in her professional life as *Good Housekeeping* piled on assignments and gave her an assistant editor as a "helper." Lyn Levitt Tornabene, twenty-three, had joined the Beauty Clinic section in 1953. Lyn considered Dare to be a consummate professional, fun to work with, and quite singular. "She was tremendously gentle and an enormously modest person. She didn't look like a New York woman at all. Much more ethereal than that, like a ghost, like some wonderful blithe spirit."

Although they were allowed to hire models, they were given no budget for clothes or accessories. Lyn was impressed that Dare had no objection to sharing the contents of her closet and jewelry box. She recalled Edie's presence at the shoots at Dare's apartment. "The mother, to me, was ever-present whether she was there or not. There was something otherworldly about them, something spooky about stepping into their lives, out of *Whatever Happened to Baby Jane?* or *Laura*. My husband remembers Dare as Blanche DuBois.

"There was something sexually that was weird. I thought, Maybe they're lovers, not mother and daughter." But she also heard about the fiancé who was killed in the war. "That was part of the whole wispy story."

If no model was available, Dorothy could always be counted on to fill in for a *Good Housekeeping* shoot. Once, Dare asked Dorothy to meet her in Central Park. Dorothy was surprised to find Dare accompanied by a dashing man she had met at one of the 58th Street cocktail gatherings. Russell Barnett Aitken had brought his own camera along; while Dare worked, Russ snapped photographs of Dare photographing Dorothy.

Born in Cleveland four years before Dare, Aitken had come to New York in 1935, having distinguished himself in various worlds,

Self-portrait as sea creature, shot in Dare's apartment
studio on 58th Street in the early 1950s.

as a ceramic sculptor, a hunter and fisherman, and a sportswriter who illustrated his pieces with his own drawings and photographs. In 1934, he left Cleveland to teach ceramic sculpture at the Old White Art School in White Sulphur Springs, West Virginia, filling off-hours playing polo at the Greenbrier Hotel. He moved to New York the next year with guarantees from two Greenbrier guests who had attended his classes that they would continue on as his students in New York. They were Clare Boothe Luce and Annie Laurie Crawford, the recent widow of George Crawford, who had been chairman of the board of the Columbia Gas and Electric Corporation. Crawford left her his fortune—his 1935 *New York Times* obituary said the company was worth 700 million dollars—and a four-year-old daughter, Martha, known as Sunny. Russ Aitken had fallen in love with Annie Laurie, but her mother, wary of gold diggers, shooed all suitors away.

In New York City, Aitken became a fixture in the social world and in the columns that chronicled it. He was described variously as a composite of James Stewart, Sir Anthony Eden, and Errol Flynn or as "the Noël Coward of the Pottery World." In 1939, *Esquire* magazine ran a profile about him under the headline AITKEN: PLAYBOY CERAMIST. He was equally at home on the African plains or in high society. In October 1947, *The New York Times* carried the news that he was off on a seven-month African safari, sponsored by the Campfire Club of America and the Adventurers Club of New York. Hiram Walker whiskey featured him in an ad wearing safari regalia and described him as "the greatest shot ever on safari" and "one of America's leading authorities on Africa."

When Russ met Dare through mutual friends, he was still courting Annie Laurie Crawford, but Aitken would always be captivated by Dare—and Edie would always be fascinated by the potential of Russ for her daughter, Annie Laurie or no Annie Laurie. The fact that he would never seek to marry Dare made him, in Edie's view, safe. She was free to play her favorite role, agent provocateur.

"I'm all for Dare meeting new men," Edie would write to Daisy, neglecting to add that she was all for Dare meeting men who would never get anywhere with her daughter.

In 1955, a new friend entered the social fold through Donald Seawell. Vincent Youmans, Jr., would become one of Dare's closest friends and allies. Seawell had met Vincent's mother on a train to New York from Maryland's Eastern Shore. They discovered they were next-door neighbors and made plans to get together there. Vincent's father, Vincent Youmans, had been a well-known composer of Broadway musicals in the twenties and thirties. His works included *No, No Nanette* and the song "Tea for Two." Anne Varley, Vincent's mother, had been a chorus girl in one of Youmans's musicals. They married in 1927. By 1928, Anne was finishing out her pregnancy in Reno as she waited for her divorce to come through. Her twins, Ceciley and Vincent, Jr., named for the father he would never meet, were born there.

When Dare and Edie visited the Seawells, Donald introduced them. Vincent, then twenty-seven, was living with his mother and dairy farming. Aside from never having really known their fathers, Vincent and Dare had in common their formidable mothers, and Vincent, too, had an extraordinarily close relationship with his only sibling, in his case a twin. Although his mother did remarry twice more after her divorce from Youmans, Vincent adopted the role in his family of little man, sensitively catering to his mother and sister's needs.

Vincent, who had bought the rights to his father's music after Youmans, Sr., died of tuberculosis in 1946, was planning to move to New York to work for a music publishing firm. When he arrived in the city, Dare, who was thirteen years older, took him under her wing, inviting Vincent to her cocktail parties and bringing him along when she was invited to Hauser's and the Seawells'. She introduced him to Blaine, who included him in weekends on Pot.

In Vincent, Dare had found someone who could provide unthreatening companionship and assistance. "She could depend on me," he said, and she did. "Everyone should have a Vincent," said a mutual friend. Their closest physical contact was dancing at El Morocco, where he discovered "she didn't have any rhythm" or was unable to loosen up enough to dance. But Vincent never asked for more.

When the black-and-white squares Dare had painted on the apartment floor and on the terrace of the apartment needed a touch-up, Vincent donned coveralls and helped out. When she had to transport lights, cameras, and models to Serendipity, a restaurant and antiques shop, for a photo shoot—featuring Vanity Fair Mills' latest leopard-print underwear—he acted as chauffeur. When Dare bought a carousel horse at Serendipity that afternoon, he returned another day to haul it home for her. (Dare named it Folly, and it stood from then on like a sentinel at the foot of her bed.)

Vincent was bowled over by Dare's beauty and her creativity. If she could not dance, Vincent discovered there was little else she couldn't do. "She could write, she could sew, she could draw. She was a pixie, a fairy, full of imagination and in another world."

Unlike other men, Vincent was willing to be a sort of playmate, never making the sexual overtures that would cause Dare to retreat or run away. He accepted her in her innocence—"She was so good: too good in some ways"—and never sought to push her beyond what he likened to a brother-sister bond. And he understood that nothing would unseat the primary relationship Dare had with her mother.

By now, the succession of men was starting to follow a pattern. In Philip, Dare had found the ultimate playmate, but he betrayed her by revealing himself to be a "real" man. For a time, Roy Wilder had seemed like a worthy replacement, as did Tony Palermo, but they all proved interested in Dare the woman, not the girl. And then there were Edie's princes for her princess: Lee Wulff and Russell Barnett Aitken. Lee had found what he was looking for elsewhere. Aitken, who married Annie Laurie Crawford in 1957 as soon as her mother died, remained in Dare's life, although always, to his evident frustration, on Dare's platonic terms.

A long chain of men made overtures. "Men did beat a path to her door," Donald Seawell recalled. "Dare was a very striking lady who seemed completely unaware of the fact. I'm sure she drove men wild and didn't realize it. She was the biggest flirt that ever lived, without even knowing she was flirting. She did it unconsciously. She was very shy. They thought she was being coy." To a degree, Dare would go along. But if an advance became sexual, she fled in terror. Once, Donald said, Blaine had called him late at night to say he had just gotten off the phone with Dare, who had called him in tears. "She had gone to dinner with some man and invited him home to her apartment afterward," Donald said. "He'd made a pass at her and she'd run out of the apartment. She ran so fast she lost both her shoes on Fifty-seventh Street."

CHAPTER SEVEN

The Books

It is an anxious, sometimes a dangerous thing to be a doll.
Dolls cannot choose; they can only be chosen; they cannot
"do"; they can only be done by.

—RUMER GODDEN, *The Doll's House*

In the forty years that had passed since their family's dissolution, Dare and Blaine's yearning for a happy, intact family had only intensified, but the trauma of their early years had left enduring scars. Unable to form the necessary attachments to adults with whom they might have explored marriage and parenthood, they both remained cut off from creating families of their own.

Women found Blaine irresistible. Many of them, after meeting him, had suddenly taken up fishing, smoking, and drinking, Blaine's main activities, in an effort to be closer to him. It never worked. He deflected them as expertly as his sister did her suitors and never achieved a sustained relationship of sexual intimacy. Dorothy, who had wanted to marry him, believed that Edie's abandonment had destroyed his ability to trust women. But she tried. Dare too had tried on Dorothy's behalf. Together they worked on an elaborate Valentine's Day card for which Dare created ten postage-stamp–sized portraits of her stunning friend. Dorothy glued these onto the interior of the card that exhorted: "Be my beau." On the back, Dorothy listed all her attributes, from her measurements to "Good disposition, friendly, cooperative, cuddly, single (not by choice), willing to travel." The last line left no room for ambiguity: "I want to be your personalized A No. 1 Valentine."

While Dare never spoke of her feelings about having children, Blaine told friends that he was against the prospect because he had no desire to bring a child into a world that he considered "an impossible, difficult place." They would only suffer. To children already in the world, he was wonderfully generous, especially to those in need of rescue. He gave money to the Save the Children and Fresh Air funds. In his will, he specified that if Dare died before he did, all he had was to be left to the Fresh Air Fund.

The siblings remained childlike themselves. Even as adults, they spoke baby talk, teased each other as children do, played children's games, and exchanged toys as gifts. It was as if they were perpetually picking up where they had left off when they were separated at ages five and three.

Blaine's feelings about the other Edith were conflicted. It wasn't that he couldn't understand his sister's love for her doll, it was her connection to Edie. He was outraged to learn that Dare had never been given a teddy bear as a child and railed against his mother, in full seriousness, for what he considered an unforgivable oversight. He was determined to make it up to his sister; while he was at it, he decided he would also buy a teddy bear for the Seawells' three-year-old son, Brockman.

It was Dorothy who was corralled into accompanying him on the 1955 trip to FAO Schwarz. "Blaine was drunk and got weird, as he always did when he drank," she recalled. "In we went. But when he saw all the bears together, he said it would be terrible to separate them because they would be lonely. With that he directed the sales-woman to pack up the entire lot, all their Steiff bears, hundreds of dollars of bears. Dare's apartment in those days was just around the corner. We walked over there, carrying all these damn teddy bears."

Dorothy found the spectacle of a grown-up brother and sister sitting on the floor surrounded by teddy bears, telling stories in imaginary bear voices, disturbing. Soon, Dare added Edith to the party—and urged Dorothy to join in. Making no effort to hide her disdain, Dorothy refused.

By the time Dorothy and Blaine left that evening, Dorothy had convinced Dare that the bears, aside from the one destined for Brockman, must be returned to the store the next morning. Dare did return all but two, a big one for Brockman and a little one for herself. For several days, though, Dare kept Brockman's bear in cus-tody and photographed the two animals with Edith. She later said she was struck by how happy Edith looked with her companions. When Blaine and Dare did present the big bear to Brockman, Dare photographed him opening the box containing the stuffed animal he christened "Dear Bear."

At home, Dare continued to photograph Edith and the little teddy bear. She liked to imagine Edith as herself and the little bear as a stand-in for Blaine. But she couldn't shake the lingering sense that something was missing. Not surprisingly, the big bear had been critical to her vision. Only with him in the picture could Dare repli-cate her own holy trinity: herself, a brother, *and* a father. She told Blaine that she intended to borrow the big bear back from Brock-man. Soon after, Blaine arrived at Dare's apartment bearing an FAO Schwarz box with a big bear in it and a note: "One does not bor-row other people's bears."

It was never Dare's intention to show anyone the photographs of her doll and the bears, any more than she would ever show anyone the countless photographs she had taken of herself. These were hermetic pursuits, fueled by a private obsession. That the photos came to be seen by outsiders was purely accidental. Donald Seawell had been so impressed with the book of Ocracoke photographs Dare gave his family for a Christmas gift in 1955 that he shared it with a publishing executive friend at Doubleday. For no particular reason, he also took along Dare's photographs of Brockman receiving Dear Bear. While Seawell thought the potential was in the Ocracoke photographs, the publisher—his name is forgotten—preferred the ones of the little boy and the teddy bear, which he thought might be suited to a book for children. He suggested that Dare speak with the Doubleday children's book editor, Margaret Lesser, and offered to set up a meeting.

The invitation alone was catalytic. In anticipation of the meeting, Dare outlined an idea for a children's story featuring Edith and the bears and planned the photographs to illustrate it. "Spring Fever" would be her first attempt to bring words to her images. Until then, if there were narratives underlying her photography, as in the earlier fictional tableaus she had taken of herself in her Hotel Bristol room, only she knew their content.

She likened the process to making a movie. "You need a story line, a shooting script, and a wardrobe department." Edith already had her name and persona, but the bears would need them as well. She christened the bigger bear Mr. Bear and decided he would assume the role of father figure. Little Bear would be the trouble-making little brother, seducing Edith into mischief. For the setting, Dare chose what had always been the sanctum—and laboratory—of her imagination, the dressing room and its vanity table and closet. She sewed costumes for Edith, composed the set, posed her inanimate cast, lit the scenes, and photographed them. She developed the fourteen photographs she chose as illustrations in the 11½-by-14-inch format she favored; when glued onto board, these became the pages of the book. She wrote out the text in her neat, childlike print on paper strips affixed to the photographs.

The story began with Edith sitting on the closet floor, peering into a hand mirror, desperately unhappy with what she sees. She complains that her hair looks dreadful and she doesn't have a thing to wear. When she climbs up on the vanity stool to get a better look at herself in the bigger mirror, Little Bear hops up beside her, proffering a daffodil, a lipstick (which he has helpfully swiveled out from its tube), a petticoat with a satin sash, and a hat adorned with roses and ribbon. All these items, he suggests, will improve her look. Edith is thrilled with her transformation. Mr. Bear, who has since joined them, is not. Perched on the other side of the dressing table, the superego to Little Bear's id, he has been taking in their foolishness with mounting displeasure. When he reaches "the end of his patience," he turns Edith over his knee and spanks her for being disobedient and for "behaving like a very vain little girl." In the end, Mr. Bear chalks up the incident to spring fever and forgives them both. With the offer to take them out for a treat, he entices Edith to put her own clothes back on.

What might in another's hands have come off as cutesy shots of a doll and teddy bears emerged as glamorous and almost noir in Dare's. The low-contrast photographs are moody, claustrophobic, and a little sinister. The inanimate toys appear startlingly, uncannily lifelike, which serves to underscore the voyeuristic thrill a young reader would feel, as if looking through the keyhole at Edith's spanking—a shameful and usually private event—and in having this chance to see what toys do when their owner is not around.

Margaret Lesser, the Doubleday editor whom Dare met in the spring of 1956, was pleased with the photographs in "Spring Fever," but she saw room for improvement in the one-dimensional story lines. She gave Dare a contract and a deadline of January 1957 to rework the story and come up with more illustrations.

Dare's final draft ran 53 pages and included 60 photographs. Edith, either on her own or with her bear companions, appears in all but five. From "Spring Fever," the story retained a dress-up scene and a spanking. But for the new version, Dare reached deeper into the reserves of her childhood memories to a place where feelings of loneliness, vulnerability, and fear lurked. These she now fastened

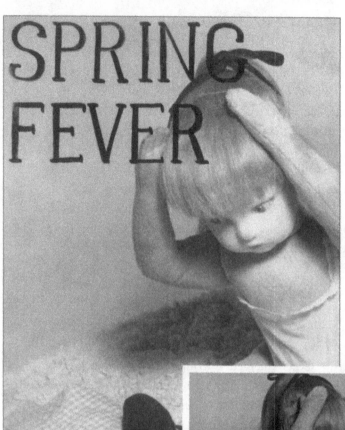

SPRING FEVER

The cover and opening scene from a mock-up of "Spring Fever," 1956, which would later become *The Lonely Doll*.

It was spring time, and Edith was very discontented. "My hair looks dreadful," she said to herself, "and I haven't a thing to wear but these same old clothes."

onto Edith, just as securely as she had her ponytailed wig. Edith became a lonely doll, as Dare had once been a lonely little girl, wishing for a brother, however naughty, to play with, and a father who might be enlisted as a reliable parent to care for them both. In this rendition of the story, Edith's wish comes true. She is rescued by the arrival of the teddy bears, delighted to follow Little Bear into transgression, even if fearful that any missteps—whether entering the adults' secret place, or dressing up in their clothes (or growing up, for that matter)—might lead to abandonment, and loneliness, anew. By verbalizing her own story it had been transformed, alchemized into a culturally viable form, into art. And now, in art, Dare had re-created the world the way she wished it to be. There is specificity to the happy-ever-after ending of *The Lonely Doll*. The father and brother teddy bears promise to stay with Edith "forever and ever!" And unlike their real-life counterparts, they do.

The photographs lend credibility to the proceedings, but an ambiguity remains. Is it possible that the arrival of the teddy bears—the entire story, for that matter—is the work of a lonely doll's imagination? This ambiguity is reminiscent of other dream worlds made real in stories like *The Wizard of Oz*, *Peter Pan*, and *Alice in Wonderland*. But while the characters in those books fear a wicked witch or an evil pirate or a pack of cards led by a queen with a decapitation obsession, Edith's fear is far more concrete. She is terrified that Mr. Bear will take Little Bear and walk out the door.

In photography Dare had found her medium, and in Edith she had found her muse. The camera provided the necessary intermediary, not just a shield to block out the world but a filter. She could use the camera to invent a universe, to control and arrange it as she wanted it to be. To the universe Edie had constructed out of fabric and makeup, canvas and paint, Dare added the elements of camera, film, Edith, and two teddy bears. Dare was coming closer to finding herself than she ever had before. Edie's muse had become an artist in her own right.

Engaged as Dare was with her book project, however, there was no thought of skipping the annual summer vacation with her mother. When Edie learned that the Seawells were headed to England that summer, she decided she and Dare, too, would go abroad; they would accept Gayelord Hauser and Frey Brown's open invitation to their house in Taormina. Before heading to Sicily, however, Edie, who had not been overseas since the 1930s, and Dare, who had not been since the ill-fated trip to visit Philip a decade earlier, would occupy themselves in England. Edie wanted to visit Bristol, to meet with Sir Philip Morris—who still had not come through with the promised commission to paint the Queen—and she wanted to see her portrait of Churchill in situ. Dare wanted to introduce her mother to Marie and Brian Sandeman.

On July 25, 1956, the Wrights and the Seawells sailed out of New York harbor on the *Île de France*. That evening, as the Seawells lay in bed, Genie, who had never been on an ocean liner before, fretted because they had skipped the lifeboat drill. Despite Donald's reassurances, she was unable to sleep. At 1 A.M., she wandered over to the cabin porthole. "A great ship is sinking," she exclaimed. The *Stockholm* and the *Andrea Doria* had collided. The Seawells ran to tell Edie and Dare, and the foursome gathered with other passengers on deck to behold the *Andrea Doria* lying on her side, blazing with lights, and lifeboats plying back and forth, packed with stunned passengers in coats thrown on over their sleepwear.

As the *Île de France* staff worked frantically to bring *Andrea Doria* passengers aboard, the group listened to first-hand reports and shuttled to their cabins to get dry clothes for the rescued. "This is history," Donald told Dare, urging her to get her camera. Dare refused. "I couldn't take pictures," she said. "It's just too tragic." Donald persisted, until she pronounced, dramatically, "I don't photograph suffering!"

Hearing of the accident, Blaine sent a cable. Dare wrote him a postcard that night which she mailed from Plymouth.

Dear Blaine,
Never again will I dare open my mouth to say all I want
is a good night's sleep and peace and quiet. What an
incredible sight that sinking ship was! The weather is hor-
rid because we swung so far north to make up time, and
I have an infected vaccination. Otherwise, all is well.
Best love, Dare.

Of the two weeks in London, the first was spent sick in bed with
colds. Once recovered, they set out for Bristol to meet Sir Philip
Morris. Edie seemed to think there was every chance that he would
arrange for the Queen to sit for her portrait on this very trip. As it
happened, Morris was away. Having told several friends in Cleveland that she was going to England to paint the Queen, she reported
on her return that she had decided to cancel the commission since
Dare had a cold. They spent the rest of their stay in London sight-
seeing and visiting Brian Sandeman and his family.

On August 15, they flew to Rome and then to Sicily. They found
Taormina a place of unparalleled beauty, and Gayelord and Frey
ideal hosts. In return they were considered equally ideal guests, for
the fact that they relished their privacy as much as they did and could
be counted on to entertain themselves. They stayed for five weeks.

Villa Apomea was as far a cry from the Wahab Village Hotel as
Taormina was from Ocracoke. They slept as late as they wanted,
awakened some mornings by the sound of the gardener knocking
almonds off the tree outside their window. One of six servants
delivered their coffee and toast as soon as they rang for it. After
breakfasting in bed or on their bedroom balcony, and perhaps a
photo session in their white dressing gowns, they would dress and
go with Gayelord's driver to tour the nearby Greek and Roman
ruins—and photograph some more—or the driver would take them
down to the bay to Hauser's beach house for a swim. In the after-
noons, they had tea in the tiled living room, cooled by breezes that

came in through the open doors, or Frey led them on antiquing expeditions in town, where they bargained for objets d'art and sumptuous old fabrics. Wandering down winding cobblestone streets, they took in the sights, if, in Edie's case, a bit too zealously. Ever since childhood, when her mother would chide her for her poor manners, Edie had been a shameless starer. She often said it was part of what made her such a good portrait painter. One afternoon, a band of children, made uncomfortable by her staring, retaliated by dancing around her and proclaiming her—in Sicilian—"The woman who looks through you."

Upon their return to New York, Dare displayed all the treasures gathered in Sicily for Edith and the Bears' perusal. She laid out the fabrics on a couch, placing one piece of tasseled brocade on Edith's head like a scarf, and photographed the scene. Dare led a busy private life with her characters. She bought them tiny toys, dolls, and stuffed animals and sat them down to write thank-you letters when they received gifts, photographing them in this pose. Or she wrote the thank-you letters on their behalf. And when they were "working," Dare talked to them as if they were real children. As she walked to the tripod after positioning them, she would call out, over her shoulder, "Now, hold still; don't move; just stand there like that."

Knowing little about book publishing, Dare had assumed she was expected not only to write and illustrate the book but to design it as well, and she spent the next few months diligently meeting the January 1st deadline. For the front cover's background, which she photographed in color, she chose the same pink-and-white gingham she had used to make Edith's dress. Inside this gingham border, she created an image reminiscent of the portrait of herself that Edie had painted thirty years earlier when they had first arrived in Cleveland: Edith seated on the floor, an open book resting between her outstretched legs.

The Lonely Doll was to be published in August 1957. In April, the book was excerpted in *Good Housekeeping*. It had been Doubleday's idea to hold off on all other publicity until after Labor Day, but Edie insisted Dare give her first interview to the hometown press, in this case the Cleveland *Plain Dealer Pictorial Magazine*, in July. Edie stage-managed the article, from the headline—MOTHER'S ARTFUL INFLUENCE—to the seven color photographs, all of which included either the image of Edie herself or one of her paintings. The text was almost exclusively focused on Edie, "who sleeps in a white satin bed in the penthouse atop the Hanna Building," and her career.

Unlike acting or modeling or photographing fashion models, creating a book was a source of emotional as well as professional fulfillment. To Edie's relief, Dare's newfound career did not seem to interfere with her ability to continue to cater to her mother's needs and so she could be unequivocally proud and supportive. But Blaine's balance was thrown off by his sister's beginning to find hers. He became unsettled as Dare's publishing debut approached, firing off angry letters to Edie once again to demand an accounting of his childhood, or at least the portion she had been there for. While Edie went along with this for a few letters, responding in a conscientious if not entirely truthful way, soon her anger, too, was aroused. "Blaine dear did it ever occur to you that Dare also suffered from a divided family? Little girls need a father as much as boys need a mother. Besides she had to take being in a boarding school for nine years. . . . Besides she never heard from her father—no letters. At least until Ivan married [Florence] you knew we loved you by weekly letters and little gifts—until our letters ceased to be answered. Ivan had every opportunity to see her if he had wished to do so."

As she ends this letter, she tells him she is working on portraits of an older, long-married couple. "I sadly think that is what I had envisioned for us. A united family growing old together—but alas! Yours, Edie. P.S. We have all three been deprived—Why?"

Blaine also asked Florence for a letter detailing what she knew of his childhood. And he wrote to air force colleagues, asking for their

A self-portrait that appeared on the book jacket of *The Lonely Doll*, 1957.

recollections of the war years. Clearly, he was hoping the information he was seeking would provide answers or inspiration. One of his war buddies wrote back to inquire if he was writing a novel. While that had always been Blaine's aim, it had been undone by his increasingly heavy drinking—irrevocably, it now seemed.

That August, Edie and Dare returned to Ocracoke. Dare planned to shoot her next book there, a story that would chronicle Edith and the Bears on vacation. Edie allowed herself to be drafted as her daughter's assistant, describing her role in a letter to Daisy as "a third hand." They decided they would rest and regroup for two weeks before getting to work.

It was an open secret on Ocracoke that the Wright women spent their days sunbathing nude. "People would come back with stories," said Lanie Boyette Wynn, Jim's mother and the daughter of the Wahab Village Hotel's managers. "They'd say, 'Oh, those Northerners!' It was kind of a tittery thing." Jake, their driver, became famous by association. When he died, a tribute in *The* (Raleigh) *News and Observer* commended him for his "judicious handling" of his charges.

> For sun bathers like Dare Wright, the author, and her artistic mother, Jake would run his truck several miles down the beach until they were beyond the sight of anyone else who happened to be on the ocean that day. When he returned to pick them up, Jake carefully beeped his horn from a discreet distance so they would have ample time to don their clothes.

That summer, the story of Dare's nude sunbathing attracted the attention of another author summering on Ocracoke. John Ehle, a young novelist from Winston-Salem, North Carolina, and a friend of Roy Wilder's, wove it into his novel, *Kingstree Island*. He put the story into an internal monologue of a local fisherman's wife:

[I]t was said a man from Beaufort almost wrecked his stunt plane flying up and down the beach looking down. She was tanning herself, and every bit of her had to be the same color. So this pilot told Jacob [the woman's husband] how he was flying over the beach and looked down and there was this woman, stretched out, face to the sun, and it looked as though she had not a stitch on. The pilot came a bit lower, for he knew this couldn't be quite what he was seeing, but when he swooped down the beach the second time, he could make out the whole form of her and see the details, and the pilot said he had never seen anything, even in the worst magazines, to equal it. So he turned his plane around and came back to a lower altitude, and the woman didn't even turn over, which would have been the least she could have done, considering the fact that her most meaningful side was turned to view; but she didn't.

Dare wasn't just stretched out, face to the sun, tanning. She was working with her mother to trip the shutter on increasingly proficient, intensely revealing—and disturbing—self-portraits. That summer's photographs were shot with a variety of films: color and black-and-white, slides and prints. Edie called them "the mermaid pictures." They feature Dare's naked, rigid, corpselike body spread out on the beach or threaded through the jagged branches of a driftwood tree or in the remains of a shipwreck. Seaweed partially conceals her breasts and pubic hair. Edie's pearls are wrapped around her neck, seashells are tangled in her long blond hair, and bluish scallop shells cover her eyes. She appears to have washed up on the beach or been left for dead.

After two weeks had gone by, and rested and tanned—all over— Edie and Dare turned to the summer's real work. Even with the help of Vincent Youmans, who had flown down for the shoot, Edie was soon worn out from traipsing all over the island with doll, bears,

Dare and Edie with Vincent Youmans, Jr., in front of his 140
Cessna. Youmans flew in to Ocracoke to help with the
shooting of *Holiday for Edith and the Bears*, 1957.

props, and camera equipment. Still, she pushed on, even when she sprained her ankle getting out of Jake's truck. She wrote Daisy her foot swelled "like a balloon, but I just kept going on it." Barely able to walk, Edie was nonetheless fiercely determined not to be left out.

Dare began shooting the photographs—in this case 48 rolls of film—with only the vague outline of a story in mind. It would begin with Edith and the Bears arriving on Ocracoke from the mainland by mailboat (as all non-flying visitors did in those days before ferry service started up), playing on the beach, and getting into some sort of mischief involving Little Bear's falling out of a boat, being rescued and punished by Mr. Bear, being forgiven, and being sad to go home.

Dare would try three different versions of this story before she felt she had gotten it right. Although the three cover versions she made depict different scenes, in each shot the wind has blown up Edith's dress and her underpants are showing.

In the first version, entitled "The Wonderful Island," Little Bear tries to entice Edith to come fish with him on the dock, disobeying Mr. Bear's orders. "We can't. We promised," she protests. "Aw, Mr. Bear's just a silly cautious old thing. Come on—unless you're scared," says bad Little Bear, in an echo of the lipstick-writing incident in *The Lonely Doll*. When Little Bear grabs a huge net to try to catch a crab, he tumbles into the water; Edith, attempting a rescue, falls in after him. Mr. Bear, hearing their cries for help, comes to save them. Then comes the scolding. Despite their promises to be good, the inevitable spanking ensues, followed by Mr. Bear's terrible threat: "How can I trust you? Perhaps I should separate you." "We'll have to do something quickly," whispers Little Bear. "Oh, yes," says Edith. "Let's do something nice for him. I couldn't bear it if he took you away and left me alone again."

This story line, far too close to *The Lonely Doll's*, was scrapped. Dare's next attempt, "The Barefoot Island," begins with Edith packing for the trip, especially excited that she'll be able to wear her new shoes. By summer's end, Edith cries at the prospect of leaving the island, especially at the thought of wearing shoes.

A beach shot in Ocracoke.

Edie and Edith outside Ocracoke's Wahab Village Hotel, awaiting their ride to the beach for the *Holiday for Edith and the Bears* shoot, 1957.

One of a series of nudes of Dare taken that same summer. Edith,
wearing a kerchief, is visible in the background.

In the third and final version, retitled *Holiday for Edith and the Bears*, the shoe business is jettisoned completely and a boat-obsessed Little Bear drives the story. Having enticed Edith into a rowboat, Little Bear drops his oar and falls overboard as he tries to retrieve it. Edith throws him a rope and saves him, but the oar is gone and they are stranded. From the dock, Mr. Bear sees them drifting out to sea, grabs another boat, and tows them back. This time, the punishment is verbal rather than corporal; instead of separating the duo, Mr. Bear threatens to separate them from their beloved island. They promise to be good, and they do get to stay—but then the holiday is over. Edith cries. Mr. Bear consoles them both by saying, "We'll come back again someday." The last photo shows Edith and the Bears on the boat bound for home; the book closes with the line: "And so they sailed away." Dare was dissatisfied with this ending but could not think of an alternative. At a cocktail party back in New York, she told guests of her dilemma. Helen Kessler, the wife of Blaine's friend Hermann, who had long ago served as Lee Wulff's confidante, suggested Dare end the book by having Little Bear ask, "How long is it till next time?" When the book came out, Dare inscribed a copy "To Helen, who had the last word."

That September, while Dare struggled with the story line of her second book, her first was flying out of bookstores. Edie wrote to Daisy: "Gosh so much ado—Wham! Wham!! . . . Edith is all over New York. They have had the biggest advance sale to shops that Doubleday has ever had on a juvenile book with one exception—a mother goose book by a famous author. They are all lit up about it." As was she. Blaine, however, expressed his ambivalence in the jumbled inscription in the copy he sent to Henry Vaillant and his wife, Janet. On the title page below the line, "Photographs by the Author," he scrawled, "To Janet and Henry without the regards of the author? Blaine (I hate the author!)." Blaine was also miffed that Edith got top billing. He felt the bears, who had been his contribution, should be the story's stars. Acknowledging Blaine's feelings on this issue in a letter to a friend, Dare wrote, "My own brother responds to Little Bear, and is always accusing me of abusing him and not featuring him enough. Just because his head is a bit loose (L.B.'s not my brother's) he says I've broken his spirit."

The Lonely Doll received mountains of publicity. The notices were positive if sometimes off-base, as in a *Cleveland Press* review, which observed that in *The Lonely Doll* Dare had "recaptured [the author's] happy childhood." Others, like the *Sioux City* (Iowa) *Globe*, got it right. "Dare Wright's uncanny skill with a camera turns her own doll and two teddy bears into a family."

Dare did not like being the focus of attention or being back on the other side of the camera. She avoided interviews whenever possible, complying only when her publisher or Edie insisted. And when she did consent to be interviewed, journalists did not find her forthcoming. It was only at Edie's urging that she spoke to Mary Rennels Snyder, whom Edie had painted when they first arrived in Cleveland and who now wrote a nationally syndicated book column called "Behind the Backs." After filling as much of the column as possible by writing about herself and the experience of being painted by Edie, Snyder managed to muster one paragraph, written in telegraphic style, about Dare:

> This sensitive, pixyish appearing Dare Wright is practical, hardworking and on her way. . . . She is shy and the only thing that frightens her is "selling myself" to publishers and editors. . . . Her living philosophy is "getting done what has to be done" and contrarily her luxury is to go out leaving all the electric lights burning. . . . It gives her a sense of luxury and probably a sense of rebellion against the dull rote of life. . . . Her favorite colors are white with a note of red and the funniest thing she can remember is when one of her pictures was labeled "BARE" instead of "DARE."

The *New York World-Telegram* and the *Sun* reporters did not do much better. When they asked, "Why the preference for dolls?"

Dare replied, "Well, they'll stand still for two–three hours for one photo—with never a complaint about wages. And all that bending over keeps a girl trim."

Otherwise, the reporters gleaned what they could from the book itself. "A picture of Miss Wright at the back of the book suggests a grown-up Edith, complete with earrings and a ponytail," noted the *Asheville Citizen-Times*. The *Park Avenue Social Register* bulletin observed that both Edith and Dare shared an "Alice in Wonderland quality."

When Dare had returned to Cleveland in 1936 in *Pride and Prejudice*, Edie had tried to interest the press in the story of a star's homecoming. Now, twenty-one years later, at age 42, Dare was indeed a star. With the release of her first book, she became the toast of Cleveland at book signings and cocktail parties, and luncheons in her honor were given by her fellow Laurel alumnae. These classmates were fascinated at the chance to reassess their most mysterious member and to see her ever-exotic mother glued to Dare's side. That had been far from the case in Dare's schooldays.

Higbee's and Halle's, Cleveland's leading department stores, fought for the chance to sponsor the book's in-store promotions. Here was an author desirable for her Cleveland roots, her dazzling looks, and because, as Edie's daughter, she brought connections to wealthy book-buying Clevelanders. Higbee's won out and both Richard Gildenmeister, in charge of their book promotions, and Anne Udin, the head of the book department, became Dare and Edie's close friends. (Dare would dedicate her fifteenth book, *Edith and Little Bear Lend a Hand*, to Anne.)

While Dare was in Cleveland, *The Lonely Doll* hit the *New York Times* Children's Best Sellers list at number fourteen of a sixteen-book list on which *The Cat in the Hat*, published five months before Dare's book, was number one. Edie wrote Daisy: "Doubleday said the market has been dissatisfied with children's books, wanted something different and this is IT. . . . All raving on the incredible action and expression she gets out of the inanimate. They say it will go on for ten years and the next the same . . . and that she will have an income for the rest of her life." To a United Press reporter, Edie crowed at having bought Edith all those years before for $12.50. "A fantastic price at the time," she said, "but it's pretty obvious we've gotten our money back several times over. We're now having her insured by Lloyd's of London."

Despite being in a highly productive period herself, with commissions to paint the portraits of several CEOs, including a second portrait of the CEO of Republic Steel, Edie groused only a little to Daisy about having to act as Dare's secretary and to "keep the house and clothes going." And Dare, only too happy to retreat to the Hanna Building studio between engagements, did her part by going on a "housecleaning spree" of Edie's studio.

It was while cleaning that she made a discovery far more exciting than the attention she was receiving for her book. Edie had *not* sent all Dare's childhood belongings to the apartment on 58th Street. Dare found one more childhood doll: Persis, a tiny German-made bisque-headed doll with a wire-strung toddler body. At ten inches, she was a little less than half as high as Edith and had blue glass eyes whose lids open and shut, a mohair wig, and an open mouth with two front teeth. Dare immediately sketched out a story:

> Ann's mother finds a little doll in a trunk in the store room. When her mother asks Ann if she would like the doll, Ann says she doesn't find dolls interesting. The mother leaves the doll on a table and Ann resumes reading a book. She is startled when a voice says, "I'm Persis. You mean you don't want me?" The little doll was sitting up. She was talking. "You're just a doll. I must be crazy. Dolls don't talk," said Ann. "I do. I talk lots. Mostly people don't seem to hear me. A long time ago, before I was shut up in that trunk, I belonged to a little girl who did hear me. . . . We had lots of adventures. You and I could too. Please let me be your doll. . . . I just won't go back into

that dark trunk! If you won't have me I'll run away." "I'll have you," said Ann. "But what will my mother think when she hears you talking?" . . . "She'll never notice. We're the only ones who'll know."

When Dare left Cleveland, Persis was carefully wrapped and packed away in her suitcase.

As she had when Edith arrived, Dare sewed Persis a new outfit and photographed her in a variety of venues and poses. This seemed to be Dare's way to explore her doll's "personality" and determine whether she would be a fitting book subject. "You can't just photograph any doll," Dare told the *Plain Dealer*. Persis's first costume was a dress with a ribbon sash, to be worn over a crinoline petticoat and lace bloomers. But after photographing her beside her sewing supplies and on her bookshelves, Dare decided the dressy look was not for Persis and sewed her a pair of striped jersey pants and a loose white T-shirt. Still dissatisfied, she stripped her of all clothes. Dare had discovered—or decided—that, unlike Edith, Persis was not interested in dressing up. She preferred to wear no clothes at all. With her short haircut, she was more tomboy, more nature girl, than Edith. If Edith was the feminine side of Dare, Persis was another side, "a little girl who likes to walk around with no clothes on," as she told Dick Gildenmeister, the sort "who loves to dance naked in the woods." Relating to Persis's rebellious streak, or just playing along, Dick expressed his approbation, always saying of Persis, "She's my girl." Over time, Dare had Persis write him many letters, such as one she wrote in handwriting even more childlike than her own:

Dear Mr. Gildenmeister:
Am I really your girl? Do you like me better in pants or frills? I love you.
Persis!

Dare was also hoping to involve Blaine, who always liked Dare better in pants than in frills, in her book ventures. He still had mixed emotions about his sister's successful career. She decided to set her next book, starring Persis, in Walton. With this book, Dare would use not only inanimate objects, her newly returned doll, and the teddy bears, but also live creatures: a turtle, a crow, a butterfly, and a bumblebee.

As the story begins, a huge turtle is making his way up to the front door of an abandoned house. He decides to look inside. But aside from some old books and a "small, small doll all covered with dust," standing on a book, her head leaning against a German-English dictionary, he finds nothing. The turtle asks the doll who she is. "I'm Persis. I've been here for years—for years and years. I don't like it here."

"Well, why stay?" asks Turtle.

"Oh, I've tried so hard to get out," cries Persis, jumping up, "but I'm too little to open the door." He lets her out. The sun warms her and the wind blows off the dust with which she's been covered. After running for a while, she soon grows hot and sits down under the shade of a daisy. A butterfly appears and suggests she'd be cooler without so many clothes. Next comes Persis's striptease, which takes place over six pages. Off come her pinafore and dress, petticoat and underwear. "How nice it feels!" says Persis, who thanks the butterfly for his good advice. She runs some more until she feels tired and settles beneath a May apple leaf and falls asleep.

When Persis awakens, two "happy bears" appear. Nice Bear is happy "because the whole world seemed good to him." Cross Bear is happy "because he had such a fine time complaining about absolutely everything." She greets them by saying, "Hello. I like you." For Nice Bear, the feeling is mutual, but not for Cross Bear. When Persis expresses her wish to go home with them, Nice Bear agrees, overruling the objections of Cross Bear, who complains bitterly about Nice Bear's plan to keep her. Despite Cross Bear's inhospitable nature, Persis is happy with the bears, especially Nice Bear, who takes her for walks and washes her in the brook.

Meanwhile, Cross Bear continues to grumble about their new companion: "She's a bother and she talks too much." Upset by Cross Bear's growling, Persis consults Turtle on how to make Cross Bear love her. "Why not do something very nice for him?" Turtle says and suggests she find Cross Bear some honey. When she finds a beehive in a tree, she is greeted by an angry bee. "That's *my* honey," he scolds, so fiercely that she becomes startled and falls to the ground, landing at the feet of Cross Bear. Nice Bear reproaches Cross Bear for letting her get hurt. Cross Bear is equally upset. "I wouldn't let any harm come to her. I love her." Hearing Cross Bear say she is loved, Persis revives. And in an echo of the ending of *The Lonely Doll*, she announces she will stay with the bears forever and ever.

Blaine and Vincent Youmans were given assistant roles on this book. They found Dare a bee, a butterfly, and a turtle, whose shell Dare scrubbed with a nail brush and polished with baby oil. The turtle played his part to perfection, but the crow, which Blaine assured her he had tamed and now intended to keep as a pet, proved uncooperative. She was not accustomed to the challenge of photographing animate subjects that, unlike her models or the dolls and bears, did not take direction and were no good at staying still.

Everyone enjoyed the shoot. Dare packed picnic lunches that she photographed her assistants eating, and at the end of each workday they all dressed up in straw hats or Davy Crockett hats and waders and horsed around in Blaine's jeep, playing like children whose mother is away.

While *Good Housekeeping* had been given first serial rights for *The Lonely Doll*, *Life* magazine signed on for the second book, excerpting five photographs and writing its own captions for the "Speaking of Pictures" section that ran in April 1958. Under the headline STARTLING REALISM IN A FANTASY, the photos are explained:

The little girl shown in these pictures is strikingly pretty, graceful and animated. She is also unusually tiny and when this fact brings closer inspection it turns out that she is not a little girl at all but a startlingly realistic doll. Her name is Edith and she is the ponytailed heroine of a picture book for children by Dare Wright coming out this summer, "Holiday for Edith and the Bears." The author got Edith as a present when she was seven years old. Proportioned after a four-year-old child, Edith was the center of Dare's childhood stories. Miss Wright became a professional fashion photographer and recently began to make up new stories for her old doll. The one told here is a photographic fantasy that wonderfully captures the reality with which every little girl surrounds her best-loved doll.

Edie, bursting with pride, wrote to Daisy, "There will be a lot of things come from this *Life* article. She has worked hard and is on top at last."

So were Dare's characters. Sales were brisk in this peak period of the baby boom. *Holiday for Edith and the Bears* made its appearance on the *New York Times* Children's Best Sellers list at number ten. Edith and Mr. Bear were featured in full-page ads for Children's Bufferin. In July 1958, the Madame Alexander doll company brought out Edith the Lonely Doll, which they continued to manufacture in a range of sizes and with slight variations until 1963, when Dare, who never liked their rendition, let the contract lapse. Some versions came in a boxed set with the book. Doubleday urged booksellers and toy stores to include both the doll and the books in their displays. The companies that made Little Bear and Mr. Bear, Steiff and Schuco, respectively, were enlisted to provide them for display as well. To their colleagues' amusement, Doubleday's all-male sales force carried the Madame Alexander Edith on their calls. That Christmas, the doll yielded $3,400 in royalties, but this didn't warm Dare to the likeness. "She [Madame Alexander] could have made a good copy but wouldn't," Dare wrote in a letter to a doll collector. "Her battle cry was 'I do not copy, I create.'"

In January 1959, the first of the foreign editions of *The Lonely Doll* came out in Italy. Edie drew the front cover of *La Bámbola Solitária: Una Stòria Fotográfica di Dare Wright* in a letter to Daisy. "Little Bear is called l'Orsacchiotto, and Mr. Bear Signor Orso— Too cute." British, Danish, Dutch, German, and Hebrew editions were also released. There was media coverage in other countries as well, especially in Germany and England. *The Daily Sketch*, a London tabloid, ran a photo spread on Edith beside the story of a woman accused of murdering her husband. Dare was amused by the juxtaposed headlines ALONE—UNTIL SHE MADE FRIENDS and WIFE ACCUSED. She gave the articles a page in her scrapbook.

Conditions on Pot had deteriorated with Blaine's drinking. Although Dare decided to shoot her next book, *The Doll and the Kitten*, in Walton, on this and all future trips Dare stayed with Florence Wakeman, a local woman Edie's age with whom Blaine had become close. Florence, who never married, had retired from her job as town telephone operator and made extra money by taking in boarders. Among her passions were people, horses (which she boarded in her barn for people in the area), and Fig Newtons. Blaine once gave her fifty pounds of them as a Christmas present. He also bought her a retired New York City police horse, a gift she refused, although no one could remember what became of the animal.

Dare and Florence's first meeting, a decade earlier, had not been auspicious. Blaine had been otherwise occupied, so Florence offered to meet Dare's bus. Florence was horrified to see a bleached blonde wearing skin-tight clothes, high heels, and too much makeup heading in her direction, exclaiming, "You must be Florence!" Florence told friends what a relief it was to run into Dare a few days later wearing a T-shirt and blue jeans, "looking like a normal person." Over time, Florence, who was a surrogate mother to Blaine, would become the same for Dare. Dare would photograph several books at Florence's home and dedicate two books to her.

The Doll and the Kitten tracks Edith and the Bears on a visit to a farm during which Edith fantasizes about taking home each of the farm animals she sees there, only to be denied every time she asks Mr. Bear's permission. Then she finds a kitten. She thinks he might consent to that, but she can never find the right time to ask. Along with the plot staple of a spanking, delivered after Edith and Little Bear open a gate and all the cows get out, there is also the rescue operation by Mr. Bear. The kitten gets lost. The little ones find him trapped in the rafters at the top of the barn. They go after him and become stranded themselves. Mr. Bear comes to everyone's aid, and in the end Edith does get to keep her kitten. Perhaps to please Edie, who had been left out of this book's production, Dare dedicated it to Noel Lawson Lewis, Edie's champion in earlier years and a cat lover. (In any case, the tribute could not have pleased Lewis, since he had died in 1950.)

Dare and Edie still made time for private play, the dress-up sessions that they photographed. Beginning in 1955, these were recorded, as always, with a still camera but also with Dare's new movie camera. For the next five years Dare took the movie camera with her everywhere, from Blaine's mountains to Edie's sea and home to Cleveland. But after shooting twenty-five reels of 16-mm film, she lost interest. Dare never mastered the moving camera as she did the still; she never learned to tell a story in this medium. A six-minute sequence shot in Edie's Hanna Building studio in 1959 comes the closest. Shot in black-and-white, the footage shares her books' shadowy, noir quality. The camera wends its way through dimly lit hallways into a stairwell and climbs the steps. Reaching the landing, it pans in on a gray metal door and a sign, written in Edie's hand: "Edith Stevenson Wright, Pent House, For appointment call CH1-3392." Inside, as the camera adjusts to the darkness, one man's face and then another come into view, floating in the air like ghosts. Once the lighting has been adjusted, these faces are revealed to belong to framed portraits. Scanning the room, the camera takes in more portraits and lingers on porcelain figurines, objets d'art, and richly upholstered furnishings. Then, coming into view through a veil of smoke, Edie appears. Seated in an armchair, smoking, sipping a drink, she wears a man-tailored blouse, trousers, flat shoes, and pearls. She is talking animatedly, as if the camera were her guest at her cocktail party. But there are no guests, only the portraits. The camera fixes on Donald Seawell in a Scottish kilt and on Dare in a princess gown, a laurel wreath encircling her head. When it returns to Edie, she is up out of her chair, standing before her easel on the black-and-white squares, waving her paintbrush wildly, as if it were a conductor's baton—or a magic wand. Turning to the palette to replenish the paint on her brush, she twirls back to the easel to stroke it upon the canvas, as reflexively as she brings the cigarette in her other hand to her mouth, draws in, and all but disappears in a cloud of smoke.

By the time the smoke has dissipated, the other Edith has replaced her in the frame. Tucked into bed, Edith clutches her own little doll. The workday is done. Edith has been put to bed and Edie, wearing a diaphanous white off-the-shoulder dressing gown, sits at her dressing table, hairbrush and makeup brush in hand, as if preparing herself to go out. Pausing only to light one cigarette after another, she admires herself in the mirror. When she picks up a hand mirror, angling it to glimpse a view from the back, Dare shoots not Edie but Edie's reflection in the dressing table mirror.

Another movie from this period features Blaine and Dare on Pot. In one scene, they take turns filming each other wearing a Mexican sombrero and serape and, in another, peering into a pool in a mountain stream, as if to catch their own reflections.

As they were both thriving professionally, Edie decided she and Dare deserved a grander summer vacation than Ocracoke. She fixed on the island of St. John in the American Virgin Islands, where Laurance S. Rockefeller, a son of John D. Rockefeller, a Clevelander, had just opened the Caneel Bay resort. Although it was expensive, rates were lower in the off season. And so at the beginning of August 1959, Edie and Dare flew to St. Thomas, where, laden down with belongings and props—including two full-length bustled period gowns and accompanying hats—they boarded a ferry for St. John. Dare had three still cameras with her, as well as her movie camera, and Edie made sure to pack the necessary art supplies. On their last trip, these had been forgotten; Edie was reduced to painting with makeup and makeup brushes.

During dinner one night, a fellow guest sent a note to their table. Clare Boothe Luce had been at Caneel Bay since mid-June, trying to complete a novel. Her husband, Henry Luce, the chairman of Time, Inc., flew down for short visits during his wife's six-week stay, but Clare was feeling alone and seeking distraction. Dare and Edie caught her eye.

Learning that Edie was an artist and her daughter artistically inclined, Clare invited them to join her in *gyotaku*, the ancient technique of Japanese fish rubbing. Dare and Clare spent hours on the beach making rubbings with freshly caught angelfish supplied by local fishermen. Edie, who would have preferred to do portraits of the Luces, did try her hand at *gyotaku*, but in the privacy of their hotel room. Dare filmed a hotel maid standing over Edie as her mother makes her rubbings seated on the floor of their room. The maid then spirits away the mess.

On Luce's next visit, Clare introduced him to her new friends, and the Wrights were invited along when they chartered a boat to visit the nearby island of Virgin Gorda. Dare filmed the boat ride, her camera lingering on the Luces, seated side by side in their bathing suits in the stern.

The only nude pictures of Dare from the trip to Caneel Bay were shot in their hotel room. Most likely, there was no place out-of-doors where they were not at risk of being seen. Edie and Dare focused instead on dressing up. They filmed each other scampering up the stairway to their room and over the ruins of a former sugar mill, hoisting the voluminous skirts of their fancy gowns so as not to trip.

While Edie and Dare relaxed in the Caribbean, and the dolls and bears rested from their labors on 58th Street, children across America pored over their images and read about their adventures in Dare's first and second books. Edith, in effigy, also made her way in the world. A postcard arrived at Caneel Bay from Suzie Vaillant, now remarried to Robert Hatt. The Hatts were traveling through the USSR that summer and visited the U.S. Exposition in Moscow. In the child's bedroom in the "ideal house," they found Edith sitting on the bed. The Madame Alexander doll had made her way to the Soviet Union, where she was considered representative enough of American culture to be included.

CHAPTER EIGHT

The Lonely Doll's Dilemma

The little lady on our cover may not be a living doll, but she's the next thing to it. She is a doll, and to hundreds of thousands of youngsters who have followed her adventures in such books as The Lonely Doll *and* Holiday for Edith and the Bears, *she's very much alive. . . . The photo on the cover was taken especially for our readers by Miss Wright, who, as you can see below, is a bit of a living doll herself.*

—American Weekly, *August 14, 1960*

The success of Dare's books had nothing to do with any calculation on her part. She did what she wanted, and it worked. As long as Doubleday gave Dare free rein, she and her publisher were on the best of terms. But Dare balked when, after the release of her fourth book, her editors stepped in with directives for future ones. Describing what she called her "squabbles" with Doubleday in a 1959 interview in *The Walton Reporter*, she said, in a petulant tone far more characteristic of Edie than of herself, "They want a series like *The Bobbsey Twins* and I don't."

This was not simply an author feeling empowered by her success. This was a single-minded artist and, beneath that, a child refusing to be told how to play. But her need to please prevailed. As she planned her next book, which she called "The Lonely Doll's Dilemma," she decided she would build it on the plot of *The Doll and the Kitten* to tell the story of what happened once Edith brought her kitten home to New York from the farm. But it would be published not by Doubleday but by Random House, which had been wooing Dare since the 1958 *Life* magazine article.

Whether Bennett Cerf, Random House's chairman, presiding over what was then the largest publisher of children's books in America—one third of its total sales volume at the time was in juvenile books—was first taken in by Dare's books or by Dare's looks, he directed Louise Bonino, the head of children's books, to extend an open invitation to the author of the *Lonely Doll* series. As Dare became more upset with Doubleday's interference, she agreed to the meeting, and at the end of 1959 she left Doubleday for Random House.

As it turned out, Random House was not offering carte blanche either, but Dare liked their ideas, especially Cerf's idea for photographic travelogs for children, to begin with *The Young Traveler's London*. For her Random House debut, Cerf decided that the travelog, which Dare retitled *Date with London*, and the next *Lonely Doll* story should be brought out simultaneously.

Dare liked Cerf's London idea because the Seawells were also planning a trip to Great Britain that summer. Brook and Brockman could pose as the young travelers, and through his wartime associations and his law firm's London office, their father was well positioned to help with logistics. Knowing the governor of the Tower of London, the head of Scotland Yard, and the Lord Chamberlain, Donald was able to secure permission for Dare to shoot in places not ordinarily open to the public, and through his work as an entertainment lawyer, he knew Boris Karloff and arranged for him to accompany them to Madame Tussaud's waxworks after hours.

As Dare readied herself for what would be a monthlong trip, she felt some anxiety over leaving Edie, but also over leaving Edith and the Bears. On the day before her departure, she rented a safety deposit box at her bank big enough to accommodate them.

In June 1960, Dare, Donald, his mother, Bertha, and the Seawell children flew to London, where they made the Connaught Hotel their base. In an eighteen-day blitz, Dare shot 1,500 photographs of Brook and Brockman at every London landmark. After their work was done, Genie, who had stayed in New York for her own work, joined them for a vacation in Scotland and the Island of Jura in the Hebrides, home to Donald's Highland ancestors.

Although Dare enjoyed the chance to photograph the Seawell children and to travel with their family, she did not like the rest of the work that *Date with London* entailed. She preferred the sort of book that told children what they wanted to know, not what was good for them. Still, researching the history of the city where she would have lived as Philip's wife did have its interesting moments. She wrote to Allie, "My head is absolutely fuzzy with the dust of ancient kings. I discovered yesterday that a 134-foot maypole once stood in the middle of the Strand, and when it finally came down Isaac Newton took part of it to mount his telescope. But I haven't found who wrote 'What's not destroyed by Time's devouring hand? Where's Troy—and where's the Maypole in the Strand?' You have to be careful not to get too fascinated by obscure bits of information."

Back in New York that fall, Dare worked on *Date*, while completing "The Lonely Doll's Dilemma," now retitled *The Lonely Doll Learns a Lesson*. Edith's kitten has joined the ménage in New York. Little Bear becomes jealous of the attention she lavishes on her new feline friend. Mr. Bear is not happy with Edith's behavior, either. As Little Bear pouts because Edith ignores him, Mr. Bear asks her, "When you were lonely, Edith, who was your best friend?" Edith faces the dilemma of how to add a new friend to the mix without betraying an old one and learns to share.

For her next book, Dare proposed an original fairy tale, in which an evil—and lonely—wizard transforms a princess into a doll. The idea, which had been percolating in Dare's photography since 1958, when she and Edie had taken photographs of Dare as a princess on the beach at Ocracoke, had reemerged during the trip to Scotland, where Dare had photographed castles "out of fairy tales." Its themes had been gathering momentum in her consciousness since her first exposure to the dark and often erotically charged world of fairy tales. Now they found voice in the only safe way she knew, in the form of a story. At forty-seven, a fully mature woman at least chronologically, Dare was clearly obsessed with the question she put into the mouth of the book's protagonist in an early draft: "What is making love?" For the first time, that protagonist was not a little girl but an eighteen-year-old.

This book could have been called "Dare's Dilemma." Its heroine is a princess, Lona, who must learn to free herself from the spell of an evil wizard, to vanquish him in order that she can grow up and be romantically—and sexually—fulfilled. If the Edith books explored a fantasized childhood with a father and brother, *Lona* was Dare's way to explore the fantasy of an adulthood with a husband and lover. And however disguised, the wicked wizard, powerful and terrifying, was Edie. This story, too, explored wish fulfillment, but of a very different kind.

Voluminous notes and four drafts detail the story as it took shape. Druth, an evil princess-hating wizard, has transformed a prince and a princess into toads. To his consternation, they are happy this way. "They didn't have to learn how to mate on the wet shore. That came naturally. They were happy as toads. Druth could not bear it."

In the next version, only the prince, named Rogain, is changed into a toad. Despondent, he tells the princess, who loves him regardless of his form, that she will never be allowed to marry a toad. " 'I can quite see my parents wouldn't like it,' " she tells him. " 'So we'll run away.' " With her prince tucked "securely in her pocket," she "lifted her skirts and ran down the endless steps, out of her castle, down the mountain, and never drew breath until they arrived safely at the shores of a lake. 'I came here because I think I've heard that toads mate in the water,'" she tells Rogain, as she carefully extracts him from her pocket and kisses him. "His long, insect-catching tongue flicked out to touch her finger, but he couldn't kiss her back. It was frustrating. 'It'll never work. We need to be the same thing at the same time,' mourned Rogain. 'Then somehow I'll be a toad,' cried the princess."

The wizard, watching the proceedings in the smoke of his magic fire, does heed her wish and she is transformed into a toad. The princess-toad is eager to consummate their love. "It's a good thing we're not wearing clothes," she observes. Jealous and determined to prevent them from getting any closer to "making love," the wizard decides the best punishment would be to turn them both "back into themselves," into their human form. "If anything will make them miserable that will," he says to himself. "It's harder being human—choices, responsibilities, they'll wear clothes, no more frolicking in the woods."

In a third draft, Dare tried out the idea of the toad as the wizard himself, whom the princess, in her goodness, could love despite his ugliness. In this version, he was not terrifying or evil but benevolent. In the end, Dare returned to the idea of the wicked wizard and the prince-toad as the object of the princess's love.

It did not take long for the theme of loneliness to find its way into the center of this story. Dare's first notes include this line: "Everything in world [does] not make up for loneliness." Even the words *lonely* and *alone* are reflected in Dare's various attempts to name the princess. She began with Aline and Alon, an *o* and *e* away from *Alone*. Later, she considered Alor. In the end she settled on Lona.

At one point Dare consulted Blaine on the story. Blaine, who had no patience with his sister's fairy-tale obsession, collaborated with her on one version. Under his influence, a fairy-tale parody emerged:

> Once upon a time there was a pale and purty princess who lived (if you could call it living) in a castle just five hundred meters above an endless and never-endless layer of clouds. The princess was purty by nature, and pale on account of the drains in her castle had been hopelessly plugged for hundreds of years. From her tip-top tower chamber, which was whisked by brisk breezes and less unbearable than the other rooms, she could survey the great undercast—or, rarther [*sic*], the top of it.

Although Blaine's take amused Dare, it in no way fit in with her vision. She formulated a new story, drawing on only a few elements of earlier drafts. Druth, an ugly and evil wizard, once scorned by a beautiful princess, is determined to take revenge on any princess he can find by casting a spell to render her as miserable and lonely as he is. The problem is that Druth has lost his touch. As punishment for an earlier misdeed, "invisible hands" have ripped the chapter on "PRINCESSES, Enchantment of" from his book of common spells. Frustrated and humiliated, Druth shuts himself in the tower of his castle, where for hundreds of years he studies what remains of his spell book, determined to teach himself how to enchant a princess. His victim will be a princess who is the great-great-great-granddaughter of his first failure. But this spell works no better than the first. In a fit of temper, he drowns her kingdom, Muirlan, under a lake and puts its populace into an enchanted sleep. He tries next on the princess of a different kingdom, Lasair, but fails again. This time he discharges his rage by burning Lasair and putting its inhabitants to sleep. Now, there is but one princess left, Lona, of the kingdom of Yarmalit. But since she is a baby princess, not worth enchanting, he decides to imprison her kingdom in a deep fog, put its people to sleep, and hide Lona away in the tower of his castle. While he waits for her to grow up, he will perfect a spell.

In an earlier draft, Dare had made notes on Druth's raising of Lona. Druth feeds Lona and clothes her and teaches her the alphabet. "But no one cuddled her or sang her a lullaby or tucked her in at night. Druth didn't know a little girl needed these things. He couldn't understand why she grew paler and silenter, but one day an odd thought came to him, 'Perhaps she's lonely.' It was an unwizardly idea, but it stayed in his head. The truth was that Druth was lonely himself, though he didn't know it. Wizards aren't supposed to be lonely. Source of all his mischief.'"

Rogain, the prince of Muirlan, the drowned kingdom, has been off seeing the world. Returning home, he finds the devastation Druth has wrought. His plan to confront the evil wizard backfires. The wizard transforms him into a toad. In toad form, but with his magic jewel affixed to his forehead, Rogain makes the first of what will be yearly visits to the imprisoned Princess Lona. As Rogain and Lona grow to love each other, Rogain becomes determined to regain his human form and save the three kingdoms from the wizard. His only hope is an "ancient witch," who might know how to undo Druth's spells. By the time Rogain finds the witch, Lona is eighteen and has grown "tall and beautiful."

The witch tells Rogain of a magic shell that will roll the waters back from Muirlan, a burning key that will enable the burned forests of Lasair to grow again, and a golden crown that will banish the fog in which Yarmalit is enshrouded. A princess, she tells him, must go alone to find them. If the princess does not give in to fear, she will succeed, and Druth's spells will be lifted. If the princess yields to her fear, all will be lost. But this is not the only sacrifice she must make. Assuming she does find the three magic objects, she must also allow Druth to enchant her, because only if he succeeds in enchanting a princess will he perish for good.

The witch asks Rogain if he knows a princess brave enough to make these sacrifices. Lona is the only princess he knows, but Rogain is distraught at the thought of Lona's sacrifice. The witch advises him to put the choice to Lona herself.

Lona accepts the challenge and Rogain offers her the only help he can, the jewel from his head. As Lona prepares to set out into the world to find the magic objects, she becomes fearful and runs back to her tower turret, where she cowers beneath the covers of her bed. Her fear empowers Druth. He sends a spell to the turret chamber. It misfires and Lona shrinks to the size of a doll. Now Lona must continue her quest despite her small size. She sews herself a miniature dress from handkerchiefs and sets off, determined never again to give in to fear.

While Druth tries unsuccessfully to frighten her at every step along the way, Lona follows the jewel, which shines when she is on the right path. It leads her through a wood, into the mountains, and to the sea, as one by one she finds the magic objects and the spells are lifted. Despite her loneliness, she perseveres.

A knight in shining armor appears to bestow the key upon her and the spell over Lasair is lifted, but when he departs, a nasty two-headed dragon threatens to eat her. She escapes and the jewel leads her to a door. She puts the key in the lock and enters to find a "windy star-filled space." Inside, a magic crown floats down to rest atop her head and the wind carries her back to her castle room. As it sets her down, she regains her true size, as her kingdom emerges from the fog.

Rogain appears and when she places the magic jewel back on his forehead, he regains his form as a tall prince. But Lona has still to carry out the last part of her assignment in order to nullify Druth's powers once and for all. Holding Rogain's hand, as instructed by the witch, she calls out Druth's name three times. Druth casts his spell and she is transformed into a toad. Although Druth lies "dead under the stones of his fallen tower," Rogain and Lona, prince and toad, must now embark on their final quest, "to learn the magic that would disenchant a princess."

The story ends happily as they succeed. "One day, hand in hand, home to their kingdom came Lona and Rogain." "There is great power in wishing" is the book's penultimate line. In fact, wishing has had nothing to do with Lona's success. Lona of Yarmalit, unlike Dare, is never reduced to passive wishing. She has acted, and unusually, for a female fairy-tale heroine. In real life, Dare of Toronto-Medford-Milford-Huntington-Youngstown-Cleveland-New York would never feel so empowered. The only way to succeed, to emerge from the fog, would be to betray the wizard, and this Dare could never do.

For the first and only time, Dare cast herself in the book. She decided she would play the princess in her full-sized incarnation, and a Lenci lady doll she had bought with her mother in Paris when she was thirteen, a boudoir doll meant to adorn a bed rather than be played with, would serve as the princess Lona under the miniaturizing spell.

Dare planned to shoot most of the photography in the castle-rich countryside of Brittany. It was arranged that Edie, who had been left out of the *Date with London* summer, would accompany Dare to Europe for *Lona*. They set aside all of July and August 1961 for this trip, in order to leave some time for rest. After all, the book's assistant was now seventy-eight.

In a letter telling Daisy of her plans, Edie wrote, "And we do have fun—minds grasp things the same way, and Dare is such a honey of good nature and optimism and so careful of me. One of our friends, who doesn't like her mother and I think is jealous, said, 'Oh, if you were together all the time you'd soon hate each other.' I actually wanted to slap her—then I felt sorry for her."

Edie, overbearing, irritable, and easily angered, did not share Dare's "good nature." As they checked in at the airport, lugging camera equipment, costumes, a doll, and their usual copious baggage, Edie had an altercation with the airline clerk, who dared to levy a $90 excess-checked-baggage charge. Dare, as always, placated her mother and smoothed things over.

They landed in Paris on July 9, where they rented a four-door Renault and, with Dare behind the wheel, headed straight for Quimper in Brittany, which was to be their base for several weeks. On arrival, they went bikini shopping for Dare. Still considered risqué on this side of the Atlantic, Edie reassured Daisy in a postcard,

"They are worn here." No sooner had the bikini been bought than storms swept Europe, and Dare wrote Daisy on her side of the postcard they shared: "I must say that a bikini seems utter madness at the moment. Wind, rain, and cold! But it was glorious when we first came, and will be again, I trust." Edie, on her side, groused about the weather. But by the last week in July the weather and Edie's mood had improved. In her next postcard Edie is raving about "wonderful sea and beach." In two homemade "books" Dare made with her photographs of this trip, it is clear that she did finally get to try out her bikini.

From Quimper, they drove southeast along the rocky coastline, stopping to photograph in one storybook village after another, beginning in Vannes, where they shot Lona climbing a ladder to a hayloft beside a *chaumière*, a thatched cottage typical of the region. Then it was on to Josselin, Vitré, and Fougères, with their medieval castles. Immersed in their work, they missed the chance to visit a popular tourist attraction, the Hôtel de Sévigné in Vitré. Three centuries earlier, Madame de Sévigné had written 1,700 letters to her daughter to combat the loneliness she felt without the beloved girl, who had married and moved to Provence.

The camera equipment was never idle. Even when they weren't working on shots for the book, they photographed each other, eating at an outdoor Breton *crêperie*, picnicking beside the road, or sunning on the beach. Nor did the cameras rest at night in their hotel rooms. Dare photographed Edie reflected in the bathroom door mirror as she reclined in the bathtub. All that is visible is her head and neck, revealing only that she wore her pearls when she bathed. Edie photographed Dare lying on the bed, a dreamy expression on her face, and sitting on the bidet in the throes of a laughing fit. Lona was also captured in her off-duty mode, undressed down to her stuffed-cotton nakedness, resting on the bidet, her long legs hanging down from its sides.

This trip combined all Dare's favorite things—traveling, working, and being with Edie, the luxury of a full two months of sanctioned

Dare, at work on *Lona*, consults her light meter, Brittany, France, 1961.

Dare on a break from the labors of *Lona*.

In costume, Dare talking with
an unknown boy in Brittany.

Edie in a hotel room during
the *Lona* shoot, 1961.

play with her mother and a doll. In the photos, Dare, three years away from her fiftieth birthday, looks half that age and spectacularly beautiful. In one of the most striking photographs, she sits on a stone wall beside a French teenage boy, wearing the white quilted gown that was her princess costume, its form-fitting bodice creating her favored "breasts on the half shell" look. Her French, learned at Laurel, was passable, so perhaps she could explain to the boy why she was so outfitted. Still, he looks dazzled by—and a little wary of—this blond apparition.

Secure in Dare's attentions, or perhaps to rub it in that she had Dare to herself, Edie wrote to Blaine, making reference to his pet toad. "Do you think 'Toad' would approve of this? Why didn't you come to protect us? We have had adventures. Dare has been wonderful with the language and the car, but tough on her—alas! We know castles to the bone and shall be glad to get home. Love Edie."

Back in New York, Dare compiled the final photographs for the book from a composite of her inventory from past trips to Ocracoke, Sicily, Scotland, and the Eastern Shore of Maryland. In this period before computer-aided photography, she created ingenious, sometimes surreal special effects by cutting and pasting the photographs and experimenting with developing techniques in her darkroom. Whereas *Date with London* was documentary in tone, Dare was released by *Lona* to the freedom of her imagination. The kingdoms in which the action takes place had no counterpart in reality; a castle in Scotland was superimposed onto a Brittany landscape.

There were still missing scenes to fill in. In Brittany, they had been unable to find a door with an old-fashioned lock into which Lona the doll might insert an oversized old-fashioned key. Vincent Youmans came to the rescue. He knew of an old church door, covered in vines, near his family home on Maryland's Eastern Shore, and flew Dare down in his 140-Cessna two-seater. Just before they took off, he used her camera to photograph his cargo, a beaming Dare sitting in the passenger seat holding Lona on her lap.

With Edie's help, Dare shot some of the remaining scenes in the Cleveland penthouse, including the scene in which the wizard transforms the princess into a doll. Dare, in a diaphanous white nightgown, cowers beneath a canopy of white nylon hanging from a gold crown on Edie's bed, her hand clutched over her mouth in terror.

In January, with still more *Lona* work to be done, Edie and Dare returned to New York together. But if Edie had proven able to make herself genuinely useful, there was an invasive aspect to her constant presence. Not even Dare's mail was her own. "Dare is going out now," Edie wrote Allie. "I am trying to answer all the letters on her desk. You bet this is a very precious time for me, even if it is hard for me to think up meals and cook. Anything done for love is good."

There was certainly no possibility of privacy when visitors came to call. When Vincent arrived on the day that Edie was assigned the job of pyrotechnics, creating the fire and smoke spewed out by a two-headed dragon Dare had sculpted out of modeling clay, Edie was in a robe with her hair set in spit curls. She excused herself, quickly brushing out her hair and donning one of her Chanel-style suits set off by a triple strand of pearls, and resumed blowing smoke from her cigarette and holding out the flame from her butane cigarette lighter.

Edie sent Daisy a print of the final shot. "The dragon has two heads and I blew the flame and smoke. . . . Poor little Lona! Both heads wish to eat her. . . . Easy to do magic in drawings—not so easy in photos—yet how interesting to see real things turned magic. Lona is *not* a doll in the story—only the princess turned small by the bad ones."

Dare dedicated the book "To My Mother." If Lona's dilemma was resolved with Druth "dead under the stones of his fallen tower," Dare's was not. The two-headed dragon was the perfect embodiment of Dare's conflict. No matter which way she went, she would be devoured—either by loneliness or by Edie's wrath—if she were to align herself with a man.

Dare continued to be sought out by friends and suitors even if almost no one seemed to know quite what to make of her relationships, both with her mother and with her doll. When Roy Wilder sent Dare a letter saying that he had married, he was surprised to hear back not from Dare but from Edie. He had not understood the degree to which mother and daughter had merged. Regardless, he recalled, "It was a hell of a nice letter. Edie said, 'Everybody should have someone to love.'"

Journalists also continued to pursue Dare, attempting to make sense of this unusual and press-shy children's book author. As always, Dare frustrated their attempts to unravel her mysteries. Desperate for some hook to latch onto, they all picked up on the story that she kept her stars in a bank vault unless they were being photographed for a book or for publicity. In a 1961 article, "Doll That Inspired Books Lives in Vault," a reporter for the *Plain Dealer* wrote:

> The loneliest doll in the world is probably one belonging to Dare Wright, creator of the "Lonely Doll" children's stories. Her doll, Edith, lives in a safety deposit box in a New York City bank. Miss Wright explained the unusual home for Edith. "It's very simple," she said. "Other people keep their valuables in a bank, why shouldn't I? Anyway, I travel a lot and I'm afraid of her being stolen."

A reporter for a 1962 *Saturday Evening Post* People on the Way Up feature also noted the bank vault arrangement but was clearly more intrigued to learn that the books' beautiful author, who had lopped twelve years off her age, was also unmarried:

> Story Teller: With the gracious cooperation of her doll friends, Dare Wright, 35, produces unusual children's books. The dolls are her characters, and for illustrations Dare takes photographs of them in beguilingly lifelike poses. Total sales of her books—the fifth and most recent was *The Lonely Doll Learns a Lesson*—exceed 200,000. . . . "I don't think of Edith as a doll," says Dare. "She was my friend when I

At a book signing at Higbee's Department store
with Richard Gildenmeister, Cleveland, early 1960s.

was a child, and now she supports me. She's a personality in her own right." Born in Canada, Dare grew up in Cleveland, Ohio, and moved on to New York when she was 20. The RAF pilot to whom she was engaged died in a crash, and Dare is still single—though not resolutely so.

A reporter from *Aufbau*, a New York–based Jewish German-language daily who came to interview Dare for "Edith und die Baren waren nicht zu Hause" (Edith and the Bears Were Not at Home), also covered the bank-vault angle, marveling at the strange family on 58th Street.

> People who don't believe in fairytales might find it difficult to follow Dare Wright's thoughts and to imagine that the blond Edith, who was born in "the land where lemon trees bloom" [Italy], could be more than just a mere inanimate doll to her lovely young mother. "We talk to her as if she were a real child," she admits. "We": that is the tall, slim Dare, who looks like Alice in Wonderland, and her petite mother, a well-known portraitist from Cleveland, whom the doll Edith was named for. She too, it seems, has a lot of fun with her "grandchild."

Dare was always relieved when Edie would take over the handling of the press, as she did when they spent six weeks in Bermuda over the summer of 1962. When the *Bermuda Royal Gazette* came to the Castle Harbour Hotel to interview Dare about her books, Edie chattered away about painting Winston Churchill, "preferring," the article said, "not to divulge much personal information she picked up from Sir Winston when she painted him"—including, apparently, the fact that she had never met him.

Edie had made it through the rigors of the *Lona* shoot without incident, but on the summer trip to Bermuda, despite, in Dare's words, "complete rest—no camera, no paints," Edie developed an upper respiratory infection she could not shake. A month after returning to Cleveland, she finally consulted a doctor, actually her dentist. Dr. Schultz sent her to see his son David, a cardiologist and director of medicine at Lutheran Hospital, the closest hospital to the Hanna Building. Despite fever, chills, coughing, and chest pain, diagnosed by Dr. Schultz as symptomatic of pneumonia, Edie fought his suggestion that she be hospitalized. He gave her antibiotics, which did bring down the fever, but her other symptoms persisted. Finally, she consented to go into the hospital, predictably arriving, as Schultz described her, "dressed to the nines."

Edie's appearance set the entire hospital agog. So did her feistiness. Patients were required to give their age as part of the admitting process. Edie refused. After much negotiation, she yielded, telling them she was sixty-nine. She was seventy-nine. But she would not give in to Dr. Schultz's attempts to separate her from her cigarettes. In those days, patients were still allowed to smoke in hospitals, and the chain-smoking Edie refused to heed her doctor's order that as a pneumonia patient she refrain.

Dare rushed to Cleveland to be by her mother's side. The appearance of this beautiful and even more glamorous daughter rocked the staff anew. Dare kept vigil at Edie's bedside while the staff speculated endlessly about the two exotic creatures in their midst.

Although she was released from the hospital after a few weeks, it took more than a year for Edie to regain her health, a situation she greeted first with annoyance and later with anger. She seemed incapable of comprehending how sick she had been. Her doctor told her he had doubted she would even survive and should consider herself lucky.

While Edie reacted to her illness with anger, for Dare it had been a deeply upsetting episode. Despite her mother's fighting spirit, she saw, for the first time, her vulnerability. Dare's hair began to fall out in clumps. Edie discussed this with the doctor and reported back to her cousin Allie, "The doctor said shock."

Now, as Edie was recovering, death was no longer an immediate threat. But the illness had upset Dare's sense of security, the promise that her mother would stay with her "forever and ever." With Edie, however temporarily, an invalid, Dare wondered whether she should remain by Edie's side or proceed with her own life. These issues weighed heavily on her mind as she contemplated both her next book and the summer ahead.

In *Edith and Mr. Bear*, the story turns on a new mantel clock that Edith breaks by accident. To avoid punishment, she runs away, making her first—and only—exploration into life on her own. In the end, she returns home, to be forgiven for breaking the clock but spanked for using matches when she and Little Bear decide to cook a surprise for Mr. Bear, to make up for her earlier transgression. "Don't ever dare touch matches again!" Mr. Bear tells them, after reinforcing his order physically.

Dare dedicated the book "To my generous and loving voluntary Godmother." This was Jane Douglass, who now used her middle name as her last, having dropped the Crawford surname to register her disgust with a father who had disowned her. Now in New York after years of living in England, Jane had appointed herself Dare's protector. Edie was not pleased by Jane's return to their lives, any more than she had been about Blaine's. But even knowing how unhappy this dedication would make her mother, Dare went ahead with it. Unconsciously or deliberately, she was reaching out to a potential mother replacement.

Dare finished *Edith and Mr. Bear* by June, in time for their summer vacation. But Edie was not well enough to travel. Oldbourne Press, Dare's British publisher, was making plans to publish *Lona* in 1964. They invited her to meet with them in London; Dare could also visit the Sandemans. After much deliberation, she decided to go. Edie was startled by this show of independence but made an effort to conceal her unhappiness at being left behind.

Blaine was thrilled by what he saw as Dare's defection. He used his sister's absence to bombard Edie with a series of letters shot through with angry reproaches and demands. Feeling vulnerable with Dare gone, Edie tried for a conciliatory tone in her responses to her son, signing one letter, "With love, your own mother," with

The first of many: the spanking scene from "Spring Fever," which would be reprised in several subsequent books, including 1964's *Edith and Mr. Bear*.

a small notation at the bottom of the page: "This is the way I sign to Dare. It may not please you." But her tone was not always so loving. She manages to put him down for his aimlessness and thoughtlessness, chiding him for his lack of concern or sympathy for her recent illness. "Dr. Schultz," she wrote, "was afraid I would go away from here—so I almost did, not from the disease but from the dehydration and lethargy caused by the drug. He says Dare is the one who saved me. That no one except one who loved and understood me could have."

In response to his request that she reproduce in charcoal a portrait of Abraham Lincoln that he had come across in a book, she replies, "It will give me great pleasure to recreate it in a monotone drawing in paint, life size on a canvas 20 x 24. I do not use charcoal since my student days. . . . I will do it in my first free time, which I am sorry to say will not be this spring. My time is fully taken by professional work patrons have been waiting for since my illness."

With one letter, Blaine enclosed an article on the Impressionists, which she took as he meant her to, as a dig at her staid and conventional society portraiture. She fired back: "Wouldn't it be lovely to paint someone with green eyes, with black eyes? Can you imagine what would happen to me? These artists are not portrait painters, so they could play—a portrait for posterity must have integrity or it is useless."

Most galling to Blaine was Edie's claim that she had pushed Dare to go to England without her, when he knew this was not the case. Edie wrote: "Dare wanted to stay here and help me but I insisted that she go and, aside from the business, have a little fling all on her own. I think it was good for her, and she had earned it by constant intensive application to work. I think she has 'had a ball'—I hope so."

As for "a ball," Dare's trip sounded more like a Philip memorial tour, with visits to Brian and Jane Sandeman and their children and to Philip's mother, Marie, on Jersey. Unless she was in the company of the Sandemans, Dare felt lost on this trip, despite the attentions of various male admirers. She wrote to Dorothy, now Mrs. Edwin

Pollack, having married a New York City police detective in 1959, that those attentions began on the boat to England, including "a gentleman of eighty" who sat with her at the captain's table, and another man who "pursued [her] diligently and with the evilest intentions." Russ Aitken came over from Paris to take her to lunch at Claridge's, and Colin Keith-Johnston, an actor who had played Mr. Darcy in that long-ago production of *Pride and Prejudice*, took her to the races at Derby Downs.

The visit with the Sandemans was a chance to meet her goddaughter, Susan Sandeman, then six, for the first time. Dare had always been an attentive godmother, sending letters and presents, including a doll, which Susan named Edith, and inscribed copies of each of her books. Susan, who admired the glamorous woman pictured on the book jackets and bragged to her siblings, "Look at this wonderful godmother I've got," was not disappointed with her godmother in the flesh. "She was a spirit, ethereal," Susan recalled. "It was almost as if, if she walked on sand, she wouldn't leave footprints. It seemed as though she was only half there, but because she was only half there she was twice as much there, if you see what I mean."

Dare left Susan with the promise to do a book with her "in mind" and a sage bit of advice, however irrelevant to a six-year-old: a warning not to tease her hair. "Dare said her hair had fallen out because she back-combed it too much," contradicting Edie's notion of hair loss as a stress reaction to her illness. In any case, Dare's hair—which had suffered the abuses of years of both bleaching and teasing—had become far less luxuriant. Edie's had too. They invested in a collection of wigs, falls, and hairpieces, copper-colored for Edie, blond for Dare. By now, Edie was never without a wig in public. Dare tended to wear some combination of a hairpiece or fall with her own hair. Yet in the pictures Clare Sandeman took of her sister's godmother on this visit, Dare wears a full pageboy-style wig.

Lona was released that fall, accompanied by the usual blitz of publicity, including ads featuring Dare modeling a line of *Lona*-inspired lingerie, three gown-and-peignoir sets with fairy-tale names: Moon Magic, Wish Come True, and Enchanted Spell. Dorothy Pollack, now working for Vanity Fair Mills, had arranged the tie-in. The critical reception to *Lona*, a magnum opus even more oversized than Dare's other books and with 50 full-page photographs and 36 pages of text, was mixed. The *Christian Science Monitor* lauded her ability to use her camera "to reveal a misty otherworld," but a writer for the *Winston-Salem Journal* called the book "impressive, showy . . . yet still a disappointment. A long, in fact much too long, fairy tale illustrated with fakey photographs. I fear Miss Wright has tried to write all the world's great fairy tales rolled into one." Blaine also gave it a bad review. In his opinion, his sister should not have attempted such a convoluted story. She inscribed a copy of the book to him: "For my beloved brother—(the bilge rat). What a toad he would have made—if he hadn't been a scupper rat. Dare."

Mothers, the most important critics, were also wary of the book, telling booksellers they found it surprisingly sexual, especially as the outline of Dare's naked body was almost visible in the scene where she turns back from the doll into the real princess.

Dare's next book, however, which she worked on in 1964 with, as promised, Susan Sandeman in mind, was a return to a story of childhood innocence. This one featured a real little girl, named Susan, and Dare's doll Persis, renamed Robin, whose sole and only occasional attire is a leaf. "Most dolls belong to little girls, and live in houses," the book begins. "Robin was different. Robin was a little doll who lived in the woods. She didn't belong to anyone, but she had more friends than she could count." When Susan comes upon her in the woods, she decides to take her home. Robin begs Susan to leave her in the woods where she belongs, but "Susan wasn't a little girl who could hear dolls talk." Susan takes the doll home and dresses her. While Robin is in bed, her collection of dolls and stuffed animals tell Robin about their happy lives with Susan. Robin says she prefers her own life. Only Sam, Susan's bear, understands Robin's wish to return to the woods, and he begs her to take

him with her. Meanwhile, all of Robin's animal friends are looking
for her. When Crow finally finds her, she begs him to take her—and
Sam—home. Crow says he'll rescue her but not Sam. He rebukes
her for making friends too fast and forces her to choose between the
woods and Sam. Having come to love Sam, she is torn. Seeing that
Robin might not go back unless Sam goes too, Crow relents and
flies them both home to the woods. Robin, having stripped out of
the clothes Susan had provided, leaves them behind along with a
note thanking Susan for her "horspertality" but explaining, "I am
going back home where I belong." Susan is shocked by the note,
and to find the doll and Sam gone. "Never again was Susan quite
sure just what a doll could or couldn't do."

Take Me Home had been shot in Walton, and now Edie was
demanding equal time. As Dare had too much work, Edie decided to
come to New York. Hating to be idle, especially now that she was
feeling better, Edie convinced Russ Aitken to commission a portrait.
This would also provide an opportunity to play her game of dangling
the unavailable Dare before unavailable men. Dare photographed the
sittings, held in her apartment, which took place over the course of
four months. Russ wore full-dress Scottish tartan. On most days,
Edie's work uniform was her white bouclé Chanel-style suit and
pearls, four-inch heels, and her copper-colored wig.

Although Russ was pleased with the portrait, his wife, Annie
Laurie, pronounced it terrible and refused to allow it to be hung
either in their Fifth Avenue apartment or in their Newport mansion,
Champs-Soleil. Russ kept it in one of the three apartments he maintained at 2 West 67th Street, a convenient place to house his world-
class collections of firearms, duck decoys, and safari trophies. The
portrait joined his considerable collection of Wright material, including photographs of Dare and seven paintings by Edie, one of them
the 1956 *Portrait of Lady with a Fan*, the lady being Dare. In 1963, six
years into his marriage to Annie Laurie, Edie had given Russ a drawing of three nude poses of Dare performing her toilette. She had
earlier painted a portrait of Russ, based on a photograph of him

Off hours: Edith and Little Bear at play with
a toy camera and their teddy bears.

hunting at the age of twenty, based on a 1930 Cleveland *Plain Dealer* article. She inscribed this painting "Russ the Great Hunter-to-Be." To accompany it, she gave him the painting titled "Dare at First Camp. Pure Joy!," as if matching the two, at least on canvas.

By 1966, with the release of *A Gift from the Lonely Doll*, in which Edith knits a too-long muffler as a Christmas present for Mr. Bear, Dare had published ten books for children in as many years. Edie reported to Allie that Bennett Cerf had told her, "Dare is now a name" and that he considered Dare "the best out of their junior department."

Dare had earned herself a secure place with her publishing house and especially with its publisher. In and among the fan letters from children and parents that filled her mailbox each day was often one signed with a variation of "Your loving publisher, Bennett." In a note accompanying the just-published *A Gift from the Lonely Doll*, Cerf wrote: "You are one of our most brilliant and certainly most beautiful authors—and I only wish that droit de seigneur rules were still in effect! As ever, Bennett."

And after taking Dare to a reception where he introduced her to the mayor of New York City, Cerf wrote: "You looked so pretty last night that Mayor Lindsay now thinks he wants to go into the book publishing business. I told him, however, that not all of our authors were as beautiful as you, and before he made a move of this sort, he'd better let us show him some of our other geniuses! . . . Come in one day soon and let your publisher kiss you!"

But if Dare was secure professionally, her hold on a sense of emotional security was slipping anew. By the late 1960s, the specters of separation and loss loomed. Blaine was essentially all but gone again, lost this time to alcohol. And although Edie had recovered from her illness, Dare had not gotten over it—or what it boded.

CHAPTER NINE

Loss

We are two clouds
glistening in the bottle glass.
We are two birds
washing in the same mirror.
—ANNE SEXTON, "Rapunzel"

Thinking to give Dare's readership a break from dolls and teddy bears but also to capitalize on her gift for animal photography, Random House suggested in the fall of 1965 that Dare try a nature book. "I'm glad to get away from dolls for a bit," she wrote to Allie.

Blaine had transmitted his love of the outdoors and animals to his sister, although she cared for them not as pets for whom she would have any responsibility but more as props to photograph. From the pigeon and the squirrel encountered by Edith and the Bears on an outing to Central Park in *The Lonely Doll*, to the fish, seagulls, and wild horses of Ocracoke in *Holiday for Edith and the Bears*, animals had already found their way into the photographs and story lines of her books, as did later a turtle, a crow, a kitten, a puppy, and a rabbit.

Dare would publish four books in the *Look at* . . . nature series, chronicling a gull, a colt, a calf, and a kitten from birth to maturity. Shot in black-and-white like the *Lonely Doll* books, they are quietly elegiac in tone. Two of the four end with the plaintive line *Look at me*.

The new photographs for the first book in the series, *Look at a Gull*, were taken at various beaches near New York. The rest were from her archives taken on Ocracoke. Dare had never produced a book without at least some assistance or companionship. Neither Blaine nor Edie were up to it now. Vincent Youmans had married and moved to Delaware. Donald Seawell was living in Colorado; in 1966 he had been named the publisher of *The Denver Post*. Dare fixed on Colorado as the locale for *Look at a Colt*, even though Donald would not be free to provide much in the way of help or company.

In early 1967, Dare began calling dude ranches in Colorado in search of an expectant mare. Lost Valley Ranch in Sedalia, two hours southwest of Denver, assured her they had a mare due to deliver in April. Dare scheduled her trip to allow a visit with the Seawells in Denver before moving on to Lost Valley to photograph the colt's birth.

When Dare arrived, however, it turned out the colt was not due for at least another month. There was nothing to do but wait. Dare settled into Hideaway, a cabin the ranch provided, and spent the days tending to the pregnant mare, learning to ride, going on long walks in the meadow with the camera as her only companion, or sunning by the pool in a tiny bikini that caused a stir in the wholesome family atmosphere of Lost Valley.

At 11 P.M., six weeks into her stay and several hours after Dare had retired to her cabin for the night, the mare finally went into labor. The wrangler dispatched Marti Saul, the ranch secretary, to Dare's cabin. Calling out Dare's name as she ran to Hideaway, Marti saw the cabin door fly open, out of which seemed to float an apparition. There, in the moonlight, was Dare, wearing a diaphanous white dressing gown over a white nightgown, her long blond hair let down. No one at the ranch knew about this side of Dare. Other than the bikini, which she had stopped wearing after the management had asked her to sport something less revealing, she dressed as everyone else did at Lost Valley, in blue jeans and a button-down shirt. Her hair was usually tied back. It took Marti a moment to recover before she could deliver the message that the birth was in progress. Marti was further shocked when Dare greeted this news by exclaiming, uncharacteristically, "Oh, shit." At 2 A.M. the colt was born, with Dare, back in her usual outfit, clicking shot after shot.

The reluctant mare had kept Dare at Lost Valley far longer than planned. She missed Edie and Blaine terribly and thought of them constantly. According to Marti, they—and Philip—were her sole topic of conversation. Otherwise, she had made the best of her forced ranch time as a chance to indulge her little-girl "horse madness" and revel in bucolic surroundings. "Sky, mountains, and flowering meadows, these were my world," she wrote, describing the place into which the colt had been born.

A real-world jolt awaited Dare on her return to New York. The Helmsley Corporation had bought 29 West 58th Street, along with several adjoining buildings, in order to demolish them and build the Park Lane Hotel. The tenants were given until the end of the year to move out. Dare was devastated by the news. After a long search, she found a new apartment at 11 East 80th Street between Fifth and Madison avenues, a charming tree-lined block with Central Park and the Metropolitan Museum of Art in view at its west end. The apartment occupied half the fourth floor of a 1910 townhouse built by Hiram C. Bloomingdale, then a vice president of his family's department store.

In letters to her cousin about Dare's move, Edie fixed on the hard work and logistical headaches the move created. But, for Dare, all that was secondary to its emotional toll. The West 58th Street townhouse had been her first New York apartment after seventeen years in dormitory and hotel rooms and it had been her home for the past sixteen years. It was the Lonely Doll's home, too. Edith had been given new life there and, in turn, had given Dare one also.

During the last days on West 58th Street, Dare immersed herself in a flurry of photography, as always her way to fasten down a moment and fix it in time. She photographed every inch of the apartment: intact, during the packing process, and after all the packing had been done. In these melancholy photographs, she called upon Edith and the Bears for "assistance," placing them before the partially rolled-up rugs to create the impression that they were finishing the job.

She also took a series of photographs of the actual moving day, shooting Edith and the Bears standing on the black-and-white squares in the stripped apartment. Little Bear and Edith look entirely forlorn. In one of this series, Edith and the Bears stand together in a cluster, their heads turned to face the camera. Edith, dressed sensibly for the gray November day, wears a white sweater, plaid kilt, and wool tights. Clutching paws and hands, Edith and Little Bear radiate bewilderment. Mr. Bear, standing straight and tall, sporting his plaid four-in-hand, exudes authority. Dare took this shot perched on the window seat, a perspective that makes them appear smaller than usual. All three are huddled on one black square as an expanse of black-and-white squares, like a giant chessboard, extends beyond them.

Eleven East 80th Street had been broken up into apartments in the 1940s. Dare's floor had originally been a bedroom floor, consisting of spacious bedrooms and closets, smaller closets, and bathrooms. In the conversion, the bedrooms became living rooms, the larger closets became bedrooms, and the smaller closets remained closets or, their doors removed, dressing rooms. Unlike the open plan of the former ballroom on West 58th Street, the new apartment was a rabbit warren of littler rooms, satellites of the living room, the centerpiece of which was the mantel Dare rescued from demolition at West 58th Street and transported to her new home in a taxi. The entryway doubled as a pullman kitchen. Dare painted the walls black and left the space dark when company came in order to obscure the less-than-elegant first impression. Just to the right of this was the living room, and beyond that a tiny bedroom with space for just a single bed, adjoining a dressing room she used as her darkroom.

The apartment wasn't big or luxurious, but all who visited remarked upon the magic Dare worked, as always, even in unremarkable interiors. As she had on West 58th Street, she did all the carpentry and painting herself. Edie, who only in her later years was generous enough to share the appellation *artist* with her daughter, wrote Allie, "That's why I call her my little Leonardo da Vinci, because she is artist, mechanic, carpenter, all the things he was, unusual for an artist."

But Dare was not able to complete her design plans just now. She had only two months to finish her next book. Although Edie had regained her strength, Dare hadn't wanted to push her. She decided to set it in Walton. Even if Blaine didn't take an active role, at least he would be nearby.

Edith and Big Bad Bill, the darkest and most frightening of the books, displays a bound and gagged Edith on its cover. On a visit to Mr. Bear's country cousins Charles and Albert, the family goes for a walk in the woods. Cousin Albert warns them about a bad bear who lives in the "dark wood." It seems he is bad because he's black and white. Good bears are brown. When the others tire and decide to head home, Little Bear asks if he and Edith may stay out. "Just keep away from the dark wood," warn the cousins.

Of course, Little Bear heads straight for the forbidden area. Edith is scared. "Then stay here alone, sissy," says Little Bear. Screwing up her courage, she follows him. They come upon a house and wonder aloud who lives there. Just then a great big black-and-white bear growls, "I live in it." They run. Big Bad Bill chases them. He catches Edith and ties her to a tree. As she screams to Little Bear to "run for your life," Bill gags her with his neckerchief. Little Bear stays to stand up to Bill, ordering him to let Edith go. Bill accuses them of being spies and says he hates noise, which he finds they make too much of. "Will she promise not to scream?" Bill asks Little Bear. Edith nods, vigorously. "Oh, thunderation, untie her then." But he will not let them go. He keeps them captive in his dark and smoky lair, in this case Florence Wakeman's barn.

Edith wants to go home, but Little Bear likes it there, so Edith adjusts and keeps house for them all. Over time, she comes to understand the source of Bill's gruffness, telling Little Bear, "I don't believe Bill is bad at all. He hasn't hurt us. I think he's just lonely the way I was before you and Mr. Bear found me. It makes people cross and mean to be lonely." Eventually, when the little ones return home and Mr. Bear suggests they invite Bill to dinner, the story ends on a bright note. But, for its author, it was proving harder and harder to stay out of the dark wood.

At eighty-five, Edie was still valiantly trying to will age away. She now favored miniskirts or a leopard-patterned pantsuit, worn with high-heeled boots. False eyelashes, long fingernails painted cherry red, and her Titian-red wig were standards. Having defied her doctor's orders to reduce her workload, she did raise her rates to $5,000 for a three-quarter-length portrait and $3,000 for a regular one. And she became less accommodating. While in earlier years she would take a portrait back, if grudgingly, to make changes if the patron found any aspect unflattering, now she held fast. Helen Bonfils had complained to Donald Seawell, her friend and lawyer, that her father Frederick, a founder of *The Denver Post*, was much taller than he appeared in the posthumous portrait she had commissioned from Edie. When Donald told Edie this, she shot back, "Portrait painters know that all great men grow six inches after death. Tell her I actually painted Mr. Bonfils two inches taller than he was." But there was a panicky quality to Edie's almost manic bouts of productivity—and an even more exteme dependency on Dare.

Dare, conscious that age was ravaging Edith too, decided to make a perfect copy, a completely new doll, one who would not have to live in the bank vault and could be used as a stand-in to spare wear and tear on the original Edith. She named the copy Replica, which she pronounced with the emphasis on the second syllable, so it sounded vaguely French. In a photograph that she took of Edith and Replica, standing beside a pile of books with their arms around each other, it is impossible to distinguish the original from the copy.

Dare wrote to Dick Gildenmeister, "Edie is painting like mad and we hardly talk to each other from breakfast to cocktail time. We've practically been hermits." But when Edie wasn't working, she didn't want Dare out of her sight. Edie complained in a letter to Allie, "Dare is out and I have an hour with nothing to do."

In New York, there was no one to paint but her daughter. When Dare was not available to pose, Edie painted her from photographs. She convinced Russ Aitken to commission a portrait of Dare. For this 1968 portrait, which she titled "Wood Nymph," Edie depicted her daughter on canvas as she saw her, decades younger than her true age, which was now fifty-three. Dare, the image of a nubile twenty-year-old, is posed leaning against the trunk of a huge tree, wearing a blouse unbuttoned to her waist, around which hangs a silver concha belt. The blouse comes just to the top of her bare and shapely thighs. She wears no pants or skirt.

Edie clearly derived a confused power from painting portraits; her subjects were more real to her in her version than in life. With portraits of men like Donald Seawell and Russ Aitken, it was as if, by re-creating them in effigy, she could obtain a power over them that she could never exercise over the men themselves. Genie Seawell had never felt cause for jealousy in her husband's relationship with Dare, but when Edie painted a portrait of Donald and Dare posed atop Folly, the carousel horse from Serendipity, Genie became uncomfortable. She asked Edie to give her that portrait and another Edie had done of Donald. Edie insisted they be paid for.

Edie, holding Edith, flanked by a portrait she painted of Dare in
the 1950s and one of herself and Dare from 1964.

When Genie did not do so, Edie refused to hand them over. Genie subsequently learned that the Wrights' cocktail hour had taken a surreal turn. They had drinks every evening with this surrogate Donald.

It was only Dare who never displeased Edie, and by now she could rest assured that Dare was hers. Men had tried to pull her daughter in, they might try still, but she knew they would never succeed. Edie could write to Allie, saying, "I would love to see her marry," knowing it was no longer even conceivable. In one letter, she boasts to Allie of Dare's current roster of suitors, including the recently widowed Nahum Bernstein, Donald Seawell's former law partner who had first met Dare during the Fenimore Cooper Marsh case in 1949. Describing him as "a recently widowed Jew—a millionaire," Edie reports that he proposed to Dare just three months after his wife died. "Dare turned him down but he tries to see her, and she accepts his invitations. He proposed that he take her for a holiday in the Islands to get acquainted. She told him she didn't go on trips with men."

Edie had no more consciousness of herself as burdensome than she did of having co-opted her daughter's life or of having aged. She sent her sympathies to Allie for shouldering the care of her elderly mother, Daisy, who had lived with Allie and her husband, Henry, for the twelve years of her widowhood. In her condolence letter after Daisy's death, Edie wrote, "You must hold in your heart what a wonderful daughter you have been—I admire you and Henry no end for your patience and fidelity—and I am worried what you hinted re: Henry's mother. Surely you can't have another such responsibility. That would be too unfair! Believe me if I ever reach such a stage, I'll take care of myself. . . . I think it a tragedy that a child should suffer for things about parents." Edie then urged Allie to hire someone to help with the care of her ailing mother-in-law: "After all you do not owe all of your lives to the last generation. You may be sure I shall never let myself be a drag on anyone. . . . Do not be put upon by a selfish old lady who probably will not appreciate—just give her someone else to boss and she will be all right."

If Edie and Dare could maintain the fantasy that they were still young, the outside world could only sometimes be counted on to concur. A boastful Edie wrote to Allie, "Dare looks like a teenager. She gets whistled at by truck drivers on the street." But her own act was less convincing. Increasingly frail, Edie had fallen in her studio. It was only because of a missed doctor's appointment that she was even discovered, after the doctor's office dispatched a building maintenance man to investigate. Because Edie had a special lock and refused to give the building a copy of her key, the worker was forced to break in. Donald Grogan, whose family now owned the Hanna Building, insisted that Edie move to a place more suitable to a woman her age living alone. He offered her an apartment in another of his properties, the Moreland Courts apartment complex in Shaker Heights, where many wealthy older Clevelanders, among them Edie's past patrons, moved when keeping up a large private home became too much for them. Edie refused his offer and arranged for her protectors to lobby Grogan to back off. Dare, the lawyer Allan Hull, and Edie's patron Fred Crawford, head of the aerospace corporation TRW, were all enlisted to plead her case to stay put. Grogan was amazed by the fight Edie waged. He always knew she had a will of iron, but she had never before turned it against him. She claimed she had a lifetime lease from Donald's father and raged at him for trying to interfere with her way of life. In the end, however, Grogan prevailed, and Edie was forced to move to Moreland Courts.

For Edie, losing this battle was a defeat and something to lie about, lest anyone think it was because she was old. Increasingly worried about her legacy, she had made Dare promise to try to convince the Metropolitan Museum to add her work to its collection. It was in this period that she began firing off letters to Joseph G. Butler III, the director of the Butler Institute of American Art in

Youngstown, whose museum collection did hold several Wrights. She detailed for him the highlights of her long career: portraits of a French general and an American ambassador for a World War I memorial building in Paris, a president, a prime minister, numerous chief executive officers, judges, bank presidents, Hollywood stars, and countless "home" portraits throughout this country and Canada. In one letter, although he could hardly have cared about this matter, she lied to explain why she was vacating the penthouse. "They are moving me from the penthouse because they are changing the roof." She enclosed a photograph of herself from 1945, noting that it "was taken about three years ago."

By now, Edie was an old woman looking back, but Dare, too, seemed to be taking stock of her life. As much as she had struggled to keep change at bay, a part of her seemed to long for it. In letters from this period, the tone is wistful. "Maybe this year will be different," she writes in one letter, or "Suddenly about a week ago I began feeling different, as though I'd turned some kind of corner." But whenever Dare felt "different" and a stronger sense of identity began to form, Edie would snuff it out, reining her daughter back in.

Dare headed to Cleveland to move Edie from the Hanna Building studio. Moves were not simple for the Wright women. They both gathered and hoarded obsessively, although Dare also purged periodically, giving the contents of her closets, knickknacks, or even photographs away—sometimes relegating them to city garbage cans. Dare did most of the work for Edie's move, inventorying the penthouse contents, some of which included her own belongings. They had always sent cast-off clothing to Daisy and Allie. Edie wrote the sixty-three-year-old Allie that they were sending her a go-go dress of Dare's. "Dare wears stocking tights with her short dresses. You are a teenage size too—isn't it wonderful?"

As they combed through their belongings, memories of more than forty years were stirred up. Dare, recognizing her mother's anxieties, sought to comfort her by proposing she write a book about Edie's work with a suitably grandiose title: "The Eyes of a Painter: The Work of Edith Stevenson Wright."

The promise of the book kept Edie appeased for a while, but she complained incessantly about hating her new apartment, despite Dare's efforts to help her mother settle in and work her magic on its decoration. As she could find no way to ease her mother's adjustment to Moreland Courts, it was a relief when summer arrived and it was time to head to Ocracoke.

The years had not been kind to their beloved island. With the advent of regular ferry service from the mainland, it had been overrun by tourists. The 1969 summer at Ocracoke would be their last. In a letter to Allie after their return, Edie complained about everything from the bad food to the cost and the crowds. "We did not benefit too much from our holiday," she wrote. "The only thing the charming way it used to be was the great fifteen-mile long beach. And oh—the damn motels and tourists. I got so weary looking at fat derrieres in shorts. . . . In fact there is too much of everything and too many people."

Dare, who always waited for Edie's party line on any subject, and then parroted it back, touched on these same things in her letter to Dick Gildenmeister, the "awful" food, the abundance of tourists, and the traffic, but she also struck a characteristically more conciliatory tone. "The sea oats and the ocean are still here. . . . we are getting sun and air, and the surf is lovely." And she wrote, "There may be a book in it, but it will have to be of an island remembered."

The altered island had inspired Dare to do a different sort of book, her first for adults, which she decided to call "Ocracoke Remembered." She planned to illustrate it from her own archive of photographs of the island's earlier days. "It will show up what this new world is doing to all the charm of the old," Edie wrote.

Even though Edie had agitated to leave Ocracoke early, she was anxious about returning to her new Cleveland apartment alone. She begged Dare to go back with her, and when Dare agreed, she wrote to Allie that this had been Dare's idea: "Dare will not allow me to go alone to face up to life in the new apartment." In order to slip away to New York for a few weeks, Dare ensured that Edie's Cleveland-based protectors were available and on call. Allan Hull, Edie's lawyer, could always be counted upon, as could Dick Gildenmeister and a new friend, Jim Irving, introduced to them by Dick. Irving, an interior decorator to wealthy Clevelanders, many of whom had portraits by Edie hanging in their homes, also lived at Moreland Courts. Jim was fascinated by this odd mother-daughter couple. He knew they slept together and came to think of them as a true couple, an almost romantic one. It was as if they formed a secret society, existing in their own world together. He liked to say it was as if one breathed off the other.

Alone in Cleveland, Edie sent a note to Dick Gildenmeister, as if to signal that she needed attention. She wrote that Dare was in New York working on the Ocracoke pictures, "Only she wishes she had her 'Mummy' to discuss them with—and 'Wow' do I!! I am so lonesome for her sweet presence."

On her end, Dare was also feeling lost. She wrote to Dick from New York that she was at work "kind of" on the Ocracoke book. "I make pictures and scatter them on the floor and stand about and look at them." But as for the approach, she was having trouble finding "a clear path." The Ocracoke project was full of conflict for Dare. If her approach was an elegy to an island that no longer existed, it would cast the island in a negative light and might offend the islanders she had known and loved for years. Nothing about a nonfiction book for adults fit with her vision. And she hated being forced to gather the facts and figures required.

Dare put the Ocracoke book aside and retreated into the world of her doll. Everywhere she turned there was an aging Edith. It had been forty-five years since Edie had brought the doll home to her from Halle's, and sixteen years since Edith had been reborn and put to work. Edith had been covered in sand and drenched in water for *Holiday for Edith and the Bears.* A hole had been poked in her mouth so that Dare could insert a thermometer in *The Lonely Doll Learns a Lesson*. She had been cleaned over and over with Dare's special method: lighter fluid on a soft washcloth. This worked well on her extremities but not on her face. By now, but for the bump of her nose and the indentations of her eyes, there was almost no face left. Dare took an eerie photograph of a faceless Edith and then got to work. She repainted her face, designed a new wig, recovered her arms and legs, and sewed new clothes. Dare loved the excuse to focus on Edith. And in order that Mr. Bear not feel left out, she made him a new tie. She took time out to answer a letter from Dick Gildenmeister, which she closed by saying she had to stop writing, "because Little Bear is tugging at my shirttails, and Edith is demanding that I dress her in some new clothes. She says she is not going to play any nude scenes no matter how 'in' it is." Dare photographed the restored Edith and sent copies to Edie. Edie sent one to Dick, writing on the back of it:

Dear Dick:
Look at my new hair, my new skin, my new fingers, and toes—and it did not hurt at all—
Love, Your Little Edith.
(This is big Edith—love from her too.)

Neither the Ocracoke book nor "The Eyes of a Painter" would find a publisher. Dare did not complete the Ocracoke book but, spurred on by her mother, she did go on to make a homemade book about Edie and her work, including photographs of 223 portraits— Dare or Edie herself had photographed almost every portrait before it left the studio—as well as 36 other shots: Edie at work, her painting equipment, her studio, pages from her scrapbooks, and photographs of the artist from childhood on. Dare never got around to identifying any of the portraits or to writing a text, beyond typing out a selection of newspaper articles chronicling Edie's career.

Edie was still chalking up achievements and working her magical ability to bring back the dead. The ninety-year-old widow of Maynard Murch, a benefactor of the Museum of Natural History in Cleveland, sobbed when she beheld the posthumous portrait of her husband she had commissioned from Edie as a gift to the museum. "You are smiling at me," she said aloud to the portrait. "You are sitting there. Why can't you get up and come with me?" Her son rewarded Edie with another commission.

In the early spring of 1970, Dare decided to "push out" another book. She filled pages and pages of a yellow legal pad as she wrestled with the idea for this story. The cast would include a kitten, a little boy who takes in the kitten, and the kitten's mother. In it, for the first and only time in Dare's books, a mother, albeit a feline one, is part of the proceedings and provides the story line's dramatic tension. "The Kitten Who Didn't Know How to Be a Cat," the title later changed to *The Kitten's Little Boy*, is the story of a kitten with an imperious mother who is forced to conceal his true feelings about belonging to a little boy. When the story begins, the kitten is about to leave his mother to go to live with the boy who has chosen him. He tells his mother of his excitement at the prospect of becoming the little boy's kitten. The mother cat is furious. She tells him cats don't "belong" to any human being. She reminds him they are cousins of the great cats, lions and tigers. In the end, the mother cat is placated when it is decided that the conventional relational order between humans and animals will be transposed: The boy belongs to the kitten, not the other way around. But this system, devised by the kitten, is all to appease his mother. Privately the kitten never troubles himself about "who belonged to whom. They belonged to each other."

As Dare worked on this text, she drew up two lists of words: "Independent, self-possessed, not servile, accept comforts, reject bondage, solitary, detached, pleasure-loving" and "torment, confused, bewildered, mixed up, perplexed, muddled, puzzled, doubtful." One list included words to describe what the kitten should be, the other, what he was. The words suggest she was working out something far more personal than the story line of a children's book.

The last two lines caused Dare the most indecision. In several drafts, the book ends: "He just loved his little boy." In the final version, she added a line: "Luckily his mother never knew."

Dare worked on *The Kitten's Little Boy* on her own, but when both the borrowed kitten and cat proved difficult to manage, she called on Russ Aitken for help. "I had to get my friend the big-game hunter to come and help handle that tiny kitten," she wrote to Dick Gildenmeister. "Then I borrowed a cat who scared me to death by vanishing up the chimney." Dare also asked Russ for photographs he had taken of lions and tigers in Africa, two of which she used in the book. In thanks, she dedicated the book to him: "For the tamer of kittens."

Random House did not like the concept of *The Kitten's Little Boy* but Dare was too invested in it to scrap the idea. In the end, the book was published in 1971 by Four Winds Press, an imprint of Scholastic. This was the third book rejected by Random House. Her editors urged her to return to the formula for which she was known. Edie wrote to Allie: "Random House have demanded another 'Edith' book, and it has to be ready by December so she is working like mad."

Edith and Little Bear Lend a Hand, originally titled "Edith for Clean Air," is the story of what the little ones do when Mr. Bear, who has had enough of the crowds, dirt, and noise of New York City, threatens to move the family to the country. The little ones beg to stay, but Mr. Bear is not swayed. Desperate to get him to change his mind, they hatch a plot to clean up the city. They dress up like hippies, borrowing from "Mr. Bear's Indian collection" (Dare's concha belts, fringed suede vest, and woven headbands), and picket in front of City Hall bearing signs saying DEAR MR. MAYOR CLEAN UP THE CITY FOR MR. BEAR—PLEASE and DIRTY AIR HURTS MR. BEAR AND ME AND YOU. No one but a television cameraman takes any notice of their march on City Hall, and they return home discouraged. But Mr. Bear has been watching the news and sees them picketing. Although he is impressed, he does not relent. They write to the mayor suggesting that if everyone did their part the city would be cleaner. They sweep and mop the sidewalk and recycle their cans and bottles. They call a hotline to complain when they see black smoke pouring from a chimney. Mr. Bear finally agrees to let them stay, "for now." They vow to continue their clean-up efforts. The book ends: "So Mr. Bear, Edith, and Little Bear stayed in their own place and tried to make it better."

Aside from the stunning photography, including panoramic shots of the Manhattan skyline taken from aboard the Staten Island Ferry with the newly built World Trade Center looming large, the story is surprisingly flat. In an earlier mock-up, Dare had envisioned a different story line. In this version, it is not Mr. Bear spearheading the idea of a move to the country, but the little ones. They are prompted by Mr. Bear's ill health—they determine the city is making him sick—and they do move. Dare was clearly confronting her concerns about Edie's failing health and the things that would have to be given up or changed to deal with it. In this version, Dare incorporated the moving-day shots. "When the movers had come and gone, the three of them stood sadly in the empty room. 'Maybe we can come back some day,' said Edith. 'When they get the air all cleaned up,' said Little Bear. 'Maybe we can,' said Mr. Bear. 'But I guess it doesn't matter where we live as long as we're all together,' said Edith."

During Edie's occupancy of the Hanna Building studio, Edie and Dare had maintained some semblance of separate bases. But Edie never adjusted to her new quarters at Moreland Courts. Working less and disenchanted with Cleveland, she saw little reason to remain there. But neither was New York an attractive alternative. Like Mr. Bear, she found it increasingly dirty and unpleasant. "Both Edie and I are looking for a new place to live," Dare wrote Allie.

Over the next two years, their summer travels doubled as scouting trips in search of a place they might move together. In the summer of 1970 they traveled to San Francisco, where a Cleveland patron had arranged a commission for Edie. Dare had hopes for northern California, but on their return Edie wrote to Allie, "Dare did not care for the California coast, so we have no plans as yet."

Dare had stayed in touch with Austin Wright, the adored uncle who had orchestrated the reunion with Blaine. Now eighty-three, widowed, remarried, and living in Victoria, British Columbia, he encouraged Dare to visit. Since the 1940s, Edie had wanted nothing to do with Austin, holding him to blame for bringing her troublesome son back into their lives. But now, hatchet buried or just desperate to be with her daughter, Edie seemed to have decided to have warm feelings for her former brother-in-law too. In a letter to Allie she gushed, "Austin is very well known in Canada, having been director of the Canadian Engineers Society, travelling all over the world for years. They have settled in Victoria because, Austin says, it is the most beautiful place and the finest all-year climate he has encountered."

Edie was not disappointed. Back in New York, she wrote, "We were treated like royalty by Austin Wright and his new, rich and charming wife. There was an interview and newspaper article about my work." It was actually about Dare's work, with a closing paragraph about Edie. But although Austin argued that Victoria would be a perfect place for them to live, they did not like it enough to consider it a new home.

The next summer's trip was not a scouting expedition. The decision to go to Russia was inspired by Edie's lifelong dream to visit the Hermitage Museum in St. Petersburg. Thinking a cruise the best way to make such a journey, they signed on for a monthlong trip through Scandinavia and Russia. As the ship set sail, Dare wrote Dick Gildenmeister: "Dear Dick: I don't believe for a moment that we're really doing this! Wish you were coming too." She closed, "Love, Dick," then crossed out the *Dick* and wrote *Dare*. Drawing an arrow from *Dick* into the margin, she wrote: "You can see the condition I'm in!" And when they reached Russia, she wrote, "Dear Dick. Don't be silly. We're not in Russia! You know it does seem unlikely. This is a beautiful city but at the same time shabby and drab. . . . The fjords were beautiful, and we've had gorgeous weather the last week through Oslo, Visby and Stockholm. The ship routine is boring though. There is a great preponderance of the very old among the passengers. . . ."

She does not mention that her own traveling companion was surely one of the very oldest, six months into her ninety-first year. Edie's postcard to Allie illustrates the extent to which she was in denial: "450 aged passengers. I am weary of canes, waddles, and humps—It is depressing. Considering the cost they must be very rich, except us. No one right for Dare to play with. No more cruises for us. Edie-Dare."

In this period, Dare's outfits became more and more childlike. Instead of the sophisticated floor-length dressing gowns she wore at home, she took to wearing rompers that were better suited to a toddler. At a midwinter dinner at the Cleveland home of Edie's doctor, David Schultz, his then-wife Judy was shocked by Dare's attire, out of place both for a woman her age and for the season. Dare looked like Alice in Wonderland in a long summer dress, her wavy blond hair—a hairpiece—falling past the Peter Pan collar and down her back. She wore white cotton gloves, which she left on all evening, even during dinner. She sat with her legs apart but crossed at the ankles, as a little girl might, and on her feet wore patent leather shoes, party shoes as Judy described them, which reminded her of a little girl's Mary Janes.

Judy found Dare shy and withdrawn and spent most of the evening trying both to engage her in a dialogue and to prevent Edie, however entertaining a conversationalist, from hijacking the discussion. She also was made uneasy by her impression that Edie was in some way trying to fix Dare up with her husband.

In this period, Dare left Cleveland and Edie only for short trips to New York or Walton, where she worked on her next two books, *Look at a Calf* and *Look at a Kitten*. For Edie, in her old age, the sting of sharing Dare with Blaine had lessened, as had her animosity toward her son, who had moved off Pot into a cabin in the neighboring town of Downsville and stopped drinking when his landlord threatened to evict him if he did not. Edie wrote to Allie: "Dare has been up in Blaine's mountains—he has been a wonderful help to her, driving all through the farm country to get what she needs such as a pregnant cat, etc. He really has proven that he does not drink anymore, and is taking excellent care of his Phoebe fishing lure, which is a great success."

The straightforward *Look at . . .* series never provided Dare the sense of fulfillment that the Edith books had. When she developed the photos for *Look at a Calf*, she must have been stunned by the photos she had taken of Blaine and those that he had taken of her during the shoot. He was now sixty-two, she fifty-nine, and although each has the physique of a much younger person, for the first time, their faces are beginning to show signs of age. Her attention drifting from the project at hand, she rifled through her archives to find photos of Blaine in his prime, movie-star handsome on Edie's first and only visit to Walton in 1946. She tacked them up on her bulletin board and, with a click of the shutter, re-created a fresh image of Blaine, untouched by time.

With so much of her focus on Edie and Blaine, Dare no longer brought the same passion to her book projects, opting instead for what was expedient. Her publisher wanted her to photograph the kittens in *Look at a Kitten* with real children, but it was difficult to find them. On an errand to Headington's, her neighborhood liquor store, Dare noticed a photograph of a little girl taped to the cash register. She asked Ida Bono, the store owner, who the child was. Ida's seven-year-old granddaughter, Gina, was only too happy to be borrowed for a shoot by the creator of her favorite books.

By mid-1974, Edie, once the human smoke-blowing machine, was all but out of steam, no longer able to fuel or maintain the illusion of the alternate world that she had once made for herself and Dare. She had filled her life with work, heeding her own admonishments to Blaine to do something creative—"The only satisfaction is in the doing"—and travel. Now she was less and less able to do either. She was at a pass not dissimilar to the one where she had found herself in in 1918 after Ivan's desertion. But her youth, her beauty, and most of her artistic talent were now gone. All that was left was Dare.

The dressing-up subsided, although not the making-up. Dare took fewer photographs of her mother in this period. Perhaps she was avoiding making any record of this version of Edie, whose excessive face paint, sloppily applied as her vision faded, gave her the look of a female impersonator—a very old one. Edie, equally loath to take in her own image, spent less time in the mirror world and tried to direct her gaze beyond herself and onto real life. She was horrified by what she found there. She wrote to Allie, "It certainly has become a frightening world! As you say the Hearst girl, the streakers—the attitude about sex, the unaccounted-for killings! The indelicate revelations on talk shows. On Merv Griffin show, one man said, 'I have a tumor on my *butt*,' another, 'Excuse me I have to pee.' From so-called famous characters. Makes one wish there were another world somewhere."

Edie still hoped to leave Cleveland, but they had yet to find a good alternative. She wrote Allie that they were trying to find a place in the country where Edie could have her studio and Dare a darkroom. The thought was to keep the New York apartment as a pied-à-terre but let go the Moreland Courts apartment to save the monthly rent. She complained that they both feel "all unsettled." "Dare cries almost every night over 'phone because she wants to be with me. So do I."

On a business trip to Cleveland in the winter of 1974, Dorothy Pollack paid a call on Edie at Moreland Courts. She was shocked to find her shrunken and wobbling so badly that she could barely walk.

When she telephoned Dare to report on the visit, Dare professed surprise at the degree of Dorothy's concern; perhaps she was incapable of seeing Edie as Dorothy did. When Dorothy insisted that Edie should not be on her own, Dare arranged to bring Edie to New York to live with her. Even so, Edie had not lost her fight. Dare expected her mother to be relieved; instead, she protested. It was as if she were being made to admit defeat. She insisted that it would be a disruption to her work, even though she hadn't had a real commission in four years.

Arguing that Edie could paint in New York just as well, Dare flew to Cleveland, packed up essentials, including Edie's easel and painting supplies, and took Edie back to New York. She also packed a transitional object, a bust of Voltaire, a copy but still valuable, of one by the late-eighteenth-century French sculptor Jean-Antoine Houdon. It was Edie's prized possession, bestowed upon her by an English admirer, Henry Talbot de Vere Clifton, whom she had met in Los Angeles in 1938.

Dorothy had also insisted Edie be seen by a doctor. Dare arranged for a house call. Edie, who had never been in the habit of paying for professional services, always turning to friends or painting a portrait in exchange, was furious at the cost—and the implied suggestion that she was in any way failing. In a letter to Allie, she railed, "He charged $50, and pronounced there was nothing to be done." In her view, there was nothing to be done because there was nothing wrong. In reality, there was nothing to be done simply because she was so old.

In New York, Edie painted every day, refusing to assume the role of invalid. Out of Cleveland, her circle had dwindled down to Dare and Dorothy. She painted Dare, looking more and more like a Kewpie doll, and decided to take advantage of Dorothy's hovering by making her sit for a portrait. Beyond these two, not only were there no more commissions, there were no more subjects. Coming across a photograph she had given to Dare of her mother, Alice Madolia Gaither Stevenson, as a young girl, she painted that. And she began an oil on board of a blue sky and clouds. It was never finished. Too weak to paint anymore, she was soon too weak to leave their bed. Dare sat by her bedside by day and at night slipped in to sleep next to her. Dorothy came each morning to spell Dare so she could attend to errands. Watching over Edie, Dorothy was amazed to see that, while she now looked every bit her age, her right hand, her painting hand, eerily retained its youthful vigor, down to the talon-like painted fingernails.

On the night of July 28, 1975, Dare and Edie settled into bed, nestling together, as usual, like spoons. In the middle of the night, Dare was awakened by a tugging around her waist. Edie's right arm was wrapped tightly around her, not at rest but clutching. Fully awake now, Dare realized that Edie was in distress. Softly, in case she was still sleeping, Dare whispered, "Edie, what's wrong?" At that instant, Edie's grasp finally released. Dare, as if frozen, stayed in the bed by her mother's side until morning.

CHAPTER TEN

After Edie

The last six months have been sad and very busy ones for me.
My mother died. It was not untimely for her, but it was
untimely for me.
　　　—DARE WRIGHT, letter to DARE BOLES, February 10, 1976

When she finally did leave the bed at eight the next morning, Dare called Jane Douglass. As Jane now lived just six blocks away, she arrived quickly and took charge. Since meeting Dare forty-five years earlier, Jane had believed the only solution for Dare would be to get Edie out of the picture. Now the job was hers. She called the Frank E. Campbell funeral home around the corner and comforted Dare as they waited for the body to be taken away. Later that morning, she accompanied Dare to meet with the funeral director. Dare said she wanted no funeral, no obituary, and would not have her mother buried. When it was explained that cremation was the only remaining option, Dare gave instructions that the ashes be returned to her.

Unable to reach Blaine, Dare called his landlords. When Bob and Shirley Homovich found Blaine, they conveyed Dare's message and their condolences and were shocked by Blaine's absence of emotion. If Blaine felt nothing at Edie's death, however, he did recognize how devastating it would be for his sister and suggested that Dare come to live near him. Dare left for Walton almost immediately, spending the entire month of August at Florence Wakeman's. "Blaine has been wonderful, and we've looked at land and houses," she wrote to Dick Gildenmeister on August 24, 1975. "It's still a little hard for me to think constructively, but it's good for me to try. The trouble is I keep wanting to tell Edie things."

The dedication of *Look at a Kitten*, which was being published that September, was prophetic. "To my brother who has his uses, with thanks." Even if he was destined to fall short as an Edie replacement, Dare now latched on to Blaine with all her force.

Allan Hull, Edie's lawyer, urged Dare to come to Cleveland to deal with practical matters, to probate the will and clean out Edie's apartment at Moreland Courts. Almost two months would go by, however, before Dare could bring herself to make the trip.

Dare was the sole beneficiary of Edie's will. The estate was valued at about $100,000, most of which was in a savings account. No mention was made of Blaine. In a letter she had written to her Aunt Daisy as Allan Hull was drawing up her will, Edie had written, "Blaine I simply won't give money. No, I concentrate on you—you always helped me to the limit, made refuge for me and Dare, and you are the only ones we feel close to." In the end, however, Edie left various paintings to museums in Cleveland and Youngstown, and to Allan Hull, but nothing to Daisy or her daughter Allie.

Despite her mother's deliberate decision to leave her son out of her will, Dare added "V. Blaine Wright, son" to every form she was given to fill out when the will was probated. This was irrelevant information, except to Dare. Although she knew it was against Edie's wishes, she sent several paintings to Blaine. Wanting nothing to do with them, he put them in storage, did not pay the bills, and lost the receipt, forfeiting his, or anyone else's, right to reclaim them.

Seeing how difficult it was for Dare to be alone at Edie's apartment, Hull spent as much time as he could with her there. She gave him three more paintings: a portrait of herself in a snowsuit hood, which Edie had done of Dare as a grown woman but based on a childhood portrait; a tiny 5-by-3-inch painting of Dare's eye, which Edie had excised from a larger canvas; and the 7-by-4-foot unfinished portrait of Dare, which had been Edie's practice portrait for the Queen and whose unfinished aspect Hull considered an apt metaphor for the life of its subject.

As Edie had paid for Hull's services through the years with paintings, there were already several Wrights hanging in the turn-of-the-century farmhouse that served as the offices of Hull & Hull. Edie had painted his portrait in 1950, and in 1968 she had given him a monochromatic portrait of Dare kneeling on a chair.

Dare shipped most of Edie's belongings to her apartment in New York. She also kept Edie's collection of old family photographs, including some of her great-grandparents, some of Edie and Ivan as children and as grown-ups, and a few of herself and Blaine from childhood. Dare rephotographed and enlarged them all, making composite prints for herself and for Blaine. She wrote "Fairly large great-grandmother" on the back of an enlarged photograph of Catherine Algeo Hicks Gaither, and "Very small grandmother" on a photograph of Edie's mother, Alice Madolia Gaither, at the age of two. She also gave Blaine the palette Edie had used to paint Coolidge, which the president had signed.

Even before Edie's death, the walls of Dare's apartment were lined with her mother's paintings. There were twenty portraits of herself, as well as one of Philip Sandeman and a self-portrait. Now a dozen more were added: two self-portraits, another portrait of herself, two portraits of David Fitch Anderson, Edie's divorce lawyer, and a portrait of Henry Talbot de Vere Clifton, the English aristocrat Edie had met in Los Angeles who had given her the bust of

Voltaire. What the walls couldn't accommodate, Dare leaned against the bookshelves or placed in storage racks. These paintings became the building blocks of the fortress Dare constructed for herself at 11 East 80th Street after Edie's death.

Many years earlier, Dare had rescued Edie's portrait of Ivan when she discovered that Edie planned to throw it out. Out of respect for her mother, Dare had always kept it out of view. Along the way, it had acquired a diagonal tear, starting in the upper right of the canvas and moving down toward the left, as if its subject had been stabbed through the heart. Now she found a place for it on the wall.

As Hull spread the news of Edie's passing, condolence letters poured in. Dare never even opened them; she just stacked them neatly on the coffee table beside the box containing her mother's ashes.

Dare did not return to work until August, a full year after Edie's death. That spring she had spent a month bedridden with what the doctor called tracheal bronchitis, which she wrote to Dick Gildenmeister, "sounds like a prehistoric beast. That's the way it behaved too! I think I have it beaten now." Her illness had permitted her to avoid facing what lay ahead; once her health was restored, she could no longer put it off.

At the beginning, Dare seemed to think that if she tried to ward off change, she could lessen the pain of Edie's loss. In every aspect of life, even down to food and drink, Dare cleaved to Edie. In 1954, Stouffer's had developed a line of frozen foods. These prepackaged frozen dinners, reminders of meals with her mother at the Stouffer's Cleveland restaurants, became Dare's sole source of sustenance. She bought them one at a time at Gentile's, a grocer down the street from her apartment. Dare's shopping list was succinct. Aside from the frozen dinners, she bought the occasional can of Campbell's soup and sometimes an avocado, a nod to Gayelord Hauser, who called avocados a "beauty-full" food and "a six-course dinner in a green shell."

At the close of each day, Edie and Dare had always had a cocktail, either in the context of a party or on their own. Their drinking was not excessive but controlled and disciplined, as was everything Edie did. After her mother died, Dare called Headington's, the liquor store where she and Edie had been customers, and asked for a delivery of the bourbon that Edie loved, even though Dare's preference had always been for white wine. When she placed the order, she told Ida Bono, the wife of the owner, that Edie had died. Ida came to pay a call. Dare seemed so lonely that Ida stayed for three hours.

For a time, many of Dare's—and Edie's—old friends reached out to the daughter Edie had left behind. Various ideas were considered for Dare's first summer without her mother. Vincent Youmans's twin sister, Ceciley, and her husband, Preston Collins, planned a trip to Venice with their son Harold, his Collegiate classmate Mark Andrejevic, and Mark's parents. Dare had met Milet Andrejevic, an artist, and his wife, Helen, through the Collinses, and they suggested that Dare come along to shoot a *Date with Venice* featuring Mark and Harold. Dare was not up to it. She wrote Allie, "I couldn't cope with the Venice book. It was just too hurried." She was, however, charmed by both boys, and when she heard that Mark Andrejevic was becoming interested in photography, she proposed to his parents that she give him one of her cameras. Mark was taken to 11 East 80th Street, where Dare presented him with two 35-mm Exakta cameras. She said he should take both, try them out, and keep the one he liked better.

Mark found it confusing to be given a gift by a complete stranger. "I thought, 'Here is this mysterious person who wants to give me a camera.' She was like a fairy godmother." He did accept her offer, however, and made a second visit to Dare's overstuffed apartment to return the camera he didn't want. She received him in blue jeans and a clingy see-through sweater. The juxtaposition of her youthful figure and dress with her much older face struck Mark as dissonant. He had listened whenever his parents and Harold's discussed his mysterious benefactress, overhearing a somewhat garbled version of the Marsh case, including the fact that Dare's defense might have rested on her virginity. And he was moved by the story of her great love, the pilot who was killed in the war.

In the end, Dare decided to spend the first anniversary of Edie's death in Cotuit on Cape Cod, the guest of Edie's patron Fred Crawford, ninety-five, who had retired as chairman of the board of TRW in 1967, and his wife, Kay, whom Dare had first met at the Hannas' Easter egg hunt in 1921. "I'm glad I'm away just now because it's just a year since I lost my Edie," Dare wrote to Allie. "It would have been hard to be right in the same place." In this rambling letter, begun on the bus to Cape Cod and completed two days after her return to New York, Dare returns again and again to the subject of being alone and its antidotes, as though trying to convince herself that they exist. Allie, seventy by now and widowed, was also confronting life on her own. "Of course it's tough to be alone, Allie. And being bored is more exhausting than the hardest work. Sometimes I think I'm lucky I have to make a living and can do it in a field I enjoy. For me work is the best medicine."

So was time spent with the Sandemans. Although they had exchanged letters, Dare had not seen any of Philip's family since her trip to England in 1963. Brian and Jane Sandeman and two of their eight children were in Newport, Rhode Island, to welcome their son David, seventeen, who was sailing in a race from Jersey to Newport. He made the trip in 43 days and set the world record for the youngest person to cross an ocean singlehandedly. To celebrate, the Sandemans decided to visit New York. They called Dare, who, uncharacteristically, invited them to come to dinner.

The dinner caused her great anxiety. Like her mother, Dare had no real interest in food or cooking. The preparations made her feel "frantic." Liz Sandeman Griffin was thoroughly disappointed by this visit to her sister's exotic godmother—from the canned vichyssoise to the absent Edith and the Bears, who were in the bank vault.

The excitement and distraction of the Sandeman visit over, Dare was off to the bank to rescue her charges. "Edith and the Bears are sitting on the couch," she wrote a few days later to Dick Gildenmeister, "and send you greetings."

She confided her sense of disorientation to Allie: "It is certainly a changing world." She went on to give a disquisition on the popularity of blue jeans and her attempts to conform to this newly ubiquitous style. She wrote that she had lunch recently with Russell Aitken at the restaurant Café des Artistes. "I was wearing jeans, and so were three-quarters of the other people. We were talking about it and I was remembering when I wouldn't have dreamed of meeting him for lunch without stockings and high heels and white gloves and maybe even a hat." Even Edith would need to adapt. "I suppose she'll have to have jeans," she wrote. To go with the jeans, Dare dressed her doll in a pair of canvas sneakers and a knitted sweater and hat.

It was a foregone conclusion that any subsequent books would be set in Walton. "I am going to do an Edith book this month," Dare wrote to Allie. "They're going to catch and learn to ride an ornery little Shetland pony." As soon as she had Edith's clothes together, Dare took off for Walton for the remainder of August to shoot the book she planned to call *Edith and Midnight*. It was Florence's neighbors who named (and owned) the pony, not Dare, but somehow the name was fitting.

In the fall of 1976, Dare met with her Random House editor to discuss the work in progress. Walter Retan thought the scale difference between the small doll and the pony would prevent the fantasy from taking off. Dare began toying with the idea of another *Look at . . .* book. She had photographs in her repertoire from which she created mock-ups of possible covers, for Look at a Turtle, Look at a Shell, and even Look at a Dandelion. But, in the end, she jettisoned all these ideas and stuck fast to her original proposal, despite Retan's objections. Without Bennett Cerf's protection—he had died in 1971—there were consequences. "R.H. [Random House] has written me off," she confided to Dick. Her agent, Bill Berger, contacted Doubleday, the publisher of her first four books. They agreed to take her back.

Despite her determination to go forward with this idea, Dare struggled with the story line of *Edith and Midnight*. In all, she wrote 148 pages of drafts for a book that would be only 38 pages long. On Butternut Island Tackle Company letterhead, Blaine tried to help, hashing out a story line that began, "On a June day at the Farm, Edith and Little Bear were playing with Pony, in the Meadow. Or rather, Pony was playing with them. The Meadow rolled in velvet green around them, spangled with daisies and buttercups, and Pony was eating clover and laughing at Little Bear and Edith, who were trying to catch him, because they wanted a ride."

The little ones catch Pony and climb up his mane, and get their ride. They discover a crow with a broken wing and rescue him and invite him "to become a member of the family." Then Blaine's story dissolves into nonsense. "Of course, Goat, the rubber-footed, helped. The agate-eyed character is most interesting. A kid is a baby goat, not a human child." Finally, he gave up. "Shucks. Over to you, little sister, and much love, Blaine."

Since childhood, when Dare had discovered that books could provide companionship and comfort, they had always been counted among her most treasured possessions. At the East 80th Street apartment, floor-to-ceiling bookshelves dominated the living room, even if many of the books were obscured by the paintings stacked against them. Over the years, she had bought valuable first editions with the proceeds of her own work and acquired hundreds of other books, including her own, in the original versions and in foreign editions. When the bookshelves were filled, she started a second row behind the first. Those titles she considered most valuable were assigned a place in the back row, whether first editions or *Tales from the Secret Kingdom*, inscribed *To Dare from Blaine, age 7*. She kept all her

A scene from *Edith and Midnight* shot in Walton, 1978. *Left to right,* Little Bear, Midnight, Mr. Bear, and Edith. This was the next to last of Dare's books.

schoolbooks from Laurel and plays she had studied in drama school or used in auditions. In many, she tucked little notes or papers, a habit begun at Laurel, when letters from Edie, old homework assignments, or a list of favorite movie stars found their way inside the covers or between the pages.

She fetishized the books, arranging them according to a system only she knew, and featuring them in many portraitlike photographic still lifes. She often included volumes from her collection in photographs that were used to illustrate her books: Edith standing on a pile of books to reach the forbidden clock in *Edith and Mr. Bear*, Persis in *The Little One* propped against books, and a self-referential shot of the cover of *Holiday for Edith and the Bears* in *Take Me Home*.

Fairy tales were well represented in her library by *The Green Forest Fairy Book* and the stories of Hans Christian Andersen, the Brothers Grimm, and Charles Perrault. So were other children's classics, including *Alice's Adventures in Wonderland*, works by J. M. Barrie, all of Frances Hodgson Burnett, all of Louisa May Alcott. *Robin Hood* in three versions, *Robinson Crusoe*, *Hans Brinker*, *Heidi*, and *Kidnapped* by Robert Louis Stevenson. She treasured her first editions of *Riders of the Purple Sage*, *The Light of Western Stars*, *Wildfire*, *Forlorn River*, and *Nevada*, all by Zane Grey, a distant relation of Dare's on Edie's side.

There was *The Forgotten Daughter* by Caroline Dale Snedeker, in which a father is reunited with his long-lost daughter. *The Dark Rose*, *La Tulipe Noire*, *Mary Rose*, and *Macleod of Dare* all stood beside one another. The last line of *Macleod of Dare*, published in 1892, was prophetic: "The new bright day has begun. It is a bright, eager, glad day for all the world. But there is silence in Castle Dare."

One of Dare's favorite books was a 1925 tooled-leather version with marbleized endpapers of *The Oxford Book of English Verse* inscribed to Edie by a woman whose daughter she had painted: "A token of appreciation for the pleasure your re-creation of my daughter has given me." Edie gave Dare the book, which she used in a class at Laurel. Dare had diagrammed the rhyme scheme by each line of "The World" by William Wordsworth. The poem's first line "The world is too much with us" could have been written to describe Dare's feeling about life after Edie.

Dare loved Wordsworth and had several collections of his work. Inside the front cover of one of them, she had written, "Wordsworth's purpose was to cast spell of imagination over commonplace deliberate theory to deal with everyday." This had been Edie and Dare's mission together, their raison d'être. But without Edie, Dare could not sustain the spell. Her new everyday world, commonplace but also frightening, was indeed "too much with" her. She had landed in the dark wood, and now there was almost no one to help her find her way out.

At sixty-four, although still looking many years younger, Dare was on a descent, not always slow and sometimes turbulent, despite the efforts of her friends to help her hold on. With Edie out of the way, Jane Douglass had more freedom to pursue Dare. Whatever the nature of Jane's love for Dare, none of Dare's friends were quite sure. Regardless, Jane was now free to invest some of her prodigious energy in her "goddaughter." She set up a joint bank account for them and drew up a will leaving Dare everything. She assumed Dare would reciprocate when she was in need. Before a trip out of town, she wrote Dare: "Darling: Nothing *is* going to happen but if it does you might need these telephone numbers. . . . Really . . . what a comfort you are—but of course none but the best will do. . . . And you are the best."

Dare's circle did not like Jane any more than Edie had. Dorothy viewed her as a parasite. Donald Seawell described her as "almost a slave in her devotion to Dare," inserting herself into everything Dare did and fawning over her. "Dare was very, very patient," Seawell recalled. "It had to be embarrassing at times."

People who met Dare in this period found her mysterious, as always, sad, and detached. She spoke in a tremulous voice, as if she were on the verge of laughing or crying. She moved somewhat jerkily, yet seemed unusually flexible and always sat with her legs tucked beneath her like a child. Her body was willowy, and there was still a loveliness about her physical presence even though her weight had dropped below a hundred pounds. An addiction to alcohol had rapidly and forcefully taken hold and eclipsed what was already a distinterest in food.

Despite her troubles, Dare's charms continued to attract others. Dare met Jeanne Frank, an art dealer and writer, at Burlington Bookshop. When she invited Jeanne for a drink at her apartment, Jeanne thought it the perfect stage setting for Dare. She remembered it as "lit only with antique sconces that gave off a faint glow just enough to see everything as if it were behind yards of fine gauze." She liked Dare immensely from the start. "You either responded to Dare or you were so conventional that you would think her too odd. She was from another world. She was very, very intelligent, but she was not of this earth. If you could imagine a fairy flying off, it was Dare."

As the friendship developed, Dare gave Jeanne a view into her life with her mother. Jeanne understood that Dare's mother was "the entire story," but she did not consider it as benevolent a story as its teller so clearly did. "They lived in a fantasy world," Jeanne observed. "All Dare wanted to talk about was Edie: where they went, who they met, how they dressed. I would think, *Was she used in that way?* It sounded as if her mother behaved the same way Dare did, except that she was manipulative and shrewd. She must have smothered Dare to death."

Dare reminded Jeanne of her book's main character. "She was Edith. Dare's voice is in all her stories. She never went beyond that. After her mother died, she could no longer be Edith. She would say to me with a bewildered look on her face, 'You know, Jeanne, life is getting so real.' Or, 'You know, the world has become too real for me. I don't belong here.'"

Jeanne invited Dare to several Thanksgiving dinners and although Dare refused all alcohol when she visited others, Jeanne suspected that Dare drank at home. "I think she wanted to escape.

If she could cut the world out, she would. The world was invading her life. She didn't want to be a part of it."

Another new friend was Jeanne Hammond, whom she had known in passing when Jeanne had been an associate art editor at *Good Housekeeping* in 1957, at which point Dare was doing her last work for that magazine. Jeanne recognized Dare in line at the neighborhood post office. Now a writer and photographer, Jeanne was mesmerized by Dare's apartment and intrigued by all the stories about Dare's life, even if some of them didn't seem quite true. "You were never quite sure with her whether you were standing on firm ground," she said, recalling an answering-machine message Dare had left for her: "Sorry you aren't there. Greta Garbo and Gayelord Hauser are coming for tea and I'd hoped you could join us." Jeanne heard about Blaine, about the fiancé in the RAF, and about Russell Barnett Aitken. When she read in *The New York Times* that Russ's wife, Annie Laurie Aitken, had died, Jeanne wondered whether he might marry Dare, until she learned of Russ's second marriage to Irene Roosevelt. But she also understood that Dare's truest love was her brother. When Dare was preparing to visit Blaine in Walton, she seemed "so excited, like she was going off to visit a lover."

Dare's circle also came to include fans to whom she was more receptive than she had been before Edie's death. They found Dare through the phone book or directory assistance. A few made pilgrimages to East 80th Street, but the majority wrote letters and called, keeping to the arm's-length relationship with which Dare was always most comfortable.

Dare answered their letters on postcards she made from photographs of Edith and the Bears and often wrote in Edith's voice. To one, whose daughter's Lenci doll had been repaired after a run-in with the family dog, Dare wrote doll-to-doll on a handmade postcard featuring Edith in blue jeans: "Dear Margie, I am so glad you are all better now. I think you look beautiful. I used to have a bonnet and a dress with frills, but just see what I'm wearing now. Stay away from dogs, Love, Edith."

In March 1979, she received a letter from a fan who shared her unusual first name. Dare Boles hoped to visit her on an upcoming trip to New York. "I wish I had a house where I could offer you hospitality," Dare replied. "Edith and the Bears would be very happy to get out of the safety deposit box and meet you."

Boles found Dare still very glamorous, and her stories thrilling. She was most impressed when Dare pointed to a chair and said, "Do you know who sat there? Greta Garbo." In a letter thanking this other Dare for her visit, Dare wrote, "It was very nice to meet you at last. All the characters are shouting for you to come back so that they'll be allowed to emerge again into the world."

But these friends and fans, never quite real to her, could not sustain her. When Dare turned up at one of Dorothy's cocktail parties in this period, Dorothy was horrified to see how disheveled she looked. She had runs in her stockings and seemed drunk and disassociated.

Blaine, her only remaining true stay, was on a downward slide of his own. In April 1978, he was hospitalized for five weeks after he fell and broke his hip. Dare spent two weeks in Walton caring for him. And Florence Wakeman, with whom she always stayed, was now eighty-four and also ill. And in June, Austin Wright, Dare's adored uncle who had brought Blaine back into her life, died at the age of ninety-one. She had kept up a correspondence with him, sending along copies of each of her books as they were released. His last letter to her was in thanks for the copy of *Edith and Midnight*. "My what a clever niece I have. I love the moral you always run through every story. Very smart. I like particularly the photograph of Edith in her nightie—beautiful. The look of excitement in the eyes of Little Bear—how do you get it? How proud we are of your work. Send word of Blaine. How I wish you folks lived within reasonable distance, so I could talk to you easily. Good night and sweet dreams."

In 1979, Dare began work on what she called "an adult fairy tale," in which she was the princess and Blaine was the prince. But she could not make it work and gave up. Casting about for ideas for her next book, she floundered for much of that year. She considered "Look at a Swan," which could take her to the Eastern Shore of Maryland with the Youmanses and Seawells, who still had houses there, but this idea too was jettisoned. Ultimately—and predictably— she opted for a story that involved the usual cast and could be set in Walton. Its story line could not have been more apt. *Edith and the Duckling*, photographed over the summer of 1980, is the story of Edith caring for a duckling after its mother disappears. When the front door is opened, the duckling walks out into "the big world." Edith and Little Bear chase the duckling and bring it home again. Finally, after Mr. Bear trips over the duckling on the staircase, he orders the little ones to put it outside to live. They comply, but place the duckling in a basin on the pond with a string attached, hoping he'll stay there. As the duckling grows up, Mr. Bear warns the little ones that the duck will fly south with the other ducks when the weather turns cold. They react in disbelief. But when the frosts begin, he does indeed fly away. Edith cannot bear to watch and buries her face in Mr. Bear's furry back. "Edith," Mr. Bear tells her, "ducks belong to the water and the sky. You've raised a fine duck. Can't you be happy to let him go where he belongs?" Edith is consoled only when Mr. Bear tells her the duckling will be back in the spring. When she asks him to promise, he replies, "I can't promise but this is home and you're his family. I think he'll be back."

As was true of her first book, published twenty-four years earlier, this one, which would be her last, didn't stray far from Dare's own story. Edith caring for a duckling after its mother disappears could have been inspired by Dare's efforts to care for Blaine, or be read as her wish for someone to take care of her. Blaine was more and more resembling a needy child, and Dare was feeling pressured by the responsibility of mothering him, especially as she was struggling with her own motherlessness. But perhaps it is less a story about Edith caring for a motherless duckling than a story about a mother allowing her child to grow up and fulfill its destiny as a separate—

Author photo for *Edith and the Duckling*, the last book in the series,
taken in Walton, when she was sixty-five.

and independent—being. This interpretation is a far more incendi-ary one. It would mean that Dare had realized her mother should have let her fly away.

By this time, neither she nor Blaine, who, like his father before him, could only walk now with the aid of a cane, could manage the logistics or multiple locations required by the earlier books. This least ambitious of them all was shot in Florence Wakeman's house and backyard and at a neighbor's pond across the road. Not only had Dare found the photographs difficult to shoot, she was having trouble pulling it together by the due date. In a letter to a fan, Dare vowed, "I'm not going to get trapped in another such deadline ever."

In July, a new paperback version of *The Lonely Doll* was released by Zephyr, a Doubleday paperback imprint. On July 25, 1980, *Pub-lishers Weekly* magazine notified its readers:

> Thousands of women will remember the joys they found as children in Wright's ingenious book when it appeared in 1957. These fans will probably want to introduce small girls they know to Edith the doll, Mr. Bear and Little Bear. Astonishingly realistic posed photos depict the toys meeting, the start of a friendship that means Edith will be lonely no more.

Doubleday was eager to line up future projects, but Dare was not inspired. Five years after Edie's death, Dare was eating still less and drinking still more, her days and nights haunted by doubts and demons. In losing Edie she had lost the armature of her identity; without the scaffolding her mother had provided, it was all collaps-ing. And so were the boundaries. Harold Collins remembered the hostess gift Dare presented to his mother at his family's 1980 Christ-mas dinner, a glass compote dish with gold filigree that she said was a family heirloom. "That struck me as very poignant," said Harold.

"I remember thinking, 'Ouch. I wish she didn't have to bring something from her own house.'"

She began giving away more and more of her things—even treasured ones—and was as likely to answer the door naked as clothed. Drinking undermined Dare's self-control and lifted her inhibitions. Her strange behavior alienated those who had earlier offered her friendship, even despite her sometimes desperate acts of generosity. She was lonelier than ever.

On a visit to New York to meet with Garbo, whose business adviser he had become, Tony Palermo, Gayelord Hauser's onetime protégé who had pursued Dare for two years in the fifties, arranged a dinner with Dare one night and suggested she might join him and Garbo the next. Dare's behavior on the first evening so shocked Tony that he withdrew the next night's invitation. Dare arrived having had too much to drink and launched into an emotional tirade at the table. "She said she ruined her whole life and we should have gotten married. She said, 'You were within my grasp at the time.' When I knew her she was the maximum introvert, but that night she was so outspoken it embarrassed me." That was the last time he saw her.

Returning home from her dinner with Tony, Dare was unable to sleep. At three that morning, she called Jeanne Frank, who wrote about the phone call in her diary:

> Dare says maybe she was a dope for not marrying him but I can't imagine her handling that. It's the love of being cared for, because she's tired fatigue caused depression and the combination throws everything out of whack. Is it a doll's house? In Ibsen, she did not choose her doll house. . . . I see this at least 60-year-old woman, her long blond hair, 20-inch waist, dressed like a doll, an exquisite one, surrounded by her stage set and I don't want to see it crumble, it would be too cruel. . . . Only death will solve her problems. It would represent peace, the surcease of

pain . . . anxiety trying to see a world she would never understand, wouldn't even know what to do with.

The world had not yet forgotten Dare. In February 1981, she was called in to meet with a new editor at Doubleday. She wrote to Dare Boles, "They seem most taken with buried pirate treasure or a haunted house." Neither appealed to her, although she did make notes for a buried treasure story, one for which she could recycle earlier photographs.

Due to inflation, Mr. Bear's savings are dwindling. No longer able to afford to live in the city, he decides to move the family to the country. "So E. and L.B. helped uproot + pack etc. 'This is fun,' said L.B., rolling up a rug. But when the movers had come and gone and all that was left of their very own home was empty spaces where their things had been, it wasn't so much fun." They move into a farmhouse that had been built by Mr. Bear's great-grandfather. Now someone wants to buy Mr. Bear's great-grandfather's property to build a subdivision. Mr. Bear has no choice but to sell. He tells the little ones it is the only way "to feed and take care of us." Edith and Little Bear aren't convinced. Surely there must be some way they can bring in some money. They could sell lemonade or rides on Midnight. As they realize they will be unable to raise enough money, "Edith put her head down on the fencepost and cried and cried."

One rainy day, while playing in the attic, they discover an old chest. Breaking the lock, they find old clothes and a smaller box with a rolled-up document inside. It is a map with a note on it: " 'I'm burying this gold under the great tree. It will be safe there. One day, perhaps my son's son or his son will find it when he needs it. I wish him well.' 'It's a buried treasure,' cried L.B. 'And it belongs to Mr. Bear and if we find it we can keep our farm,' cried Edith. 'Does the map show where the tree is?' " There Dare's notes trail off.

Financial concerns and a move to the country were on Dare's mind in this period. Dorothy, who saw Dare "in her apartment drinking herself to death," was trying to convince her that such a move might be a solution to her problems. Dorothy suggested they buy a property in South Egremont, Massachusetts, together. She drove Dare up to look it over, but nothing came of it.

Along with everything else that Edie had passed on to her daughter were her anxieties about money. From earliest childhood, Dare had understood money problems to be a force that could separate a family, and they had. The economy was now in a downturn, and soon after Dare's meeting with Doubleday the government began cutting funds to public schools and libraries. As these made up 80 percent of children's book sales, Doubleday canceled dozens of projects and cut their children's book department by two editors. Dare was having trouble conceiving a new Edith book, but now Doubleday was also equivocating about wanting one. Dare wrote in frustration to a fan, "They may not even want the Edith book which they'd had me working on plots for for two months."

In any case, Dare had lost her passion for the books. She had arrived at a place of regret; work, "the best medicine," had lost its healing effect. So had the prospect of a visit from a member of the Sandeman family. When Teresa Sandeman, next to youngest of Brian's eight children, called to say she was in New York and would like to pay a call, Dare begged off with the excuse that her apartment was too much of a mess. Teresa offered to come help her straighten up. Dare declined. When Teresa told her father that Dare had refused to receive her, he became concerned. He wrote to Dare several times but there was no reply. Teresa's attempted visit was the last contact Dare ever had with a member of Philip's family.

While Edie was still alive, her patrons would talk during long sittings of current events, and through these reports Edie kept up, in her way, with world affairs; this information would filter down to Dare. But after Edie's death, contact with the outside world was sporadic at best. Dare turned to television for company. She wrote Allie, "If I'm alone, I watch the news. I enjoy some of the old movies, and *Mas-*

terpiece *Theatre*, and some of public television. I occasionally watch soap operas when I'm doing something that only employs my hands. I know actors on some of them, and there are some excellent performances, if only the stories weren't so dragged out. I guess they can be an addiction. I know that Tallulah, if she had to miss certain ones, would hire someone to watch them for her and report."

She rarely read newspapers although friends sent her clippings, a few of which she saved in a box: an article about Ocracoke sent by Dorothy, an article written for the *New York Times Magazine* by P. L. Travers, the author of *Mary Poppins*, in which she quotes a line from the Nestor section of James Joyce's *Ulysses*, "My childhood bends beside me." This line was marked with an asterisk as well as the handwritten words *I like this*. And there were two clippings relating to the case of Russ Aitken's stepdaughter Sunny von Bulow, whose husband Claus stood accused of overdosing her with insulin, leaving her in a coma from which she never emerged.

Dare had also followed the case of the imprisoned Jean Harris, then serving fifteen years to life in a maximum security prison in Bedford Hills, New York, for the murder of Dr. Herman Tarnower, the "Scarsdale Diet doctor." Dare told a friend she was forwarding a gift subscription of *New Mexico Magazine* to Jean Harris when she was done reading them. Dare had learned that Harris was from Cleveland and that she and her two sisters had attended Laurel. Harris, nine years younger than Dare, said she hadn't known Dare at Laurel, nor had she known Dare's books. And she never received copies of *New Mexico Magazine*, although it was possible that they had been sent to her. She believed that the prison staff, resentful of the high volume of mail she received, would often throw out full bags of it.

In 1982, Cathy Lawson, a young West Virginia mother of two daughters who was trying to track down one of the *Lonely Doll* books, contacted Dare. Cathy's daughter Natalie was showing signs of speech and learning disabilities and did not share her older sister's passion for reading and being read to. Only when Cathy read aloud from one of Dare's books would Natalie join in.

Cathy found Dare happy to converse and generous with her time and with gifts, the first of which was *Edith and Mr. Bear*, the book Cathy had been unable to find. Dare sent a copy of the German translation, *Edith und Herr Bar*, as she didn't have any spare copies of the original. Along with the book she enclosed typed-out pages of the text in English in a plastic cover tied together with a white ribbon. She also sent photographs of Edith with each of her co-stars, a puzzle, and a photograph of one of Edie's paintings. Over the next ten years, Cathy and Dare communicated through a weekly Saturday phone call and through letters. In one of these, Dare wrote, "Things keep happening—bad things to people I care about."

In 1982, Blaine, who chain-smoked like his mother, was diagnosed with lung cancer. When he refused treatment, the doctor told him he would not have long to live. He asked Dare to accompany him to Florida for the winter. She declined. That fall, Jane Douglass died at the age of eighty-six. The funeral was held at St. Thomas Church, where Dare and Philip were to have been married. Dare did not attend, despite nearly fifty years of friendship and the fact that all of Jane's belongings had been left to her.

Dare wrote to Dare Boles from Walton in October: "I'm up here seeing my brother before he takes off for the winter. I only have four days. I meant to come earlier but wasn't able to. I may have mentioned Jane Douglass, the old lady I've known since I was nine, who has been so ill for the last year or so. She died, and I had a lot of responsibility for coping with things. She left me her personal effects, which meant I had to take care of clothes, objects, and papers. She had three stacks of files each six feet high, some things going back to the twenties. She lived in a hotel and they would only allow two days for everything to be cleared out. A lot of the research, letters, etc. will go to the Lincoln Center Library and a museum theatre collection. It was an almost impossible job—dealing with a lifetime in two days. I did manage, but I don't think I was ever so exhausted in my life."

She ended this letter as she often did: "I ought to re-read this to see if it makes sense, but I don't dare. Love, Dare."

With Blaine away for the winter, knowing it was just a matter of time before she would lose him altogether, and with Jane gone, Dare was coming unglued. But because she concealed her drinking, everyone who knew her had a different theory of what was happening. And Dare's penchant for storytelling didn't make it any easier to sort out the truth. When Allan Hull visited one day, Dare couldn't manage to unlock the door. He heard her becoming increasingly frantic on the other side. He had to borrow a screwdriver from a neighbor to remove the door panel. Once inside, he was stunned by the condition of both Dare and her apartment. "She was loaded," he recalled, and surrounded by the wreckage caused by her drinking. At some point earlier, she had fallen on the coffee table and it had split in two. "It was just sitting there like a shipwreck," he recalled. When he proposed trying to repair it for her, she said she didn't want anything changed.

After he returned to Cleveland, he asked his daughter, Kathy Hull Stropoli, who lived in New York, to look in on Dare. On these visits, Kathy said she found Dare to be at once childlike but also "a ship going down very quickly." She could see that Dare was not eating and said her behavior was becoming increasingly bizarre. On several occasions, Dare tried to give her Edie's ashes.

Then came fantastic stories of what Dare described as "muggings," horrible attacks in which she claimed to have been knocked down on the street, beaten, her purse stolen. Sometimes she said she had been thrown in a trash can by her assailant. Some acquaintances, especially those in long-distance phone relationships, took these reports at face value. After all, New York was a dangerous place, and Dare, fragile and defenseless, would be an easy target.

In reality, no one was doing anything to her, good or bad. Perhaps she was expressing what she had never been able to before, confabulating a feeling of being punished, mistreated, manipulated, and controlled by Edie. Reality, a shaky concept for Dare at the best of times, had blurred beyond recognition.

Allie recorded her impressions of what was happening to Dare from information gleaned from phone calls. "Dare had several bad falls. Getting on a streetcar, she was pushed off, fell in the street; another time while going up the steps to the art museum, two boys chasing each other knocked her down and she was hurt; another time she was posting a letter, and a man grabbed her purse and knocked her down on the sidewalk."

Dare was telling these sometimes elaborate stories over and over, to anyone who called. But none of those who saw Dare in this period suspected the problem was alcohol. One day a neighbor found Dare lying on the floor in the building lobby. There was no assailant. She was simply drunk and had fallen.

Jeanne Hammond had not known of Dare's drinking. She explained away her behavior as the result of being overwhelmed not only by the loss of her mother but by Jane's death, Blaine's worsening condition, and even Russ's ordeal with his son-in-law and Sunny von Bulow's situation. When Dare called Jeanne to say she'd been mugged, Jeanne was surprised by Dare's request to come over. Jeanne told her it made no sense for an injured person to venture out and that she would come to her. Dare persisted. When Dare arrived, she appeared to be beaten and her hand was covered in blood. She had made no attempt to clean it. Seeing how horrified Jeanne was, Dare laughed and said, "Your doorman almost wouldn't let me in."

Even more disturbing to Jeanne was the time Dare called to say she'd been walking on Madison Avenue the day before when a taxi swerved up on the sidewalk and hit her. The driver had taken her home. This time, Jeanne rushed over to Dare's apartment. Dare seemed unscathed, but Jeanne was puzzled at a bizarre display before the fireplace. There were bottles of every kind of liquor, neatly lined up. When Jeanne asked about this, Dare told her that the taxi driver had just been by with this gift.

"She was constantly getting mugged, beat up, black eyes, face bruised," Jeanne noticed. "But I felt she was courting it, wandering around after dark, looking bleak and absent. She wasn't coping."

Now Jeanne began to question everything about her friend. How was she even supporting herself? Might Russ or someone be keeping her? Was she a prostitute? Was a physically abusive relationship the explanation for all her bruises? She wrote a letter to Dare saying she couldn't see her anymore. "I gave up on her. I felt I was being pulled through a wringer for no purpose. Maybe her mother had sheltered her so much that she couldn't cope with life. I couldn't tell if she was drinking or in deep psychological trouble." Jeanne did see Dare once again, by chance, on the street. "She was walking on Madison Avenue. The look on her face was blank. She was wearing high heels and a tight black dress. It looked like it was left over from the night before."

By 1983, Jerry Mayro, the owner of the Burlington Bookshop, stepped in to help. He took a set of keys to Dare's apartment and her checkbook so he could handle her finances. Soon after, he had Dare admitted to the Smithers Alcoholism Treatment Center on East 93rd Street. After a few days, she simply walked out. Jerry was standing on Madison Avenue opening the gate to his bookshop when he thought he heard her voice saying, "'Oh, hello, Jerry,' all airy-fairy, very proper and waspy." He turned to see her walking by. She didn't stop. A few minutes later, she was back. She had discovered she didn't have the keys to her apartment and needed Jerry's set. When Jerry had Dare admitted to Smithers for a second time, she "escaped" again, this time running the thirteen blocks home in her nightgown, barefoot despite the snow on the ground.

Dorothy tried to monitor things. Traveling often, she always left contact information in case of an emergency. Dorothy was on a business trip when Dare called to say, "I just want to hear your voice before I die." Dorothy flew home that afternoon, heading straight from the airport to Dare's apartment. "You could barely get in there," Dorothy recalled. "Her apartment was like a fortress." Seeing Dare's condition convinced her that Dare was not going to do anything precipitous. She had chosen a slower method: drinking herself to death.

Dare found no safety—or peace—in her fortress. She longed to escape. She told a friend from Walton that she had taken a letter to the mailbox, as though this were a major accomplishment. "She kept saying, 'I need to get out in the world. I need to do something in the world again.'"

In 1985, Dick Gildenmeister visited Dare for what would be the last time. He didn't call in advance but announced himself on the intercom. Dare buzzed him in, and when he got off the elevator on her floor he was greeted by his old friend standing stark naked in her doorway, as if in the persona of Persis, the doll who didn't like to wear clothes, the doll he had always loved best.

By that summer, Blaine was approaching the end, alone and bedridden in his cabin on the Homovich property. He refused to be hospitalized or to touch the meals that Shirley Homovich brought him every day. All he wanted, Blaine told his few visitors—the Homoviches and Florence's niece and nephew—was to see his sister. Finding her absence incomprehensible, Bob called Dare repeatedly. "I told her her brother was dying and how much he wanted her with him. What I was saying didn't seem to click with her." More likely, it clicked all too well. Dare could not bear to contemplate the loss of Blaine. If she didn't see him in this condition, it was far easier to deny that he was dying.

A few days later, Blaine himself called. "He begged her to come visit him," recalled Barbara Hann Quimby, Florence's niece. Dare told him she could not. "She wasn't strong," Barbara said, "and she just couldn't bear to see him. He wanted her to come so bad and she wouldn't."

On July 22, Bob Homovich corralled another volunteer fire department ambulance driver into helping him take Blaine to Delaware Valley Hospital. Blaine died there the next day, six days before the 10th anniversary of Edie's death. Blaine's friends decided that Dorothy Brandt, the Walton woman who had known Blaine for more than fifty years and Dare for almost as long, should be the one to give her the news. Dorothy meant to discuss practical concerns: funeral plans and estate matters. In fact, there was no discussion as Dare could not speak. "Dare wept uncontrollably," was all Dorothy could report.

CHAPTER ELEVEN

Disenchantment

What is the worst of woes that wait on age?
What stamps the wrinkle deeper on the brow?
To view each loved one blotted from life's page,
And be alone on earth as I am now.
　　　　　—BYRON, "Childe Harold's Pilgrimage"

Blaine had not wanted a funeral. Joe Hann carried out his wish to be cremated and have his ashes scattered over the Atlantic Ocean. As promised, Blaine's will, drawn up by Donald Seawell, left most of what he had to Dare or, if she predeceased him, to the Fresh Air Fund. His estate was valued at $50,000. Dare and George Vaillant were named co-executors. The island, valued at $650, went to Joe Hann by default as neither Dare nor George Vaillant wanted it. Dare did not want her role as co-executor, either, and signed it away to George. Half of the Butternut Island Tackle Company royalties were left to Dare, the other half to be divided between George, now a psychiatrist teaching at Harvard and at Dartmouth Medical School, and his brother Henry, a doctor in Concord, Massachusetts.

When George cleaned out Blaine's cabin, he took Blaine's collection of Dare's books and the fishing creel that had once hung over the bed where Edie and Dare had slept. Joe Hann, Florence's nephew, asked Bob Homovich to cart everything else to the Downsville dump. Bob, who had developed a deep affection for Blaine, could not bring himself to do this and packed up Blaine's papers, books, and photographs to store in his house.

Blaine had been well-liked, even in the small towns of Walton and Downsville, where what Bob called his "staggering drinking" had been no secret. Those who knew his story had compassion for him: abandoned by his mother, separated from his sister, losing his father quite young, feeling guilt because so many of his World War II compatriots died in the war while he survived, failing as a writer. "Traumatic events shape our lives forever," George Vaillant said.

Blaine had lived as marooned as he felt, a recluse on an island of one. His only success had been the fishing lure; his only real love was for his animals and the sister who had been returned to him, but with broken wings. George felt that Blaine tried hard for Dare. But he could not or would not continue his mother's work of maintaining her fairy-tale world, and he wasn't interested in anyone doing that for him. He threw all interested women back, like so many fish. With their walking papers, he gave them earrings made from a pair of Phoebe lures.

By the time Blaine died, the butternut trees that once proliferated on Pot were dying off from disease, and the high springtime waters of the Delaware River had flooded the island so often that all that was once man-made was gone. Except for a few planks of rotten wood, Blaine's two-story cabin on stilts had washed away. Still, living beings sought out the island. The Hereford cows who grazed in the pasture on the opposite bank liked to wade across to Butternut, drawn there in cold weather for protection. The island had drawn Blaine there for the very same reason. As Jim Robinson, a childhood friend, once said, "Blaine was a very lonely man, but he was always looking for a quiet place."

In Blaine's baby book, the page for Baby's First Step shows Blaine photographed taking his—*literally*, Edie has penned in, *at one year and one day*. Beside another photograph of him at one year and seven months, Edie wrote, "Quick, independent. (Just like Daddy.)" Perhaps this was the trait his mother had most disliked in him, that he was independent, so like Ivan and so unlike Dare.

Dare wanted no part in the settlement of her brother's estate or in the disposal of his belongings. Nor did she want Blaine's possessions or his money. They would not bring her brother back. With Blaine's death, she lost all will to live. She made no attempt to disguise how disconsolate she felt. When anyone asked how she was, her stock response became, "Blaine has died and now I am all alone." It seemed to Dorothy Pollack as if Dare "was just evaporating." Allan Hull was shocked to observe how she "seemed to have lost her hook to anything." Thinking photography might be a comfort, he suggested she get out her camera. "I won't know how to do it," was her reply. It had been several years since Dare had touched a camera or entered her darkroom. She never did either again.

Existing photographs, however, took on an even greater importance for her after her brother's death, especially those of Blaine, Ivan, Edie, and Philip. If there was no one left living, surrogates were still there on photographic paper, finally able to be arranged, to sit beside one another—and stay with her, as she had always hoped they would in real life. Dare lined them up on the couch, like guests at a cocktail party, and talked to this ensemble, together at last.

As for her other cherished companions—Edith and the Bears— she visited them occasionally in the bank vault, but they were rarely brought home to her apartment. Replica, Persis, Lona, and a few Spare Bears, as she called them, were stored away in a chest in her living room.

While she left Jerry Mayro to handle her bills, every check Dare wrote herself was made out to Headington's liquor store. Sometimes, when the apartment felt too oppressive, she sat outside on the building's front stoop or even on the sidewalk itself. Or she walked up to Central Park, where she sat on a bench, framing an image with her hands and making a clicking noise, as if to capture an imaginary shot. When homeless people who frequented the benches there tried to befriend her, she was amenable. Sometimes she invited them back to her apartment. Sometimes she spent the night on a park bench.

Professional developments, even without Dare's hand in them, continued apace. In 1985, the Rothschild Doll Company in Southboro, Massachusetts, came out with replicas of Edith and Mr. Bear. Dare saved the announcement: "New for 1985! Dolls and Bears from the enchanted world of EDITH the Lonely Doll. Based on the classic children's book series from the creative genius of author Dare Wright."

In November 1985, Dare Boles's article "The Lonely Doll—Not a Bit Lonely" appeared in *Doll Reader* magazine. It was the most comprehensive article ever written about Dare's inanimate cast. Its author made what would be her last visit to Dare just after the article came out. She found Dare emaciated and in a confused state.

In May 1988, Dare fell and cut her head on Edie's bronze bust of Voltaire. She managed a phone call with Donald Seawell's daughter Brook (now Brook Ashley) before falling unconscious in a pool of blood. Brook notified the police, and had Dare transported to the hospital by ambulance. When she was to be released, Brook arranged for Christine Corneille, a nurse's aide from St. Lucia, to take her home and care for her until her strength returned.

When Christine arrived each morning, she found the apartment littered with abandoned glasses containing the remnants of milk or orange juice spiked with bourbon. Dare, she observed, spent her time drinking and conducting running conversations with her photographs. Christine was horrified. "Sometimes she would talk to a photograph of Philip all day long. She would say 'Why, why, why?' How she pined over that man. She would also talk to her mother, saying 'Edie, Edie, Edie.' She would sit and talk to those stupid pictures until I couldn't take it anymore. I told Dare, 'It's not normal. You cannot be talking to a picture.'"

If all that was left was alcohol and ghosts, Christine was determined that Dare would be better off without them. She hid the photographs. Twice, Dare asked Christine if she knew what had happened to the pictures. Both times, Christine lied and said she did not know. "And that," recalled Christine with evident pride, "was the last time she asked." Later, she moved Edie's ashes from the coffee table in the living room to a high shelf in the darkroom.

Getting Dare to stop drinking turned out to be harder. Dare was expert at what Christine termed "playing hide-and-seek with the bottle." It was a game, like dressing up, that Dare had played all her life.

As the weeks went by, though, Christine came to realize there was more than alcohol and ghosts. There were visitors, a constant stream, and almost all undesirable. "All sorts of people would ring the buzzer," Christine said. "I came to hate the sound of that bell."

To Dare, these were her friends from Central Park. To Christine, these were vagrants who might be dangerous. When she would tell the visitors to go away, Dare would protest. "That is my friend, Christine. Let him in." Despite Christine's lectures, the "friends" kept coming. Like Robin in *Take Me Home*, Dare made friends too easily. She loaned them money, and they stole as much as they "borrowed." Almost anything left of value that was not safely hidden away disappeared.

Christine tried to think of other ways to ease Dare's loneliness. She took her to the park herself so she could supervise Dare's contacts. "She would see the dirtiest homeless man and she would say to me, 'Isn't he handsome?' The filthiest-looking person, that is who Dare would respond to." Christine took Dare home to Brooklyn for holiday dinners. She brought her grandniece, Nicole Regis, to visit. Nicole liked to make Dare up and braid her hair. It amazed Christine that Dare would put up with this; she even seemed to enjoy it.

But Dare was not as patient with Christine's attempts to alter her eating habits or her lectures on proper nutrition. Dare could be convinced to eat a Stouffer's dinner every night and a few carrot sticks or a piece of toast during the day, but apart from that it was a losing battle.

Dare received the rare old friend who came to visit sitting on the couch like a china doll, dressed often in a lavender turtleneck and jeans, a long blond wig, and a circle of rouge on each cheek. When Allan Hull came to visit, he broke down and cried. He later recalled, "I realized they had lived a fairy tale and now it was over." Vincent Youmans, one of her last visitors, brought her a bouquet of anemones, her favorite flowers. She accepted them with a smile and threw them in the trash can.

In 1992, yet another enterprising mother, this one from Cleveland, called Dare. Cathy Niswonger had rediscovered her favorite books from childhood on a trip to the public library with her young son. Learning that all the books had fallen out of print—*The Lonely Doll* was the last to go, in 1991—she became determined to see if she could make the case for reissues. She found Dare through directory assistance. At first, Cathy did not detect the condition of the woman on the other end of the line. When Dare reacted with disinterest to her idea, Cathy wrote an open letter to *Doll Reader* magazine, asking if there were others who would like to see the books in print again and, if so, to contact her if they were willing to write letters to Dare's publishers. She received hundreds of letters, which she collected in a ring binder along with notes she took when people called. While Cathy waited to see if the letters she forwarded on to Dare's publishers might achieve results, a friend coincidentally happened to invite her to New York. Surprisingly, Dare agreed to a visit.

In the photos Cathy took that afternoon, Dare wears no wig. Her hair is white. She is pale and emaciated. Her teeth are broken. She is drowning in a loose-fitting smocklike dress that looks like prison issue. In the background, Edie's portraits of Dare as a child with a Dutch-boy haircut, Dare as a magnificently beautiful young woman, and herself in a gossamer-blue gown are visible. On the couch beside Dare is the drawing of Philip Sandeman. And on a shelf behind her is a stack of her nineteen books, including the ten Edith books with their gingham spines, all in different colors. The woman seated before them looks as if she could barely lift a book, let alone write and illustrate one.

Dare rallied for Cathy, patiently answering her questions. Asked how she created the illusion of Edith sleeping with her eyes closed, as Edith's painted-on eyes were permanently open, Dare told her she had made little felt eyelids with eyelashes to set over Edith's eyes. Asked how she staged the temperature-taking scene in *The Lonely Doll Learns a Lesson*, Dare explained that she poked a hole in Edith's mouth, inserted a real thermometer, and sewed her mouth back up again when she'd gotten her shot. Cathy decided she didn't want the other secrets of Dare's magic revealed. "Tell me," she asked, "they are all really alive, aren't they, Edith and the Bears?"

Dare's mouth broke into a wide smile, and her eyes started to sparkle. "Ah," she said. "You've found us out."

On weekdays, Christine continued to come. But in the evenings or on weekends, Dare would still wander up East 80th Street to the benches by the Metropolitan Museum of Art or into Central Park. When Christine arrived in the morning to find Dare gone, she would head straight for the park. Often, she found her there asleep on a bench.

Christine chided Dare endlessly for frequenting the park and bringing street people home with her. Like a child, Dare could not understand that Christine's prohibitions were for her own good. Or perhaps her longing for company was so overpowering that she determined to find a way around her nurse.

When Christine began to detect signs that Dare was letting these people sleep in her apartment on the weekends, she advised Brook to arrange for weekend care as well. Marie Simon, Christine's friend from St. Lucia, was hired. When Marie arrived one morning, Dare did not answer the doorbell. Thinking to go back down to the street to call from a pay phone, Marie rang for the elevator. Just then, the door to Dare's apartment flew open and out bounded a disheveled-looking man. As he pushed past Marie into the waiting elevator, pulling a grocery cart behind him, Marie slipped into Dare's apartment and slammed the door.

The place was in complete disarray. Crouched on the living room floor in the darkness was Dare, shaking and muttering softly, "Where's that crazy monster?" She seemed to be in shock. As Marie soothed and examined her, she realized Dare had put up quite a struggle. She was covered in scratches and bruises. Marie dressed her wounds and called Christine, who arrived as quickly as she could. Together they took Dare to Lenox Hill Hospital. The doctor's examination revealed that Dare had been raped.

After that, Christine came to live with Dare, sleeping on the couch in the living room, with Marie relieving her on the weekends. In the mornings, Christine would awaken to find her charge already up, preparing a glass of orange juice to serve her, just as she had always done for Edie. Dare drank no alcohol on Christine's first day in residence. Just as she had forgotten the photos, Christine said, "she completely forgot about the drink. It was loneliness that was causing Dare to do all that drinking. The lady was crying for help."

For a time, the visitors from Central Park kept coming. "I was so scared of that doorbell. If it was raining, they would ring in the middle of the night. They wanted a dry place to sleep." But as they learned of Christine's presence, they stopped coming.

Each day Christine would help Dare dress and then take her out for a walk. They would battle over her getup. Dare would insist on wearing one of her blond wigs, although by now she didn't care whether it was on straight or how tattered it might be. "She would throw a wig on her head, half slipping off. I would say 'Oh, Dare, I can't stand that wig.' She said, 'If you're ashamed to be seen with me, then just walk on.'" Gradually Christine threw away all the wigs, and Dare forgot about them also.

In February 1995, a little more than two years after the rape, Christine took Dare for a medical checkup. During a medical procedure, Dare suffered respiratory failure. She was sent by ambulance to Lenox Hill Hospital, where a tracheotomy was performed. Dare remained in the hospital for several weeks, at which point Christine was notified by the hospital administrators that her charge would have to be moved to a long-term-care facility. Dare was admitted to Goldwater Memorial Hospital on Roosevelt Island, a two-mile-long sliver of land in the East River, in May 1995.

Epilogue

It is a labour in vain to recapture [our own past]: all the efforts
of our intellect must prove futile. The past is hidden somewhere
outside the realm, beyond the reach of intellect, in some mate-
rial object (in the sensation which that material object will give
us) which we do not suspect. And as for that object, it depends
on chance whether we come upon it or not.

—MARCEL PROUST, Overture to *Swann's Way*

At the end of November 2000, Christine went home to St. Lucia for a week, and Brook Ashley, Dare's legal guardian, left on a trip abroad. I had already made plans to visit Dare on December 3, her eighty-sixth birthday, but now both called to ask me to go in their stead. Dare's condition was noticeably worse. As I left, I was asked to stop at the nurse's station to review the emergency contact information in Dare's chart. They had Christine's phone number and Brook's; now they added mine. I returned a few days later. Dare slept throughout my visit.

On January 25, 2001, at 8:30 P.M., the phone rang. An unfamiliar male voice asked to speak with Nathan Jean. "Yes?" I replied, annoyed at what I assumed was a solicitation. "Dr. Yee, Goldwater Hospital." A split second passed before I caught up.

And just as I had, he said, "Dare Wright expired." On his rounds, just a few minutes earlier, he had discovered she had no vital signs.

The following morning I called *The New York Times*, fulfilling my promise to Brook. The obituary ran on February 3.

> *Dare Wright, Children's Author*
>
> Dare Wright, a photographer and children's book author whose best-known work is "The Lonely Doll," died on Jan. 25. She was 86 and lived in Manhattan.
>
> Ms. Wright's story about Edith, the lonely doll, befriended by a pair of teddy bears, was first published in 1957 by Doubleday and illustrated with Ms. Wright's photographs of her own doll.
>
> Ms. Wright wrote eight [*sic*] more books about Edith and the Bears.
>
> The first book never lost favor, especially with young girls, and in 1998 Houghton Mifflin reissued it.
>
> Born in Thornhill, Canada, Ms. Wright was the daughter of Ivan Leonard Wright, a theater critic for the *Toronto Globe*, and Edith Stevenson Wright, a portrait painter.
>
> She graduated from the Laurel School in Cleveland in 1933 and moved to New York, where she worked briefly as an actress and model before a successful career as a photographer.
>
> No immediate family members survive.

Dare's body was sent to a crematory in Brooklyn. Brook asked Winkie Donovan to retrieve the ashes. Winkie brought them back to her apartment, where she placed them on a bookshelf, as fitting a resting place as any for Dare.

A decade before her last hospitalization, Dare sent the Lawsons a 2,500-piece jigsaw puzzle. It took Cathy and her daughters four months to assemble it. Of course, they'd known all along where they were headed: They were re-creating the image of three teddy bears depicted on the cover of the box. I, too, had been given a puzzle. Unlike Cathy's, however, mine had not come in a box; I could not refer to the image that I was striving to create. Only now did I realize that from the moment I laid eyes on the book jacket, I had that image in front of me. The Lonely Doll was Dare.

The story of *The Lonely Doll* was in large measure Dare's own story. In the book, a tour de force of wish fulfillment, she found a way to make things right, providing her alter ego, Edith, with love and rescue in the form of two male teddy bears, the father and brother whose real-life counterparts she had lost when she was young. She ceaselessly sought that rescue in her own life, which was spent posing, playing dress-up, and retreating into fantasy in order to remain her mother's "good and precious daughter," as if holding on to her mother and her mother's love depended on that.

I came to books very young. My mother worked in a bookstore before my birth, and both my parents were committed readers who read aloud to me from an early age. We proceeded avidly from *Pat the Bunny*—I was fascinated to look into the book's mirror and see myself reflected back—to *Goodnight Moon*, the sight of whose talismanic objects (the comb, the brush, the bowl of mush) flooded me with a sense of comfort, as did the incantatory rhythm of those words. In my favorite photograph of myself from childhood, taken when I was three and still an only child, I sit on my father's lap, "reading" to him, while he pretends to be riveted. The book, *God Is Good*, which I had picked out myself at the bookstore, is upside down.

Books not only comforted me, they intrigued and enticed me, belonging, as most of them did, to the enviably sophisticated province of the grown-ups. They seemed to carry the same fascination for my parents that toys did for me. I studied the rows of them on a full wall of shelves at one end of the living room, stretching all the way to the ceiling. But they were beyond my reach in every way; until I was five, I didn't know how to read.

Apart from books, my greatest passion was for dressing up. There was a manic energy to this. I don't know what fueled it. Maybe it was a primitive form of storytelling, because I know there was always an accompanying story line in my head: something about being big and grown up, and grown up in just the way I planned to be—glamorously. My own mother struck me as surprisingly disinterested in all the appurtenances to which she, as a grown-up, was entitled. She used makeup, for example, so sparingly. I preferred to pile it on, as I did the costume jewelry that various of my parents' female friends and relatives bestowed upon me when they learned of my obsession.

By the time *The Lonely Doll* entered my life, I was spending less and less time on my father's lap. Since the *God Is Good* period two little brothers had arrived, competing with me for that privilege. And God, I had come to realize, wasn't entirely good. My second brother was plagued by problems from birth. When he was a year old, the doctors finally put a name to what was wrong. The words they used—*mental retardation*—meant nothing to me, although I understood they were bad. My grandparents on my mother's side arrived from Oklahoma to console my parents. With them they brought a gift for me.

While the grown-ups conferred in the living room, I escaped into my new book. I studied the pictures. It was the first book I read to myself and I read it over and over and over. But there was a creeping awareness that even if the only place I wanted to be was inside this book, this was not where I belonged. I belonged in the living room where the grown-ups were whispering. Suddenly, it seemed, there were so many secrets.

I studied their faces, looking for clues. I remember my parents holding my baby brother in their arms, scrutinizing him with worried looks on their faces. I didn't understand what upset them so. Blond and blue-eyed while the rest of us were dark, he looked like an angel to me, or like an exquisite, if fragile, little bird. It troubled me to observe how the others persisted in their notion that something was wrong.

I can't be sure when I lost my fierce attachment to *The Lonely Doll*. I do know that somehow, with the remarkable carelessness of a child, I lost the book. But most important, I lost, if temporarily, my hook to the transformative powers of stories. My brother's story, a story I didn't like, was eclipsing all the others. When Wendy Darling asks Peter Pan why he came to her nursery window, Peter, who has just explained to her that he lives with the Lost Boys in Never Land, tells her of his quest. "To try to hear stories. None of us knows any stories." And Wendy replies, "How perfectly awful!"

As I look back at my childhood now, I see myself as a lost girl and my brother as the boy who would never grow up. With my brother's diagnosis, my story—our story—looked "perfectly awful." At that moment came *The Lonely Doll*. For a while, I think it became my life raft and rescued me. By the time I was eight, my brother was becoming harder and harder to manage. My dreams of his miraculous transformation—might he not get better?—were not coming true. At four, he could hardly talk.

I knew he knew he was different. I knew he didn't want to be that way. I understood that he had no words to say any of this, or to ask why it was so, and that was why he acted out. I didn't blame him.

What I did not know is that my parents had decided to follow the doctor's advice that it would be best for my brother to live in a home for developmentally impaired children. This happened at the end of that summer, which we spent in a rented house in the country near what was always called his "school." Every day, my mother took him there "to play." But how could I have not known this was in preparation for the day he would be taken there—and left? By the time I did figure this out, it was too late.

On that day, an unlikely babysitter arrived in the person of my uncle. This time, both my parents put my brother in the car. And then I knew. Restrained by my uncle, I stood, stunned, in the driveway as they drove away. As the car disappeared from view, I felt a snapping feeling in my chest. I guessed it was my heart breaking in two.

Later, my parents tried to comfort me. Explanations were given. But I could not comprehend.

From that time forward, I lived in books. I found they always helped me to make sense of and order my world. I didn't spend much time with those I had loved earlier, however; fairy tales, especially, no longer worked for me. I didn't feel protected or safe. I didn't want to know about children being eaten by witches or giants or wolves. I had no interest in evil spells. But in missing those fairy tales, I also missed their essential lessons: that obstacles can be overcome, that things can work out.

My brother, as it turned out, was not completely lost. We visited him on weekends, taking him out for a few hours, or sometimes, over holidays, for a few days. We took trips to hospitals when he had surgery. The arc of these visits haunts me still: the joy at seeing him, the feeling of time stretched out before us to be together, and the gradual realization that the togetherness would soon end and, once again, we would have to leave him behind. I still can't say goodbye without feeling overcome by sadness.

Every goodbye felt like a rerun of the first one. Now it was him, not me, standing—in his case, so brave and dignified—in a driveway as we drove away, as we abandoned him—over and over. When he didn't cry, I knew he was trying not to as hard as I was. My parents expressed relief; he was adjusting. When he did cry, it was ghastly and we all cried, all the way home.

As we drove away, I would watch out the backseat car window as he would get smaller and smaller before disappearing anew. Each time, it felt as if some part of me split off and stayed behind with him. But it wasn't only that I ached for him and missed him. It was also that I was frightened. If you are not good, I thought to myself, you too might get sent away.

I began my journalism career in my twenties. I married in my thirties. I thought about having a baby, but even less than halfheartedly. I knew too much about what could go wrong. And childhood, as I remembered it, even if it was someone else's, was not a place I would want to revisit. I decided my body would make the decision for me. And while I waited to see what would happen, memories of my childhood, not forgotten as much as buried, began flooding my consciousness. That was when *The Lonely Doll* made its reappearance in my mind.

All biographies are in some way rescue operations, if not always selfless ones. At times, in my attempts to intercept Dare's story before it too was lost, I thought I might, in some way, release her. I hadn't thought of all the ways that writing it might also be a way to release myself.

By the end of my journey, I had discovered many, many women who spoke, often with deep emotion, of the powerful attachment they too had felt for *The Lonely Doll* when they were children. In some cases, the book stayed with them—literally—on their passage to adulthood. In others, the book itself was lost along the way. Some had gone to great lengths to find it again, which explains why, among book searchers and rare book dealers, demand is high and waiting lists are long. Copies in good condition command hundreds of dollars. People bid furiously for Dare's books on eBay.

In 1996, through a licensing agreement made with Dare's agent, a doll design firm, Haut Melton, brought out an $895 boxed set, including a felt Edith doll, a teddy bear, and a colorized limited edition of *The Lonely Doll* in a small format. A less expensive version was later made available.

In September 2001, Houghton Mifflin reissued *A Gift from the Lonely Doll*. It joined *The Lonely Doll* and *Edith and Mr. Bear* on bookshelves all over the country; the rereleases had found a ready and enthusiastic audience. There are over 100,000 copies in print today. *The Lonely Doll* is in its ninth printing.

In the fall of 2003, the Madame Alexander doll company brought out a new Edith doll. Dare would not have liked it any more than the one that came out in 1958; this version, with its Barbie-doll blond hair and small round eyes, is a very unconvincing Edith.

As for the real Edith, eighty as I write this, she is at Brook Ashley's home in California—with the Bears. Dare would have been happy to know that Edith is not alone.

Notes and Acknowledgments

Something hidden. Go and find it. Go and look
behind the Ranges—
Something lost behind the Ranges. Lost and
Waiting for you. Go!
> —RUDYARD KIPLING, "The Explorer"

Were it not for the people who brought her to life for me through their vivid recollections, I would have returned from the Ranges empty-handed, and this portrait of Dare Wright would be no more than a blank canvas.

Aside from newspaper and magazine articles, there is no secondary source material available on either Dare or her mother, Edith Stevenson Wright. My impressions were formed and facts drawn from interviews with relatives, friends, and colleagues. No one who met Dare ever forgot her, and yet no one who met her ever came away with the feeling that they truly knew her. But for their willingness to share their impressions, I am deeply indebted to them all. In particular, I thank Dare's lawyer, Donald Seawell; Geary Anderson, his assistant at the Denver

Center for the Performing Arts; and Seawell's daughter and Dare's executor, Brook Ashley.

What follows is both an expression of my gratitude for the help and encouragement I received and notes as to my sources.

Prologue

The information in this chapter is based on conversations with Brook Ashley; the late Winkie Donovan; Dare's nurses, Christine Corneille and Marie Simon; and Anita Silvey, the former publisher of children's books at Houghton Mifflin.

Chapter One: Beginnings

The information about Edith Stevenson Wright's family history was gathered from interviews with family members and from articles that appeared in newspapers and magazines in Toronto, Canada, and in Youngstown and Cleveland, Ohio. I am deeply indebted to Judith Jorg Johnson for sharing the essays of her mother, Alice (Allie) Pearl Whiteside Jorg, as well as the correspondence between her grandmother, Daisy Gaither Whiteside, and her mother with Edie and Dare. She also supplied a cache of family documents and photographs.

I also thank Suzanne Heil Norton, Judy Johnson's second cousin and the granddaughter of Edie's uncle, Charles Thomas Gaither, who provided information about Gaither family history, Craftstone, and letters and family photographs.

The information about Ivan Leonard Wright's family history came from A. Meade Wright, the son of Ivan's brother Austin. Meade also provided family photographs and documents.

Ivan's poem "The Want of You," which first appeared in the *Toronto Mail and Empire* in 1906, was later anthologized in *The Best Loved Poems of the American People* edited by Hazel Felleman (Garden City, N.Y.: Doubleday, 1936) and in *The Family Book of Best Loved Poems* edited by David L. George (Garden City, N.Y.: Doubleday, 1952).

For information on Edie's Youngstown Courthouse commission, I thank Ed Black, file clerk and "Designated Courthouse Historian," and Robert A. Mastriana, architect of its 1991 renovation, who rediscovered the paintings in the courthouse attic and decided they should hang in the rotunda once again.

Algeo Stevenson Zinkan's daughter, Algeo (Posie) Zinkan Day, generously provided a family photo album and scrapbook, as well as memories of her aunt and cousin. I also thank her sons, Frederick Stevenson Day and Ronald Day. Bettie Zinkan Vajda, the widow of Algeo's son Ted, was helpful in supplying family lore. The children of Algeo's son Gaither—Peter Zinkan, Sonya Zinkan Babchuk, Chris Zinkan, and Charlie Zinkan—graciously shared information about family genealogy and Edie's paintings.

I am indebted to Shirley and Bob Homovich, Blaine's landlords in Downsville, New York, who ignored instructions to take Blaine's possessions to the town dump after his death. The collection of artifacts they preserved—ranging from Blaine's baby book, his report card from the Collegiate School, his short stories, and his correspondence with his sister, mother, and stepmother to photographs, World War II memorabilia, and even his hand puppet, Bongo—provided many missing puzzle pieces.

Anne Berard of the Milford (Massachusetts) Town Library helped locate information about the Wright family's sojourn there. Paul Curran tracked down information about the fire that destroyed the Medford (Massachusetts) house belonging to Dr. Alonzo Shadman. Dr. Shadman's grandson, Bruce Meyer, combed through his grandfather's effects and shared the wonderful photographs of Edie and Dare he came across in his search.

For information about Florence Jeanette Cobb Wright, I thank her niece, Barbara Hann Quimby, and Joy Hann, the widow of Florence's nephew, Joe, who shared recollections and family photographs. I also thank the office of the registrar at Bucknell University, Florence's alma mater.

I am indebted to Donald J. Petit, city planner with the Cleveland

Landmarks Commission, for all manner of assistance, from maps to census reports, and for chasing so willingly after wild geese.

For information about Emily Arms Aull, I thank Emily's daughter, Charlotte Aull Finstad, and Pamela L. Pletcher, archivist at the Mahoning Valley Historical Society.

Tales from the Secret Kingdom, by Ethel May Gate, was published by Yale University Press in 1919. I thank Aldona "Jinx" Gobuzas for sharing with me many of Dare's childhood books, and also for her steadfastness.

I am grateful to Edward Enright for research done in Toronto, Canada, and to Laura Weaver of the Thornhill Historical Association.

Chapter Two: Cleveland

For information on notable Clevelanders and Cleveland history, I referred to the online *Encyclopedia of Cleveland History* maintained by Case Western Reserve University and the Western Reserve Historical Society. *Cleveland: The Making of a City* by William Ganson Rose (Cleveland and New York: World Publishing Co., 1950) was also a great help. I consulted *The Cleveland 200: The Most Noted, Notable, and Notorious in the First 200 Years of a Great American City*, edited by Thomas Kelly et al., with an introduction by Dick Feagler (Cleveland: Archives Press, 1996).

For information on the Stouffer restaurants in Cleveland and the Stouffer family's patronage of Edie, I thank Marjorie Stouffer Biggar.

The information on Dare's early schooling came from Wendy Sechrist of the Cleveland Heights School District. Kay Saxon Crawford, who attended that long-ago Easter Egg hunt at the Hanna home and later married Edie's patron Frederick Crawford, also helped with school information and provided photographs and recollections.

Dare's years at Laurel School were brought to life through the tireless efforts of Julie Donahue, director of alumnae, and her former assistant, Alicia Reale, who unearthed yearbooks and other memorabilia from the period. Julie led me on a school tour of both the old and new Laurel campuses. She also led me to four of Dare's schoolmates, who in turn helped me find others: Elizabeth Newell Chamberlain, Marjorie Cast Danforth, the late Helen Kuhn Ekstrom, Eva Tuttle Hawkins, Lee Wilson Lockwood, Elizabeth (Betty) Hitchcock Rose, the late Grace Hanford Thurston, Marguerite Vliet Vaughan, and the late Mary Yost. I thank them all. I also consulted Ethel Andrews's *Roots and Branches: The First Fifty Years of Laurel School* (Shaker Heights, Ohio: Laurel School, 1958) and Hope Ford Murphy's *Educating the Independent Mind: The First Hundred Years of Laurel School* (Shaker Heights, Ohio: Laurel School, 1998).

Anthony Phelps, archivist of the Rowfant Club in Cleveland, provided information on Noel Lawson Lewis. *The Fabulous Interiors of the Great Ocean Liners in Historic Photographs* by William H. Miller, Jr. (New York: Dover Publications, 1985) was a help in learning more about ocean liners in the period that Edie and Dare traveled to Europe.

I thank Chris Edmondson, Interlibrary Loan Librarian at the Cleveland Museum of Art, for the research she did on Edie and for her hospitality.

I also thank the following institutions and their staff members:

The Cleveland Public Library: Margaret L. Baughman, Photograph Collection; John Skrtic, General Reference; Evelyn Ward, Literature Department; Stephen Zietz, Fine Art and Special Collections.

The Cleveland State University Library: Bill Barrow, Special Collections.

The Public Library of Youngstown & Mahoning County: Louisa Berger.

The Western Reserve Historical Society: Ann Sindelar, reference supervisor.

The Mahoning Valley Historical Society: Pamela L. Pletcher, archivist.

Fairleigh Dickinson University Library: James Howard Fraser.

National Library of Canada: Martin Ruddy.

Mark Piel and the entire staff of the New York Society Library.

The entire staff of the Tompkins Square branch of the New York Public Library.

Information on Jane Douglass came from her nephew William Haggard Crawford, Glenda Crawford, and Lovelace and Tom Howard, as well as from the Yale School of Drama, where she studied playwriting in 1941–42, and from the Theater Collection at the Museum of the City of New York, where her papers were donated.

Chapter Three: New York

For information on the American Academy of Dramatic Arts and Dare's attendance there, I thank Meg McSweeney.

For information on the Art Students League and Dare's attendance there, I am grateful to Stephanie Cassidy. Dr. David J. Soloway allowed me to quote from his 1994 homage to George B. Bridgman on the 50th anniversary of his death.

Ian Schrager's office was helpful in providing information on the American Women's Association clubhouse, now the Hudson Hotel.

Information about the fire that destroyed Edie's portrait of Calvin Coolidge appeared in the Cleveland *Plain Dealer*, March 8, 1935.

For information on the career of Eugenia Rawls, I am most grateful to Donald Seawell and the Library at the University of North Carolina at Chapel Hill, where their papers were donated.

For information on Sam Katz, I thank his son and grandson, Elmer Balaban and Bob Balaban. See also *The Making of the Wizard of Oz* by Aljean Harmetz (New York: Alfred A. Knopf, 1977).

For information on Edie during this period, I thank the children of Dr. Holly Broadbent: Dr. Holly Broadbent, Jr., Ann Broadbent Holden, and Marion "Pinkie" Broadbent Philbrick. I also thank Donald Grogan, who, with his father, Tim, managed the Hanna building and bought it from the Hanna family in 1959.

I thank Amelia Lizak York, Edie's waitress at Fred Harvey's, for showing me the charm bracelet and the photographs that Edie gave to her and for sharing her recollections, and her daughter, Jackie York, of the Playhouse Square Foundation in Cleveland, for arranging our meeting. I also thank Drew Rolik, archivist for Tower City Center, Cleveland.

For information on Blaine in this period, I thank his lifelong friend, Walter Breckenridge, and his son, John Breckenridge; as well as Susannah Vaillant Hatt's children: Dr. George E. Vaillant, Dr. Henry Vaillant, and Joanna Vaillant Settle. See also George's book *Adaptation to Life* (Cambridge: Harvard University Press, 1977).

I am grateful to Frank Lorenz of Hamilton College for information on Blaine's application and his one semester there.

Meade Wright provided valuable information on the reunion of Dare and Blaine that was brought about by his father, Austin.

For interviews, photographs, and other documents, I am indebted to the family of Philip Sandeman: his brother, Brian Sandeman, Brian's daughter, Sue Sandeman, and her sister, Elizabeth Sandeman Griffin. See also Ned Halley's *Sandeman: Two Hundred Years of Port and Sherry* (London: The House of Sandeman, 1990).

Chapter Four: Making Family

I thank Roy Wilder, Jr., for his encouragement and his insight into his friendship with Dare.

Arthur A. Lavallee, president of Acme Tackle Company, generously provided information on the Phoebe lure. He estimates that twelve million Phoebe lures have been sold since they were patented in 1949, with an approximate retail value of $17 million. They are still manufactured today. Royalty payments, which supported Blaine during his lifetime and a percentage of which went to Dare during hers, are still paid to Blaine's heirs, George and Henry Vaillant.

For background on Ocracoke, as well as for photographs and gracious hospitality, I thank Lanie Boyette Wynn; her son, Jim Wynn; her daughter, Jean Wynn Cox; and Alton Ballance and his brother, Kenny. Alton's book *Ocracokers* (Chapel Hill, N.C.: University of North Carolina Press, 1989) was a great help. I also referred to the following books in Dare's library: *Ocracoke* by Carl Goerch (Raleigh, N.C.: Edwards & Broughton Co., 1956) and *The Cape Hatteras Seashore* by David Stick and Bruce Roberts (Charlotte, N.C.: McNally and Loftin, 1964).

The book that Edie reads in one of Dare's photographs, *A Pinch of Poison*, was written by Frances and Richard Lockridge (New York: Frederick A. Stokes Co., 1941).

For information on Philip's work at London Films, see Michael Korda's *Charmed Lives: A Family Romance* (New York: Random House, 1979).

I thank Lavinia Emmet Fleming for sharing information about her friendship with Philip Sandeman and his relationship with Dare.

For background on Edie's portrait of Churchill, which today hangs in Churchill Hall at the University of Bristol, I thank Michael Liversidge in the department of History of Art and Dr. Alan Rump, the custodian of Churchill Hall. See also Yousuf Karsh, *Faces of Destiny* (Chicago and New York: Ziff-Davis Publishing Co., 1946).

Chapter Five: After Philip

I am indebted to Dorothy Tivis Pollack Horwitz for her help in identifying the subjects of Dare's photographs and for the many hours we spent discussing her friendship with Dare, Blaine, and Edie.

Annabelle Prager provided background on the Fenimore Cooper Marsh scandal.

I thank the late Wanda Ramsey and her husband, Robert, for their recollections of Dare's West 58th Street apartment, and Wanda's sister Iza and daughter Daphne for helping me date the *Good House-keeping* shoot in which they appeared.

I thank Donald T. Grogan for wonderful stories about his association with Edie and for taking me to the Hanna penthouse on my visit to Cleveland.

Further information about Dare's modeling and photography career came from the Library of the Fashion Institute of Technology.

Dare Boles offered information on Edith before her transformation; she also shared with me her correspondence with Dare as well as reminiscences of her visits to Dare's apartment on East 80th Street. See also her article "The Lonely Doll—Not a Bit Lonely" in *Doll Reader* magazine (November 1985, pages 204–208). Big Bad Bill (see chapter nine) now lives with her in Glen Allen, Virginia.

Chapter Six: Behind the Little Green Door

For information on Gaylord Hauser, I thank his nephew, O. Robert Hauser, and Anthony Palermo. See also John Bainbridge's *Garbo* (New York: Holt, Rinehart and Winston, 1971) and Karen Swenson's *Greta Garbo: A Life Apart* (New York: Charles Scribner's Sons, 1997).

For recollections of Blaine, Dare, and Pot, I thank Helen Kessler, the widow of Hermann Kessler.

For information on Lee Wulff, I thank his sons, Allan Lee Wulff and Barry Wulff. See also Lee's book *Bush Pilot Angler* (Camden, Me.: Down East Books, 2000).

For information on Russell Barnett Aitken, I thank his widow, Irene Roosevelt Aitken, Chris Edmondson and Henry Adams at the Cleveland Museum of Art, and Laura Hilbert at the Cleveland Institute of Art. I also consulted the catalog for the 2003 Christie's New York sale of the Russell B. Aitken Collection of Silver Trophies, Vintage Firearms, Antique Arms and Armour, and Militaria and the Sporting Library with Related Material. See also his *Great Game Animals of the World*, a Giniger Book (New York: Macmillan Co., n.d.).

For her recollections on working with Dare at *Good Housekeeping*, I thank Lyn Levitt Tornabene.

I am grateful to Barbara and Vincent Youmans for sharing photographs and reminiscences of their friendship with Dare. See also Gerald Bordman's *Days to Be Happy, Years to Be Sad: The Life and Music of Vincent Youmans* (New York: Oxford University Press, 1982), and Zelda Fitzgerald's *Save Me the Waltz* (Carbondale and Edwardsville: Southern Illinois University Press, 1967, p. 45).

Chapter Seven: The Books

My thanks to former Doubleday book designer Diana Klemin for supplying details of the production of *The Lonely Doll*.

Dare's quote likening the making of her books to the making of a movie appeared in "It's No Fairy Tale, This Tale of Toads and Dolls" by Kenton Robinson, *The Hartford Courant*, May 8, 1981.

Arlette Schriber provided background on Dare's work in Walton.

I thank Stefano Savona for a wonderful night ride across Sicily from Palermo to Taormina, and for masterful sleuthing required to help me find and gain entrance to what was once Gayelord Hauser's Villa Apomea, now owned by Vittorio Sabato. I thank Mr. Sabato, in turn, for finding Giuseppe Caltabiano, once Gayelord's houseboy, now proprietor of Ristorante Il Corsaro, where we all shared a memorable lunch.

I quote from John Ehle's *Kingstree Island* (New York: William Morrow and Co., 1959, page 110).

I am greatly indebted to Richard Gildenmeister, who shared an extraordinary cache of letters, as well as photographs, and many stories of a long friendship.

Dare Boles provided useful background on Edith and Lenci dolls in general and on Persis. See also Dorothy S. Coleman's *Lenci Dolls* (Riverdale, Md.: Hobby House Press, 1977).

I also thank: Barbara Barstow, librarian in charge of Children's Services at the Cuyahoga County Public Library, for providing photocopies of Dare's books that I did not have; June Egan, for information on Florence Wakeman and for the invitation to visit Florence's house (now June's), where Dare stayed and shot several books; and Sylvia Jukes Morris, for information on Clare Boothe Luce. See also her book *Rage for Fame: The Ascent of Clare Boothe Luce* (New York: Random House, 1997).

Chapter Eight: The Lonely Doll's Dilemma

For information on Random House children's books in 1960, see Louis Menand's "Cat People," which appeared in the December 23 & 30, 2002, issue of *The New Yorker*. See also the Bennett Cerf Collection at the Rare Book and Manuscript Library of Columbia University.

The information on shooting *Date with London* came from interviews with Donald Seawell.

The author of "Time's devouring hand" was James Bramston. See *The Art of Politics*, published in 1729.

My thanks to Dr. David Schultz for information on Edie's stay at Cleveland's Lutheran Hospital during her illness and for supplying hospital records.

I am grateful to Susan Sandeman for information on Dare's 1963 trip to England and for providing photographs from that visit.

And I thank Irene Roosevelt Aitken for information about Russ's collection of Edie's paintings and for bequeathing them to me.

Chapter Nine: Loss

The information on Dare's time at Lost Valley Ranch in Sedalia, Colorado, came from interviews with its owners, Bob Foster, Sr., and Bob Foster, Jr., and former staff members Marti and Charles Saul.

Information about the origins of 11 East 80th Street came from "Town-House Block Returning to Single-Family Use," an article by Christopher Gray in *The New York Times*, May 17, 1998, and from an interview with Mr. Gray.

I am indebted to the late Allan Hull, Edie's lawyer and Dare's friend, for filling in so many pieces.

I also wish to express my gratitude to Rebecca A. Davis, Kathy Earnhart, and Samantha Kimpel of the Butler Institute of American Art in Youngstown for information on the portraits by Edie in their collection and for sharing with me the correspondence between Edie and Joseph Butler III, former director of the museum. Thanks also to Louis Zona, the institute's director, for giving me a copy of Joseph G. Butler, Jr.'s *Recollections of Men and Events: An Autobiography* (New York: G. P. Putnam's Sons, 1927).

My thanks, too, to Jim Irving for sharing reminiscences of Edie and Dare in the Moreland Courts period.

Chapter Ten: After Edie

I am grateful to Gene Schultz of the Frank E. Campbell Funeral Chapel and to Sandra Malitz for helping me locate Edie's will and estate records, and to Dick Moore, whose company, The Bonfoey Picture Framing Co., framed all of Edie's paintings and appraised the paintings in her estate.

For more on Gayelord Hauser, see his *Mirror, Mirror on the Wall* (New York: Farrar, Straus and Cudahy, 1963). His treatise on avocados appears on pages 85–86.

The information on Dare in this period is based on interviews with the following, whom I thank: Helen Andrejevic, her son Mark Andrejevic, Harold Collins, Kay Saxon Crawford, and the late Jenny Bell Whyte.

For information on Dare's last two books, I thank Elizabeth Retan, widow of Walter Retan, head of children's books at Random House from 1966 to 1978, and Jenny Frisse Fanelli, who worked with Walter; thanks also to Jeanne Seely Cherniak and her mother, Helen Seely, formerly of Walton, whose horse, Midnight, starred in *Edith and Midnight*.

I thank Jeanne Frank for sharing her diary entry and Natalie Buck for Dare's letter to her daughter, Barbara.

I am grateful to Jean Harris for talking with me. It was thanks to Shana Alexander's *Very Much a Lady: The Untold Story of Jean Harris and Dr. Herman Tarnower* (Boston: Little, Brown & Co., 1983) that I learned Harris had attended Laurel School. I also consulted Harris's own book *Stranger in Two Worlds* (New York: Macmillan Publishing Co., 1986).

For insight into Dare's years at 11 East 80th Street, I am grateful to Cathy Lawson, Linda Ruskoski, Kathy Hull Stropoli, Jed Feuer, Alexandra Hughes, Astrid Schumacher, Evelyn Semler, Jeanne Hammond, the late Jerry Mayro, and Jane Trichter.

Chapter Eleven: Disenchantment

My thanks to Robert MacGibbon, who unlocked the gate on his property adjacent to Butternut Island so that Jim Robinson could take me to what was left of "Pot." I thank Jim for a lifetime supply of original Phoebe lures, as well as butternuts, for which Butternut Island, later Pot, was named. Sallie and Jim Crawford and Anna Sulger at the Ogden Free Library in Walton were also kind enough to talk with me.

Much of the information in this chapter came from Dare's nurses, Christine Corneille and Marie Simon. They both have my gratitude.

I thank Cathy Niswonger for sharing her vast collection of Dare Wright memorabilia, including photographs and books.

Epilogue

In this chapter, I refer to the following books:

J. M. Barrie, *Peter Pan and Other Plays* (New York: Oxford University Press, 1995).

Margaret Wise Brown, *Goodnight Moon*, a 50th Anniversary Retrospective by Leonard S. Marcus (New York: HarperCollins Publishers, 1997).

Dorothy Kunhardt, *Pat the Bunny* (New York: Random House—Golden Books, 1940).

My thanks to Hannah Rodgers of Houghton Mifflin for information on the three books by Dare that they have reissued.

I would also like to thank Clevelanders Ginny Carroll, Gladys Haddad, Harriett R. Logan, Dr. Robert Phelps, Molly Schultz Slenker, Thelma Smith, and Christeen Tuttle; also the following people, either painted by Edie or descended from those painted by her: Grace Grasselli Bowman, Ann Hoyt Jones Carr, Priscilla Ide, Jean Moseley, and Louise Marshall Prescott.

Everyone I know heard much too much about Dare during the years I worked on this project. I thank Llewellyn Gibbons Smith, who became an unwitting expert on Dare Wright, for his understanding and for our trips to Walton and Ocracoke.

For the constancy of their support, I thank, in particular, Patsy Cummings and Joe Logiudice and Noel and Richard Prince. I am grateful to the MacDowell Colony, especially for sanctuary; to Judith Reiberg and George Diggle, especially for heat; to Susan and Chip Kessler, especially for couches; to Mus and Stephen White, for guidance; and to Jay Jennings for reading.

I also thank Christa Balzert, May Castleberry, Michael Gallagher, Penelope Green, Rachael Horovitz, Henry R. Kaufman, Dr. Michael Lockshin, Marcia Paul, Izhar Patkin, and Thomas Renart.

Joyce P. Smith has my immense gratitude for unflagging support and hard work.

I am indebted to Alice Quinn at *The New Yorker* and to Pamela Cannon, Katie Hall, and Susanna Porter at Random House for an almost-home; to Rob Spillman, Elissa Schappel, Win McCormack, and Holly MacArthur at the literary magazine *Tin House* for the best home imaginable; to Jacki Lyden at NPR's *Weekend All Things Considered* and Susan Burton and Ira Glass at *This American Life*.

Boundless gratitude to Jennifer Barth and Sam Douglas at Henry Holt, and to Amanda Urban and Ron Bernstein at ICM. I also thank Tom Nau, Rita Quintas, Kenn Russell, and Paula Russell Szafranski at Henry Holt, and Christina Capone, Dylan Kletter, and Boris Undorf at ICM.

My thanks to my family and to my grandparents, Ruth and William Elson, for the gift of *The Lonely Doll*.

Books by Dare Wright

The Lonely Doll (Doubleday, 1957)
Holiday for Edith and the Bears (Doubleday, 1958)
The Little One (Doubleday, 1959)
The Doll and the Kitten (Doubleday, 1960)
Date with London (Random House, 1961)
The Lonely Doll Learns a Lesson (Random House, 1961)
Lona, a Fairy Tale (Random House, 1963)
Edith and Mr. Bear (Random House, 1964)
Take Me Home (Random House, 1965)
A Gift from the Lonely Doll (Random House, 1966)
Look at a Gull (Random House, 1967)
Edith and Big Bad Bill (Random House, 1968)
Look at a Colt (Random House, 1969)
The Kitten's Little Boy (Four Winds Press, 1971)
Edith and Little Bear Lend a Hand (Random House, 1972)
Look at a Calf (Random House, 1974)
Look at a Kitten (Random House, 1975)
Edith and Midnight (Doubleday, 1978)
Edith and the Duckling (Doubleday, 1981)

Re-releases

The Lonely Doll (Houghton Mifflin, 1998)
Edith and Mr. Bear (Houghton Mifflin, 2000)
A Gift from the Lonely Doll (Houghton Mifflin, 2001)

Illustration Credits

Chapter Four
[90] DW/BA
[94] DW/BA
[96] Private collection of Blaine
Wright/Courtesy of Robert and
Shirley Homovich
[97] Private collection of Blaine
Wright/Courtesy of Robert and
Shirley Homovich
[105] DW/BA
[107] DW/BA
[116] DW/BA

Chapter Five
[118] DW/BA
[126] Private collection of Jean
Wynn Cox
[131] DW/BA
[131] Courtesy Maidenform
Worldwide
[131] Courtesy of *Cosmopolitan*
magazine

Chapter Six
[134] DW/BA
[142] DW/BA
[142] Wendy Hilty/*Good
Housekeeping*
[144] DW/BA
[146] DW/BA
[149] Perry Cragg, from DW/BA
[151] DW/BA

Chapter Seven
[156] DW/BA
[162] DW/BA
[168] DW/BA
[171] DW/BA
[172–173] DW/BA

[175] Both DW/BA
[176] DW/BA

Chapter Eight
[190] DW/BA
[201] DW/BA
[202] DW/BA
[203] Both DW/BA
[207] Courtesy of Richard
Gildenmeister
[211] DW/BA
[216] DW/BA

Chapter Nine
[218] DW/BA
[226] DW/BA

Chapter Ten
[242] DW/BA
[251] DW/BA
[258] Photograph by Blaine Wright/
Courtesy of Thelma Smith

Chapter Eleven
[270] DW/BA

Epilogue
[280] DW/BA

Notes and Acknowledgments
[288] DW/BA

CPSIA information can be obtained
at www.ICGtesting.com
Printed in the USA
LVHW022102300721
694160LV00007B/396

9 780312 424923